THE IONIAN ISLANDS
TO THE ANATOLIAN COAST
A SEA-GUIDE

By the same author
THE ADRIATIC
THE AEGEAN
THE TYRRHENIAN SEA

DARDANELLES: A Midshipman's Diary

*To the memory of Madge, my wife, who often accompanied
me at sea and made attractive sketches of ships and
coastlines to embellish this book*

First published 1982
by John Murray (Publishers) Ltd
50 Albemarle Street, London W1X 4BD
Printed in Great Britain by The Camelot Press, Southampton
Photoset by Keyspools Ltd, Golborne, Warrington, Lancs

British Library Cataloguing in Publication Data
Denham, H. M.
The Ionian Islands to the Anatolian coast:
a sea-guide – (Denham sea guides)
1. Greece, Modern – Description and travel –
Guide-books   2. Turkey – Description and
travel – Guide-books
I. Title
914.95′0476   DF727
ISBN 0−7195−3949−8

THE
IONIAN ISLANDS
TO THE
ANATOLIAN COAST

A Sea-Guide

H. M. DENHAM

JOHN MURRAY

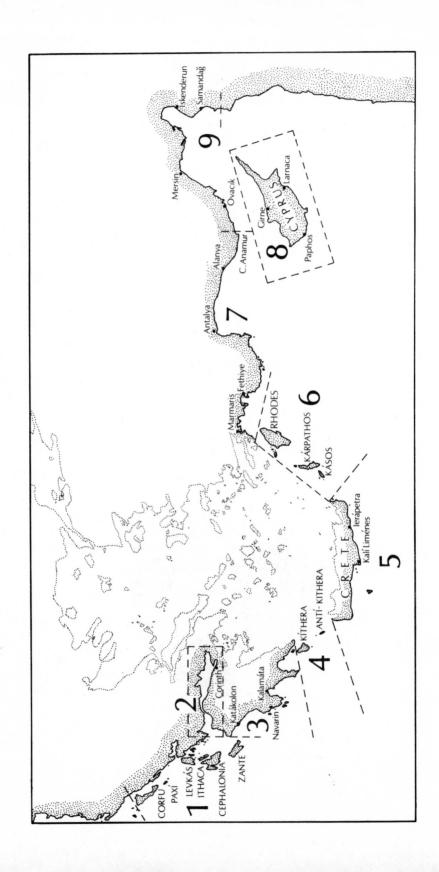

Contents

Illustrations

Sources of Illustrations

Sketch-maps by Zillah Pettit and Aydua Scott-Elliot, c.v.o. Drawings by Madge Denham. Title-page drawing by David Knight. Photographs: 1, Syndication International; 3, 4, 5, Walter Ingham; 6, 18, 32, Paul Popper Ltd; 7, 10, Yeletzes; 8, M. Chroussaki; 9, Nick S. Stournaras; 12, Spyros Meletzis; 13, K. Raphaelidis; 14, 17, Paul Myloff; 15, V. & N. Tombazi; 19, J. Allan Cash; 20, 22, 23, 24, 28, 29, 31, John Marriner; 26, 27, Capt. P. Courtenay.

Preface

This book replaces the second edition of *The Ionian Islands to Rhodes* and *Southern Turkey, The Levant and Cyprus*. It includes the south Anatolian coast of Turkey and a brief reference has also been made to Cyprus, where, in 1980, parts of it were again practical to visit in a yacht.

I feel specially indebted to Mr Robert Carter, Mr Davson, Mr Kenneth Marsh, Mrs Janet Sanso; Wing Commander Neville Bulpitt; Mr John Marriner for his extensive photographic studies; Mr and Mrs Brotherton; Commander John Guard; and Mr Walter Ingham, all of whom have helped me with new material concerning the many changes in recent years.

As regards south Anatolia and Cyprus, I am grateful to Mr C. A. Hunter. I refer particularly to the late Mr Andreas Cariolou, a most experienced diver and a mine of knowledge on parts of Anatolia and all the coast of Cyprus; to Mr and Mrs Burgess of *Sinbad Seven*; and to Mrs Jehane West for considerable help with most of the Anatolian coast.

This book is not intended to be a substitute for British Admiralty Charts and *Sailing Directions* and neither author nor publisher accepts responsibility for any consequences of the material being used instead of such official publications.

H.M.D.
1982

Introduction to Greek Coast

Crossing the 70-mile Otranto Strait from the heel of Italy one reaches the outlying islands off Corfu. The remaining six Ionian Islands, extending nearly as far as Crete, are mountainous and attractive. On reaching Cephalonia, a decision must be made whether to turn eastward into the mountainous Gulfs of Pátras and Corinth or to continue southwards, following the open west coast of the Peloponnesus to Cape Maléa. Crossing the Kíthera Channels one comes to the steep southern coast of Crete – no place for a sailing yacht – and reaches the eastern gateway to the Aegean and Rhodes.

Place-Names. In medieval and subsequent times, the names most commonly used for islands and ports were those given by Venetians and Genoese: Kérkira became Corfú; Zákinthos, Zante. Although some of these names still appear on a few of the older British charts, they are unrecognizable to the Greeks, to whom Cape Matapan is now always Taínaron and Navarino is Pílos. New British charts conform to the Greek Hydrographer's names, the transliteration from Greek to Roman alphabet being in accord with the Permanent Committee ruling on Geographical Names. In this book such well-known places as Corfu, Crete, Rhodes, etc., I have written according to our British custom, but to make sure that the place may be easily found in the index, I have in most cases inserted the alternative name. For less well-known places the spelling of the modern Greek name is used with accents added to help with pronunciation.

A glossary of geographical terms and other words used in place names will be found near the beginning of the Admiralty *Sailing Directions*. Some of the most common are:

Ákri	Cape	*Nísos, Nísoi*	Island, Islands
Áyios-iou, Ayía	Saint	*Órmos*	Bay
Kólpos	Gulf	*Palaiós*	Old
Levkós	White	*Pétra*	Rock
Limín	Harbour	*Potamós*	River
Mávros	Black	*Skála*	Small port, quay
Megálos	Big	*Stenón*	Strait

ENTERING GREECE

Ports of Entry. A yacht must enter and leave Greece only at one of the following Ports of Entry:

West Coast: Corfu, Préveza, Argostóli (Cephalonia), Pátras, Itéa, Zante, Katákolon, Pílos (Navarino), Kalamáta and at Rhodes in the S.E. Gateway.

The Aegean has a dozen ports, including the yacht harbours at Piraeus, listed in the author's *The Aegean: A Sea-Guide to its Coasts and Islands*.

Anti-Pollution. A Greek law forbids vessels in ports and bays, or sailing within Greek waters, to jettison any liquid or solid waste materials. It is essential during a vessel's stay in port that toilet outlets and outlets for waste products must not be used. Garbage disposal should be packed in nylon bags and handed to Garbage Disposal Service or put in garbage cans provided.

Transit Log. At the Port of Entry, a Transit Log will be issued. It acts as a 'ship's passport' and eliminates further formalities at subsequent ports. The Transit Log is valid for a calendar year; unlike the French Green Card and the Yugoslav Permit of Navigation, it covers but one visit to Greece and must be surrendered before leaving Greek waters.

Passports. It is sensible to have all the crew's passports stamped on arrival. If they leave Greece in the yacht, it will have been superfluous; if they should have cause to leave by public transport or by road, the absence of an entry stamp may cause embarrassment.

Taxes on Foreign Yachts. Law 438 of 1976 prohibits foreign yachts from engaging in the charter business in Greek waters without a permit. It also states that private foreign yachts not engaged in the charter business are to pay U.S. $15 per ft of length overall from the completion of one year's stay in Greek waters. Periods spent in Greek waters are aggregated: each time the total reaches 12 months the tax becomes due. Many yachts avoid the tax by leaving the country before it becomes due, and on return apply for a new Transit Log.

Harbour dues were imposed in certain ports in 1980; these were based on time spent in Greece and on tonnage.

This tax is described as a yearly special contribution to the port funds of the country for services rendered by the port and other installations. Anyone contemplating a winter lay-up in Greece would be well advised to ascertain whether this special contribution is then being levied in the manner now intended, because it would make a significant addition to the cost.

Port Officials are usually to be found at each port in Greece; even in a small port there is normally both a Customs Office and a Port Authority. In very small places the local policeman sometimes acts on their behalf. The harbour officials dress like the Navy, although they are not sailors, nor are they administered by the Admiralty. On a yacht's arrival a 'sailor' from this office will usually direct the yacht to a berth and will then ask for the Transit Log.

Yachts' Mail. It is normally quite safe to have one's mail addressed c/o Harbour Master at any significant port that the yacht may be visiting.

Arrival by Public Transport. The easiest way to join or leave a yacht in Greece is to choose a port with air connection with Athens.

The diagram illustrates the services usually running in the summer; the link from Igoumenítsa to Ioanína is by bus. When planning air travel, it is useful to know that there are two terminals on opposite sides of Athens Airport; Olympic Airways uses the western terminal for all its flights, international and internal; all other airlines use the eastern terminal, and for a passenger the only way to go from the one to the other is an expensive taxi ride round the outside of the perimeter.

Car ferries run to Italy and to Yugoslavia as follows:

Brindisi—Corfu—Igoumenítsa—Pátras—daily.
Otranto—Corfu—Igoumenítsa—daily exc. Sunday.
Dubróvnik—Corfu—Igoumenítsa—twice weekly, mid-week.

But services within Greece are frequent and punctual; the bus terminal may be recognized by the initials K.T.E.L.

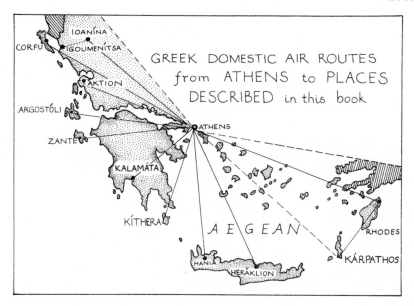

GREEK DOMESTIC AIR ROUTES from ATHENS to PLACES DESCRIBED in this book

PILOTAGE

Charts. Interesting information both on pilotage and archaeology can be gleaned from the older Admiralty charts based on the British surveys of the last century. At sea, soundings can be seen to have changed in consequence of silting and earthquakes; on shore, many of the ruins so carefully recorded by Beaufort and his contemporaries have since disappeared. Although it is obviously unwise to navigate on any but the most modern charts* available, anyone interested in the area is advised to retain or collect early Admiralty charts.

Metric charts of the coasts of Crete have recently been published, but because most of the Admiralty charts of the area described in this book still use feet and fathoms, they have been retained in this edition to avoid, or at any rate minimize confusion.

Sailing Directions. It is important to consult the Admiralty *Sailing Directions*. *Mediterranean Pilot*, Vol. III, covers the Ionian Islands, the west coast as far as Cape Taínaron and the Gulf of Corinth; Vol. IV covers the rest of the Greek coasts and islands.

---

* When ordering a new chart, it is wise to stipulate the title as well as the number, as Admiralty are apt to change numbers in the course of time.

Time. Greek Standard Time is G.M.T.+2. From April to October there is an hour of daylight-saving time.

Tides and Currents. Tides are scarcely perceptible. Currents are variable, their direction and strength depending mainly on the direction, strength and duration of the wind. In settled summer weather they can, for practical purposes, be ignored.

> In the Ionian Islands, prolonged northerly winds cause a rise in the water-level of about a foot, and southerlies the converse. In the Corfu Channel, between Corfu and the mainland, this rise and fall is increased to 3–4 ft and the current can there attain 1½–2 knots, but this is rare in summer.
>
> In the entrance to the Gulfs of Amvrakikós and Pátras currents have attained 3 knots. (See *Sailing Directions*.)

Winds. As in all hot countries the winds result partly from differences of pressure and partly from changes of temperature. The latter causes the familiar day and night breezes which normally result in little or no wind in the morning, a sea-breeze starting early afternoon and a calm or very light off-shore air at night. The usual summer winds off the coast described in this book affect the following areas:

Corfu Channel. There is often quite a brisk little N. wind in the narrows between Corfu and the mainland, otherwise calm in the morning with light N. to N.W. winds in the afternoon. By night and in the early morning there may be a very light easterly land-breeze from the mainland mountains.

Corfu to Cephalonia. An area of frequent calms and light variables, but when there is a brisk wind it is likely to be between N.E. and N.W.

Gulfs of Pátras and Corinth. Calm in the morning, W. or S.W. in the afternoon.

Zante to Kíthera. N.W. around Zante, becoming more westerly, somewhat stronger and more consistent as one goes southward.

Kíthera Channel. Off shore the westerly day breeze predominates. In the Kíthera Channel the strong Aegean Meltemi diverts the breeze to the N.E. after midsummer.

Crete to Rhodes. Along the north-west coast of Crete N. and N.W. winds predominate, and at Rhodes westerly winds. The south coast of Crete is renowned for the sudden strong squalls which sweep down from the mountains.

Weather Forecasts (see diagram opposite)

Hellenic National Radio   728 kHz   (412m)
    0145 G.M.T. (whole of Mediterranean).
    Forecasts in English, French and German at 0430 G.M.T. on 728 kHz (First Programme) and subsequently at times that vary from year to year.

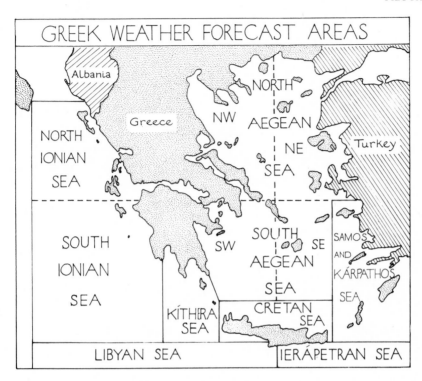

GREEK WEATHER FORECAST AREAS

Coastal Radio Telephone stations (in recent years)

Athens ⎫
Heraklion ⎬ on 2182 Kcs. at 0345, 0945, 1545 and 2145 G.M.T.
Chios ⎪
Limnos ⎭

Prohibited Areas are, or should be, marked on the chart. They have been extended in the last few years, particularly off Crete. Those whose charts have not been kept corrected can obtain the necessary information at Room 410, 2 Filellinon Street, Piraeus, where charts can also be bought.

In addition to the prohibited areas, there are also exercise areas where, from time to time, firing and bombing practice takes place. Warning of this is given at short notice by radio:

Athens 728 kHz at 0233, 0833, 1233, 1633, 2033 G.M.T.
Corfu 1007 kHz at 0233, 0833, 1233, 1633, 2033 G.M.T.
Pátras 1511 kHz at 0233, 0833, 1233, 1633, 2033 G.M.T.
Haniá 1511 kHz at 0333, 0833, 1333, 1733, 2133 G.M.T.
Rhodes 1493 kHz at 0333, 0833, 1333, 1733, 2133 G.M.T.

Special forecasts of dangerous weather changes are broadcast on 2182 Kcs at 3 minutes past the hour and half hour.

SUPPLIES

Fuel and Water

The Greek authorities have issued a list of Supply Ports at which fuel and water can be obtained. At many places they have always been available for fishing boats, but now they are usually supplied by pump and hydrant at quays marked by blue and yellow diagonal stripes. At major ports diesel fuel should be available without tax, but recently supplies have been uncertain, as is the method of payment. In theory, one exchanges foreign currency for drachmas at a bank and obtains a special form of receipt which must be handed over to the fuel supplier. In 1981, however, at Gouviá the Shell Station was demanding foreign cash, refusing even travellers' cheques. Others were equally difficult.

Food and Drink

Shopping. Small villages are likely to have a general store with a limited selection of tinned goods and perhaps eggs, cheese and a few vegetables. Larger villages have a butcher, a baker and several grocers and greengrocers.

Fish and Meat. The following are usually available:

Fish		Meat	
Tsipoúra	French Dorade	*Arnáki*	Lamb ⎫
Sinagrída	Sea Bream	*Hirinó*	Pork ⎬ – often good
Barboúnia	Mullet	*Brizóles*	Chops
Maríthes	Whitebait	*Bon Filet*	Steak (fillet)
Octopóthi	Octopus	*Moskári*	Veal
Calamári	Squid	*Nefró*	Kidney – usually good
Astakós	Crawfish		
Garídes	Prawns		
Palamída	Tunny		

Fruit and Vegetables. Early in the season there are oranges, cherries, loquats, apples, beans, peas and courgettes.

Some of these begin to go out of season in May and are followed by tomatoes, cucumbers, aubergines, lettuces, peaches, apricots and figs. Later there are grapes and melons.

Wines and Spirits. Wine is obtainable everywhere in bottles or in small carafons; sometimes it is to be had on draught, which used to be better but is now being officially discouraged because of isolated cases of adulteration. There are many brands; *Deméstika*, red and white has wide distribution and is safe, but it is more entertaining to try the wine of the locality, such as the black wine of Ithaca. *Retsína* is to be found everywhere though it is only native to Attika.

Local vermouth and brandy are passable aperitifs.

Oúzo (a form of *Raki*) is the local spirit and is obtainable everywhere on draught.

'Fix' beer and other brands can be bought nearly everywhere and are excellent.

Bottled soft drinks, either with water or as concentrate, are exceptionally good.

Duty-Free drinks and tobacco are readily available at Piraeus for yachts over 40 tons net registered. Elsewhere their acquisition is too slow and involved to be interesting.

Restaurants. In all the small restaurants in Greece it is quite in order for the customer to enter the kitchen and choose his dish from the wide copper pans spread out on the charcoal stove – generally there are chicken, lamb stew, stuffed tomatoes, savoury rice, and fish soup, etc., all looking most inviting, as well as Turkish dishes such as *dolmádes* (meat and rice in vine leaves); *moussaká* (a sort of shepherds' pie with cheese on top), and *pastícche* (baked macaroni with meat and cheese). Usually there is a charcoal grill, and lamb cutlets or fish cooked on this is a safe bet, but be sure to say 'without oil' (*óhee ládhi*) when ordering or you will find cold olive oil has been poured over your grill. Fish is almost invariably good and fresh. Never order your whole meal at one time, or you will find that the dishes will be brought all together, and by the time you have eaten your first course the second will be congealed. Sometimes restaurants have little dishes of yogurt, and also delicious *baklavá* (honey cakes with almonds).

Ice, often much appreciated by the small yacht, is nowadays seldom available.

General Information

Health. The incidence of typhoid and tetanus varies from year to year in certain places described in this book, but there is always some, and it is sensible to be inoculated.

Practically all the well-known medicines and drugs can be bought in Athens and possibly in the few big towns mentioned, but nowhere else, so it is advisable to have a well-stocked medicine chest. The *Yachting World* diary gives an excellent and comprehensive list which covers most eventualities. Two useful additions are sulphathalidine and lomotil, especially for newcomers to the Mediterranean, who, inoculated or not, are sometimes afflicted with what is vaguely known as 'stomach trouble'. Kaolin powder is also recommended. As a result of refrigeration and of improved water supply this malady has become less common. Nevertheless, it is prudent here as elsewhere to wash all fruit and vegetables that are to be eaten raw, and to avoid a chilled stomach. Twilight is very short and the temperature sometimes drops correspondingly fast, so it is sensible to take an extra garment ashore in the evening.

Nowadays in Greece there is no trouble in finding a doctor on the larger islands, and even in the smaller places there is generally a qualified medical practitioner, a chemist, or at any rate a midwife. *Sailing Directions* mentions the hospitals to be found at the larger ports; in most of the Ionian Islands the hospitals are modern and appear to be efficient.

Berthing. In Greek ports yachts normally berth with an anchor laid out to seaward and stern to the quay; small yachts mostly berth bows to quay.

This method of securing has certain advantages: the yacht's side does not get rubbed by the quay; one has some privacy from the gaze of onlookers; but, perhaps more important still, one is less likely to be invaded by cockroaches or other vermin which sometimes frequent the quayside. In this unfortunate eventuality, the only successful way to eliminate the pest is to purchase Fumite tablets (obtainable through Boots the Chemist), and having sealed all apertures, ignite the tablets as directed and leave the yacht for 24 hours.

Repairs and Laying-Up. For any work below the waterline a yacht must be professionally slipped; in a tideless sea one cannot dry out for a scrub! During a cruise it may be necessary to make good some misfortune which is beyond the scope of ship's resources. It is then a matter of chance whether or not outside help can be obtained. At many islands and small ports in Greece there is a boatbuilder, or a joiner's shop or a mechanic in the village willing to help; sometimes quite unexpectedly one comes across a caïque sailor who has experience in making sail repairs.

Although the National Tourist Organisation of Greece now issues a chart denoting certain ports where repairs to a yacht can be undertaken, one should realize that few places here or elsewhere in the eastern Mediterranean have had previous experience with high-grade yacht work.

Wooden yachts usually winter afloat; those made of G.R.P. are often laid up ashore. The more sophisticated places are usually expensive and in the others the language problem is a deterrent to those who do not speak Greek or have a knowledgeable local friend. The possibilities include:

Island of Corfu. A few yachts lay up afloat in Gouviá Bay, but there should be a caretaker aboard or a reliable gardienage arrangement made: this is difficult to come about. Facilities of a marina are to be provided, but no engine repairs or slipway is planned.

At Levkími in the south of the island a yacht-yard to accommodate and slip large yachts is planned.

Rhodes. The modernized 'Nereus' yard with a 60-ton travel-lift, storage space and moorings for wintering afloat is described under the heading of Rhodes (p. 138).

Aegean. Yacht-yards and a choice of winter berthing arrangements are described in *The Aegean*. 'Olympic Yachts' would be the first choice and Piraeus the last.

Places. During the last 15 to 20 years most inhabited places on the west coast have become larger – many hamlets have become villages, a few villages small towns – in some places populations have doubled. This is in contrast to some of the Aegean island populations which have shrunk considerably.

Chartering. Some firms advertised in the yachting press now charter small sailing yachts (4 people). Usually a flotilla of 6–12 yachts make a fortnight's cruise, putting in at a safe harbour each night. Yachts can also be chartered to sail independently – 31 to 35 ft suitable for 6 or 9 persons.

Size of Yachts. Over the years the tendency has been for yachts to become smaller. Today 20 tons would be considered a large yacht, 10–12 tons a medium-sized yacht, and up to 8 tons small; or in terms of length: over 35 ft large, 26–35 ft medium, under 26 ft small.

Fishing. Off the shores of Greece a variety of fish is caught both by day and, when the moon is down, by night. An attractive sight at many a small port is the evening departure of the *grigiá*, the mother-ship towing the net-boat and five 'ducklings' – each fitted with two large gas lamps. They usually remain on the fishing ground all night, not returning to harbour until the sun is well above the eastern horizon.

Tunny, which people now believe spawn in the central Mediterranean, are caught in that area in long and complicated nets, called *mandragas*, usually laid off prominent headlands in Sicily and Tunisia. Only small numbers of tunny visit the eastern waters, although in Greek and Roman days they were a constant source of food for the people.

Fish generally are becoming scarce, and consequently expensive. The reason for this scarcity is both because of the small-mesh net and the use of dynamite.

Of the non-edible fish two very unattractive species are sometimes seen:

Mackerel-sharks up to 12 ft in length are sometimes met with off shore. Usually seen on a steady course, they seldom go close to the land, although every two or three years one hears of someone being attacked. Sting Ray, Torpedo or Electric Ray are very occasionally met when bathing off a shallow unfrequented beach. This is especially so in spring when the young are being hatched, and it is easy to step inadvertently on a ray half buried in sand. A sting may have serious consequences and should be dealt with at once and the poison extracted.

There are also to be seen occasionally flying-fish which are fascinating to watch. Although seldom airborne for more than about 15 seconds they have been estimated to fly at 35 knots and to make flights of 200 yds or more.

Dolphin is the great companion for a yacht in open waters. When sailing on a steady course a whole school may suddenly be seen approaching at high speed effortlessly rising and dipping through the waves. Having reached the yacht they will surround her and amuse themselves swimming backwards and forwards under the keel with a knowing upward look at the humans peering down at them from the upper deck. When tired of this game, another spurt and the shoal is gone, their course being marked by splashes receding into the distance.

There are two species of dolphin in the Mediterranean, the bottle-nose and the common dolphin; the latter can be recognized by the long, narrow beak and somewhat finer features, dark brown back and white belly with stripes of grey, yellow and white on either side; when full grown they can be 8 ft long, and are immensely powerful swimmers capable for a short while of making 30 knots, although a cruising speed of about 15 is preferred. Being mammals they must surface at intervals to take in air; this they do through a crescent-shaped hole in the head, like the blow-hole of a whale. The beak is purely for catching the fish on which they live.

Local Craft in Greek Waters. The lugsail rig – 'standing and balance lug' – was until recent years to be seen everywhere in Greece. No more are being built and nowadays the few *trehandíri* still to be seen off the west coast and Ionian islands are power-driven with steadying sails when needed.

I

The Ionian Islands
and the Mainland Coast

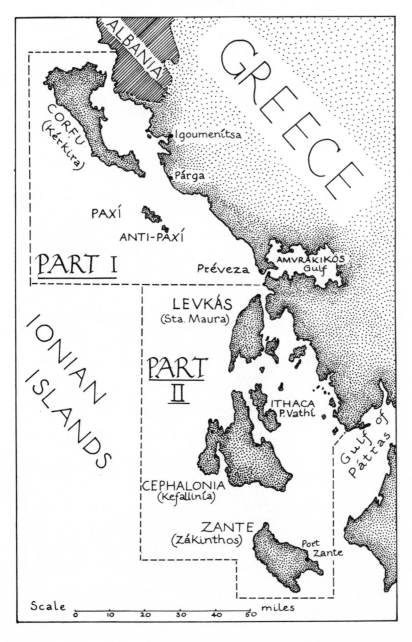

ALBANIA

GREECE

CORFU
(Kérkira)

Igoumenítsa

Párga

PAXÍ

ANTI-PAXÍ

PART I

Préveza

AMVRÁKIKÓS
Gulf

IONIAN
ISLANDS

LEVKÁS
(Sta. Maura)

PART
II

ITHACA
P. Vathí

Gulf of
Pátras

CEPHALONIA
(Kefallinía)

ZANTE
(Zákinthos)

Port
Zante

Scale

0   10   20   30   40   50   miles

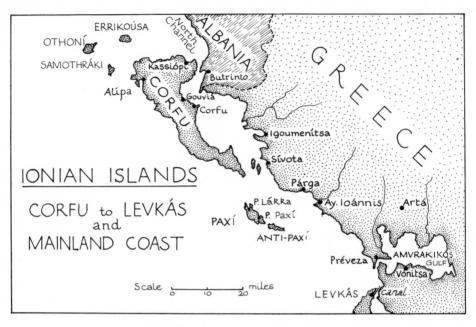

IONIAN ISLANDS

CORFU to LEVKÁS
and
MAINLAND COAST

Scale 0 10 20 miles

ISLAND OF CORFU (KÉRKIRA)
Port of Corfu
Gouviá
Garítsa Bay
Dassiá
Kalámi, Agní, Kouloúra
Ay. Stéfanos
Kassiópi (Imerolía)
Alípa
Áy. Spirídonos

OUTLYING ISLANDS
Óthoni (Fanö)
Errikoúsa (Merlera)

ISLAND OF PAXÍ
Lákka
Lóngos
Port Paxí (Gaios)
Mongonísi Anchorage

ISLAND OF ANTÍ-PAXI

ADJACENT COAST
Ftélia
Paganiá
Igoumenítsa
Liyiá
Islets of Sívota and Ay. Nikólaos
Moúrtos
Párga
Áyios Ioánnis
Fanári
Cape Kastrosikiá Anchorage
Préveza

AMVRAKIKÓS GULF (ARTÁ)
Vónitsa
Kópraina Bay and Menídi
Karvasará Bay
Loutráki
Salaóra Bay

I

The Ionian Islands and the Mainland Coast

PART I: CORFU, TO LEVKÁS, AND THE ADJACENT COAST

The Island of Corfu

Spread like a shield upon the dark blue sea.
Odyssey v.281

Since Hellenic days, when its traders set out to found colonies on the Mediterranean shores, Corfu has almost continuously played its part in maritime history: Thucydides* refers to 'that splendid armament which was destined to perish at Syracuse'; 400 years later Octavian's ships passed *en route* to Actium, and here again after another twelve centuries Don John of Austria led his fleet from Corfu to annihilate the Turks at Lepanto.

Later Corfu, together with the other six Ionian Islands, was for four centuries under the sovereignty of Venice whose influence is still in evidence in the names and features of some of the inhabitants as well as in much of the architecture. When Venice fell in 1797 these islands passed to France, then, after changing hands a number of times, to Britain under a Protectorate which she maintained until 1864, when they reverted to Greece. As a Protectorate the Ionian Islands operated a number of trading vessels sailing under their own flag. This flag had the emblem of the Lion of St Mark with a small Union Jack flag recessed into the top corner of the luff – a symbol of British protection against piracy.

During the First World War the Serbian army was evacuated here, and a memorial to those who died was erected on Vido Island, which is sometimes visited by Yugoslav warships. In 1920 the town was bombarded by an Italian

---

* *Victory song was sung, the pouring of libations brought to an end, and the fleet moved in column out of harbour. Once open water was reached . . . they pressed on with all speed for Corcyra.* History of the Peloponnesian War (6.32).

warship, and in the Second World War was occupied by the Italians and Germans.

With a population of 36,000, Corfu town, capital of the Ionian Islands, is largely Venetian in architecture with some French houses on the seafront and British Georgian public buildings by the Palace Square. A legacy of the English is the game of cricket, and on the occasion of a visit by one of H.M. ships the local club usually turns out an Eleven. Ginger-beer can also be bought.

The country, with its many villages, is beautiful with luxuriantly wooded mountains and everywhere green with colourful shrubs and wild flowers. The large unpruned olive trees, gnarled and very old, are a legacy of the Venetians; their oil is still good today.

Climate. The summer temperature reaches well into the nineties, yet the climate is not oppressive. In the spring the place is known for its humidity and in winter for its heavy rainfall. 'There is no winter' wrote Edward Lear, who made many visits to the Ionian Islands, writing and painting with much enthusiasm.

Winds on the eastern side of Corfu seldom conform with the official forecast for the Ionian Sea. During the summer nights and well into the forenoon there is invariably a gentle easterly land-breeze followed by a calm; but towards noon a light N. to N.W. 'day-breeze' predominates, occasionally coming in from N.E. Sometimes this light breeze may be whipped up into a fresh mistral. Only on about one day in four can a S.E. breeze be expected.

A weather forecast in French, German, Greek and English is transmitted daily on the Greek National programme (see p. xiv).

Approaching the Island. A yacht may be fortunate in approaching Corfu in the early light when few sights can be more beautiful than the distant Pindus mountain range described by Byron in *Childe Harold's Pilgrimage*:

> *Morn dawns; and with it stern Albania's hills,*
> *Dark Suli's rocks, and Pindus' inland peak,*
> *Robed half in mist, bedw'd with snowy rills.*

Chart 206 shows the Corfu Strait, the northern passage of which was closed to navigation for twelve years after the mining of H.M. Destroyers *Saumarez* and *Volage* on 22 October 1946. Since no diplomatic relations exist between Britain and Albania, the shores of the latter should be avoided by yachts – even in daylight. When approaching from westward by night Albania's mountain villages, lit by a blaze of electricity, may be seen a great distance off.

Near the narrowest part of this strait – a mile across – may be seen a few small houses of the Albanian outpost at Butrinto. The Venetians maintained it as a port until Napoleon's time, its defences having given it the title of 'The Key to Corfu'. Nothing of the defences now remains; only a customs house and some fishermen's cottages can be seen; but a couple of miles inland are the excavations of a small Graeco-Roman town. The river, which flows from a large lake, enters the sea at Butrinto after passing over a shallow bar. The whole area was famous for an abundance of game and, until the Second World War, was visited annually by British shooting parties.

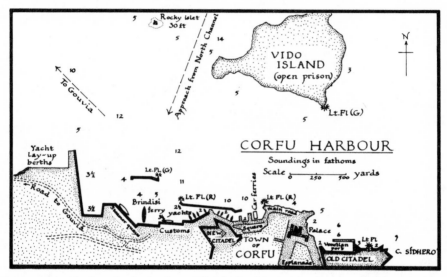

For convenience the above sketch-plan shows Vido Island and Rocky islet about 500 yds closer to Corfu than they actually are.

The Port

Berth. See Chart 725. The Venetian galley port is reserved for swimming contests. Yachts should therefore make for the Commercial port where berths are allocated at the yacht station eastward of the steamer quays. This is not always an agreeable place to lie, especially in strong N.W. winds when it can be dangerous. It is, however, possible for some yachts to berth inside the detached mole, recently improved and strengthened, but the depths of nearly 2 fathoms cannot be depended upon, and the place can be smelly. Caïques are continually moving in and out.

In the event of bad weather from the N. and N.W. it is advisable to move to Gouviá, or alternatively to proceed round Cape Sídhero into Garitsa Bay and anchor south of the citadel.

Officials. A Port of Entry – Harbour, Customs, Immigration and Health. There is a naval commandant and a British Vice-Consul.

Facilities. Fuel and water at the yacht station. A number of restaurants and tavernas, provision shops, banks and modest hotels are within 10-min walk. Ice from a factory also 10-min walk, but delivery can be arranged. Electrical and engineering work is available near the quay. A 5-ton crane at the Customs quay. Chandler and chart agents are on the waterfront; also the local wine shops. A yacht-yard (Mike & Nikos) has recently been set up on the west of the port. Two trolley slipways and one skid-cradle. Showers available.

The more fashionable part of the town, with restaurants, cafés, better shops, cable office and travel agencies, is by the Palace Square – 20-min walk.

Communications. Daily ferry service with Brindisi, Igoumenítsa and Pátras (for Athens) – frequent car-ferry to Igoumenítsa; coastal steamers and cruise ships call regularly. Air connections with Athens and Italy; frequent flights to London.

The Town. Following the coastal road towards the town one comes to the large English palace of St Michael and St George. Built of sandstone brought from Malta in 1816, part of this building is now used as a museum for Greek and Roman finds, and also a collection of Ming. The palace looks out upon the spacious esplanade which, being raised high above the sea, provides beautiful views across the massive citadel known as the 'Old Fort' towards the mountains of Epirus on the mainland coast opposite. The sides of this large square are flanked by a long façade of 18th-century three-storey French architecture whose tall arcades not only form an appropriate background for naval and military ceremonial parades, but also blend themselves most propitiously into the gay café-restaurant life where Corfiots come to foregather here in the cool of the summer evenings. The present-day Corfiots have sprung from families much intermarried with Venetians during the earlier centuries of Italian influence. There is also in Corfu town a small Jewish community, much reduced after the German exterminations in the Second World War.

Shore Excursions. A number of places on the island are easily accessible by taxi or bus. Apart from Paliokastrítsa on the N.W. coast and a number of bathing beaches on the north coast, there are some interesting places to be seen just south of the town.

Kanóni or 'One Gun Battery' (its former English name) overlooks the spacious lagoon of Khalkiopoúla, the former harbour of the Corcyran–Athenian fleet more than 2,000 years ago. At that time it was deeper and more extensive, for it is only recently that the airport has reclaimed much of its inland area. From the Tourist Pavilion at Kanóni one can enjoy the well-advertised view across the two islets guarding the entrance to this shallow but picturesque lagoon.

> **Anchorage.** The southernmost of the two islets, Pondikónisi or Mouse Island, has 2-fathom depths close northwards where a yacht may anchor temporarily in pleasant surroundings. This, however, is no longer a peaceful anchorage, as it lies exactly in line with the airport runway.

On the hillside of the tall peninsula which divides this lagoon from the sea lies the site of the early Greek fortified capital at Ánalypsos. This stronghold continued until medieval days when the Venetians came to build the new city and the New Fort. Most of the stonework of the ancient city was then used as a quarry. Towards the sea lies *Mon Repos*, which was the country residence of the Greek royal family, and was originally built some decades ago as a country-house for a British governor. It was here that Prince Philip was born in 1921. The estate runs down towards the sea where there is a pier. Above this is a spring of fresh water which was used by the wooden ships of the Royal Navy early in the last century.

The *Achilleíon*, now a casino, was built originally as a summer palace for the Empress Elizabeth of Austria, and was used some years later by Kaiser Wilhelm II for his spring holidays. The vaunting inscription set up by the Achilles' statue, 'To the greatest of the Greeks from the greatest of the Germans', has now been removed.

Emergency anchorages in event of strong N. to N.W. winds at Corfu Harbour:

Gouviá. Three miles N.W. of Corfu. The north anchorage in this bay affords all-round shelter.

> **Approach.** Chart 725 and sketch-plan. From Goúvinon Island steer about N.N.W. for the islet off Cape Komméno. On reaching a position 200 yds from the islet, turn westwards towards the conspicuous hotels and village on the point. Then steer about W.S.W. passing through the channel (its S. side marked by small buoys) towards a quay and galley sheds partly obscured by trees. Southward lies the marina, and northward a safe but restricted anchorage.
>
> **The Marina**
> **Berthing.** Care should be taken to select a safe quay especially if intending to leave a yacht here for the winter. Safest berth is W. side of main pier. The top of the quay ledge is apt to overlap the deck of the yacht and in the event of disturbed conditions this can seriously damage the yacht. In fresh easterly winds yachts have complained that despite careful fendering conditions

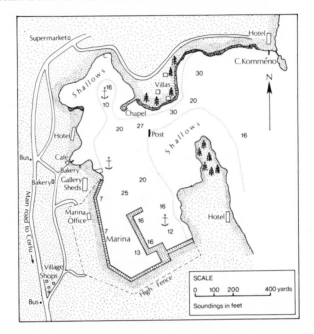

can be dangerous. A holding-off anchor is often necessary. Berth alongside main pier or stern-to at the quays.

Facilities. Water by hose alongside marina office, but only after paying for a three-day stay. No supply of diesel fuel or petrol. No facilities for hauling out, but see under Corfu Port; a first-class Perkins engineer in the area – apply marina office. There are shops in the village nearby and bus to Corfu town.

Anchorages. The most sheltered, and also the most attractive, berth is in the northern corner of the bay beyond a conspicuous white chapel, but the space with 2-fathom depths on a mud bottom is very restricted. There is a jetty 300 yds northward and a supermarket on the main road. There is also good temporary anchorage off the loading pier near the galley sheds. A freshwater spring suitable for laundry is near the short pier, also a bakery and the bus to Corfu.

Getting ashore by dinghy at either of these anchorages is difficult on account of the soft mud. Apart from the hotel quay, it is recommended to try the small boat basin. There are shops and restaurants in Gouviá village, but the drinking water is obtained from wells. A half-hourly bus service reaches Corfu town in 15 min.

Garítsa Bay, on the south side of Cape Sídhero, provides useful shelter in strong northerly winds if the yacht harbour should become untenable.

Anchorage is close southward of the old British garrison church of St George, recognized by its handsome Doric façade. There are depths of 4 fathoms on mud; good shelter from N. and W. The above-water rocks can be seen. A mole forming the Navy's small-boat and swimming harbour may be used on the outside for berthing yachts. In event of wind shifting to S.E. a yacht can move over to shelter in a small, recently dredged yacht harbour at Anemómilos, but anchorage close off is shallow with weed.

In Corfu Bay

Dassiá, an open bay by the Club Méditerranée close northward of Gouviá, is pleasant as a temporary anchorage if one anchors in the southern corner. In calm weather a yacht may anchor close off the beach where there are small hotels, restaurants and tavernas.

Kalámi, Agní and **Kouloúra** (the latter recognized by the white Venetian mansion) are attractive coves all shown on Chart 726. Kalámi is the best choice; anchor in 4 fathoms at the head of the bay. The bottom is thin weed on sand. A small *pension*, once the house of Lawrence Durrell, can provide a meal. Kouloúra, the most attractive, is impractical as a secure anchorage.

Ay. Stéfanos, close to the narrow strait, has good anchorage on sandy patches, but is open to wash from passing ferries and motor-boats. Two tavernas, small pier.

Outside Corfu Bay

Kassiópi (Imeroliá), lying on the north coast about 2 miles west of North Channel, is incorrectly shown on the new Greek Survey (Chart 726).

A short mole protects a very small harbour where it is possible for a medium-sized yacht to berth in settled weather, but it can be crowded with local craft.

Berth. Secure head or stern to the mole and lay out a kedge. The bottom is largely weed and boulders.

Facilities. There are some shops and a couple of tavernas.

The ruined fortress on the headland was built by the Angevins of Naples in the 14th century. The Venetians, later in possession of Corfu, fearing its capture by the Genoese, destroyed it. Kassiópi was formerly a Homeric site and later a Roman settlement. It was here that the emperor Nero 'danced and sang' during his travels in Greece.

The other bays on the north coast shown on Chart 726 are not recommended for yachts on account of the discomfort caused by the afternoon day breeze.

Alípa and **Áyios Spirídonos** on the west coast are suitable anchorages in settled weather, but entirely open to south. Alípa is the better and more spacious anchorage – 3 fathoms on a sandy bottom. A short mole has been completed recently affording protection for about 20 yachts, but this is not shown on the chart which also lacks details of many buildings including a government pavilion, restaurant and bars. The place is now overrun by tourists on account of near-by Paliokastrítsa. The monastery should be visited and those with sufficient energy should ascend the steep track leading to the castle of St Angelo, high above.

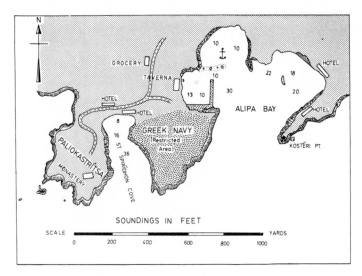

The Outlying Islands of Óthoni (Fanó) and Errikoúsa (Merléra)

Both these islands are partially cultivated and wooded with small hamlets inland. The anchorages are on the south coast and can be identified by a few small houses on the waterfront.

Óthoni is tall (1,300 ft) and green on the south side and is the more interesting of the two.

Approach should be made with caution in order to clear the rocky shoals (less than 6 ft) which lie 3 cables south of the anchorage. Coming from the east a yacht should pass southward of the shoals and turn towards the land when the eastern edge of the cliffs bears east of north. The southern shore may then be followed at a distance of half a cable until reaching the anchorage. Coming from the west there is no difficulty; the S.W. point of the island is lit and there is deep water half a cable off shore. A breakwater extending from the E. side of the bay in a westerly direction was recently being completed.

Anchorage can be found in depths of 2–4 fathoms in the western half of the bay on a clear sandy bottom. One should not proceed east of the little settlement of Ámmos where the sea-bed becomes rocky and there is a small and very shallow (3 ft) caïque harbour cut into the rocks. Shelter in the bay is good except in southerly winds.

In the event of having to seek shelter on the north side of the island, anchorage in 4–5 fathoms on a bed of clean sand may be found towards the eastern end of the bay opposite a cleft on the hillside; this is nearly a mile west of the eastern point of the island which is dangerous on account of protruding underwater rocks. In strong southerly winds strong gusts sweep down upon this northerly anchorage.

Part of the small population live in villas on the wooded hillside during the summer months. A rough road leads up from the settlement at Ámmos, making a pleasant walk through wooded country.

Errikoúsa lies relatively low compared with Óthoni; it has a very small population, and attracts a few summer visitors.

Approach. At both headlands of the bay underwater rocks extend further than the chart implies.

Anchorage. Rocks protrude above the sandy bottom on the west side of the bay near some bollards. The N.E. corner is better and the water is very clear. There is no suitable anchorage on the north side of this island.

At both these islands police are the only officials. As regards facilities, Óthoni has a small bar and a summer taverna. Bread, eggs, fish and sometimes crawfish can be bought. Errikoúsa cannot offer so much. At both islands water is from wells.

Both these islands are renowned for their crawfish, many being sent to Corfu by local caïque, which maintains daily communication (6 hrs) with Corfu.

About 1,000 people live in Óthoni and barely 1,000 in Errikoúsa but the populations are dwindling as the young men leave to seek a livelihood elsewhere. In summer one or two yachts call when on passage to or from Italy.

There is no particular history attached to these islands, but, during the British occupation of the Ionian Islands a subaltern's detachment was stationed at Fanó which was then popular in spring for the quail shooting.

Farewell Corfu

Go in thy glory o'er the ancient sea
Take with thee gentle winds
thy sails to swell.
JOHN WEBSTER, Yacht *Wanderer*, 1850

Leaving Corfu and proceeding southwards, one reaches after 12 miles the low-lying Cape of Levkími with its 30-ft light-tower protruding from the N. end of an area of saltpans. Some 2 miles south of this cape is an insignificant light-tower shown on the chart, and nearby a shallow canal is being dredged, leading towards the village of Levkími where a new yacht-yard was planned. In 1981 there was a project to build it south of Levkás Canal instead.

Island of Paxí

This little island only 5 miles long, of oval shape and well-wooded, has three attractive and safe havens for a yacht under all conditions.

Here and at several small Ionian ports there has recently been much congestion with tourist charter flotillas.

Lákka is a broad but shallow sandy bay with a growing hamlet, lying in attractive surroundings and having good shelter.

> **Approach.** Charts 206, 723. *Sailing Directions* describe the approach; no difficulty by day. Depth on the sand-bar is 11 ft and this increases towards the quay where it is 2–3 fathoms close off.
>
> **Anchorage.** Small yachts berth or anchor off the quay, being careful not to encroach on the ferry berth. Shelter is excellent, there being only a slight swell in the afternoon breeze.
>
> **Facilities.** The hamlet is no longer primitive, fresh provisions being obtainable; there are restaurants, tavernas and cafés. Fresh water usually available from a pump. Corfu ferry calls. Bus to Port Paxí.

Lóngos, consisting of a few houses tucked into the corner of an open bay, may look uninviting from seaward, because of the ugly disused factory building on the north side of the village; but closer in it appears as an attractive little fishing harbour, clean, colourful and relatively unspoiled.

> **Approach.** Chart 723. Care should be taken to avoid the Paxí Reef, lying about 4 cables off shore. There are also some rocks close to the point on the southern shore.
>
> **Anchorage** is on a sandy bottom with patches of weed in 2 fathoms. A small yacht may berth close inside a short mole (10 ft) affording some shelter from east.
>
> **Facilities.** A couple of shops and tavernas. Bus service between Port Paxí and Lákka calls nearby.

Port Paxí (Gaios) is a charming 2-fathom creek with a growing village at its head. It is the main base for a yacht flotilla company and there is also a dinghy sailing school; it is apt to be crowded during the tourist season. (See upper plan, opposite.)

1 Corfu: coastal view from Paliokastrítsa

2 Párga: village with its Venetian fortress

3 Moúrtos: looking south across new quay in foreground

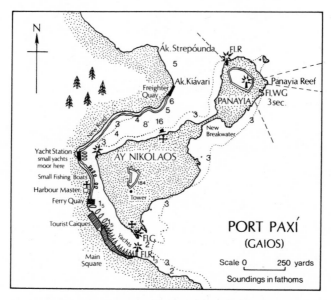

N

Ák. Strepóunda   Fl.R
5

Ak. Kiávari
Freighter
Quay.   6
5
3
4   8   16
4
New Breakwater

Panayia Reef
Fl.WG
3 sec.
PANAYIA
3

Yacht Station
small yachts
moor here

AY NIKOLAOS
3
3

Small Fishing Boats
Harbour Master
Ferry Quay   1
5
Tourist Caiques

184
Tower

Yachts
2
Fl.G
3
Main   Fl.R
Square   2   1

PORT PAXÍ
(GAIOS)

Scale 0   250 yards

Soundings in fathoms

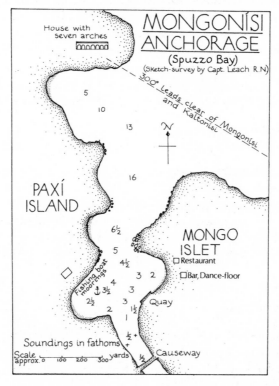

House with
seven arches

MONGONÍSI
ANCHORAGE
(Spuzzo Bay)
(Sketch-survey by Capt. Leach R.N)

5

10

13

N

16

300° Leads clear of Mongonísi
and Kaltonísi

PAXÍ
ISLAND

6½

MONGO
ISLET
Restaurant

5
4½
Bar, Dance-floor
3   2
4
Fishing boat moorings
3½   3
2½   2   3   1½   Quay
1
½
Soundings in fathoms   ½

Causeway

Scale
approx. 0   100   200   300   yards

13

Approach. See plan on Chart 723. Yachts drawing more than 5 ft must use the northern entrance. The southern entrance, though lit, is used only by local craft. If approaching from the mainland coast care should be taken to avoid the Madonna Shoal, lying in position $2\frac{1}{4}$ miles east of Madonna Lighthouse. Here the Venetians once lost a treasure-ship and in 1817 two British frigates struck.

At the northern entrance a new breakwater now joins the islet of Panayía with Ay. Nikólaos. This is to provide some shelter at the quay recently constructed for the Corfu ferry-boats off Ak. Kiávari. (N.W. of the breakwater the holding is poor.)

The southern entrance, though sometimes lit, is used only by yachts and local craft (mid-channel depth is reported as being 6 ft).

Berth opposite the village square off the recently lengthened quay, or on either side of it with the anchor laid out eastward. There is room for at least 20 yachts in depths of 1–2 fathoms.

Officials. Harbour Master in former British Residency.

Facilities. Several provision shops, a chandler/ironmonger which also serves as a bank, some good tavernas and two discotheques. Water is available from a small water truck when the water taps are turned off. Daily ferry to Corfu, bus to Lákka. A summer hotel lies about one mile southward along the coast. Small yachts sometimes winter here.

The little houses and church form a charming setting to the square. The only tall house was once the British Residency, and here Gladstone spent a night in 1858 when visiting the Ionian Islands. A road leading from the village to the top of the hill provides a pleasant walk with views over the island. One may also land on the islet, among the ruins of the fortress.

Close to the S.E. corner of Paxí Island is a deserted islet which is joined to Paxí by a short causeway. The inlet thus formed making a suitable yacht anchorage.

Mongonísi Anchorage, named Spuzzo Bay on Chart 203 (see plan, p. 13), provides suitable shelter in pleasant surroundings. Recently spoilt by tourism.

Approach. The prominent house standing on the northern point of the entrance gives a lead into the anchorage.

Anchorage may be found in convenient depths in the inner basin opposite a quay with tavernas and restaurants. It is well sheltered and normally not crowded at night. Up to 20 yachts may secure to the quay and to rocks and staging to the west of the bar and restaurant. There is, however, a disco and it may be noisy until the early hours of the morning if the anchorage is crowded.

Island of Antí-Paxí

This island is small with only a few score of inhabitants; it is of no particular interest. The anchorage is in the bay on its eastern side where fishing craft sometimes haul up. Supplies are obtained from Paxí when weather permits. The island grows some vines from which a small quantity of palatable sparkling red wine is produced.

On the east coast are some wonderful bathing beaches frequented by tourists during the day.

ADJACENT MAINLAND COAST

On the chart may be seen a number of bays along this mountainous coast, some are well sheltered according to the direction of the wind and make an interesting anchorage for a yacht.

Under summer conditions a land-breeze springs up at dawn, lasting for 3 or 4 hrs, followed by a calm. The N.W. breeze begins to be felt towards noon.

Following the shore southwards from the Albanian frontier, richly wooded mountains rise steeply above the coast, and opposite Corfu there are a number of anchorages, few of which are used, as yachts usually prefer the attractions of Corfu. The two most northerly bays are Ftélia and Paganía.

Ftélia, being so near the Albanian frontier, should be approached very carefully; pilotage information is lacking. It would be prudent to consult the Harbour Master, Corfu, if contemplating a visit.

Paganiá is an almost deserted bay with a few farmhouses.

> **Approach.** Beware of treacherous above-water rocks in front of dwellings. (They are *not* an islet with a ruin as stated in *Sailing Directions*.) Depths generally 4–5 fathoms; anchor in 4 fathoms, soft mud, poor holding, mountain squalls.

Igoumenítsa. Chart 723. A small port under the Pindus range lined by a sandy shore off a plain of olive groves. The town has become important as a terminal for the Italy–Greece car-ferry service. A Port of Entry without interest.

> **Approach.** Chart 206. This broad bay has a narrow channel marked by three pairs of buoys near the outflow of the river. Here the current occasionally flows swiftly.

> **Berth.** A broad quay, for mooring the car-ferry and other steamers, has sufficient space for a yacht to berth on the shoreward side where it is well sheltered, except from the N.W. breeze, but there is sometimes a great demand for berthing space.

> **Facilities.** In the village fresh provisions and fuel may be bought; there are three or four small hotels and restaurants. A daily bus service reaches Athens in 8 hrs. The large car-ferry takes 10 hrs to Brindisi, and there is also another car-ferry to Corfu running several times daily.

The port lies in a pleasant setting, but has no particular interest other than the scenery. One can drive by taxi or bus to Ioánina, an ancient town on the lush shores of an elevated lake. There is a bus connection with Préveza; also a short excursion to be made to the ancient site of Dodóni. N.W. of Igoumenítsa the anchorage of Váltou has been recommended.

Liyiá. Chart 723. A deserted bay three miles W. and N. from the entrance to Igoumenítsa. Though the surroundings are agreeable the place is without interest.

> **Approach.** Proceed northward from Prasoúdhi islet, then anchor about one mile eastward near the northern point of the peninsula. Excellent shelter.

On the east side of Corfu south channel are the uninhabited islets of **Sívota** and **Áyios Nikólaos**; tall and wooded they stand out against the mainland.

The outer islet Sívota is separated from Áyios Nikólaos by a channel affording only 3-ft depth at its southern end, and Áyios Nikólaos has a bar with only 4–5 ft separating it from the mainland. High on the N.W. of Sivota is a 20-mile light (Gp.Fl.3).

> **Anchorages.** There are none on the two islets, but on the mainland there is a choice of three pleasant places to stay for the night.
>
> (a) Moúrtos, the northern bay with a few small houses lining the waterfront, has a pier (4½ ft depth) projecting from the N.E. shore off which a few medium-sized yachts can berth. The afternoon breeze from N.W. blows into the bay but causes little disturbance. Corfu ferry calls in summer.
>
> (b) The close-by bay is separated from Moúrtos by a hill with olive trees and a few ruined houses. Anchor inside the mouth in convenient depths and fair shelter. No signs of life.
>
> (c) South Bay, usually approached from south (except by small yachts) because of the shallow channel bar, affords convenient depths of 2–3 fathoms on a sandy bottom. A road crossed by a causeway lies at the head of the bay.

> **Facilities.** The only habitation is at Moúrtos where sometimes bread and fruit may be bought.

From seaward there is no sign of the Customs House or village referred to in *Sailing Directions.*

Known as the Swine Islands in antiquity, these two islands supported a mainland village where Moúrtos now stands – the 'continental Sívota' of Thucydides, where the Corinthians once erected a memorial, no longer to be seen, to commemorate a sea battle.

Only 100 years ago travellers reported the presence of deer and wild boar; and at the beginning of this century these islands and the other places on the coast already referred to, were well known to shooting parties from the large yachts that came here in early spring and October; the abundance of game – quail, snipe, woodcock, partridge and duck – continued to attract shooting parties until recent years.

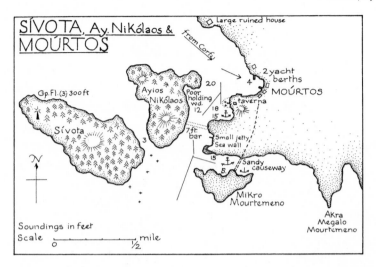

The steep mountainous coast trends to S.E. for 12 miles until reaching Párga.

> *On Suli's rock and Parga's shore,*
> *Exists the remnant of a line,*
> *Such as the Doric mothers bore.*
> BYRON, *Don Juan*

Párga. A delightful village standing on the slopes overlooking two pleasantly sheltered bays (see Plate 2), becoming a tourist resort since 1980.

Approach. Plan on Chart 723. The prominent objects mentioned in *Sailing Directions* are easy to discern. The pier is in constant use all day.

Anchorage. Though a few yachts prefer the more eastern of the two bays on account of easy access to the town, it is far more comfortable during normal fine weather conditions to anchor in the sandy western bay. By anchoring to seaward of the ancient mole one avoids the discomfort of the swell caused by the day breeze and enjoys bathing from the yacht. There is also this alternative:

The ancient mole has been extended for a distance of 200 yds in a northerly direction; it is mostly made of rough stone, some of which protrudes under water. A short pier has been built from the opposite shore beneath the Club Méditerranée. The area thus enclosed forms a small harbour, with 10-ft depths in the middle, making it possible for a few medium-size yachts to berth inside. Holding near the molehead is poor.

Officials. Harbour Master and Customs.

Facilities. Near the waterfront are shops well stocked with fresh provisions. There are restaurants, tavernas and two modern hotels. Fuel at the pierhead. Ice can be bought. Bus communications with Levkás and Igoumenítsa.

17

The ruined Venetian castle dominates the village whose inhabitants, together with those of two neighbouring hamlets, number about 2,000. They are mainly engaged in the cultivation of olives. The village with its winding streets, old white houses and stairways is charming and quite unspoilt. A summer camp for tourists has been built on the slope near the convent on the high ground of the western bay. East of Párga is an open bay with modern hotels.

Áyios Ioánnis. Chart 723 (plan). Lies in a beautiful mountainous setting and is suitable as a summer yacht anchorage, provided the wind keeps north of west. Anchor on the west side in Skulíki Cove. The bottom (mud) shelves steeply and a warp ashore may be necessary.

There are no habitations, but a road with bus communication passes above leading to Párga.

Fanári Bay, open to winds between S. and W.; apart from a discomforting swell after the day-breeze, it is sheltered from other quarters. It lies by a flood-plain formed by two rivers; its position can sometimes be located at a distance by the ruins of a castle on the mountains $2\frac{1}{2}$ miles eastward of the entrance. The bay is constantly silting.

> **Anchorage.** Chart 723. Proceed towards the north corner, according to draught, and although there is much less water than charted, there is sufficient depth for small vessels to swing to an anchor.

There is a good bathing beach in the S.E. corner of the bay near the mouth of the river Ákheron, but the sea is cold and discoloured by river water. This is undoubtedly due to the same spring referred to by Pausanias and was also remarked upon by the captain of one of Nelson's frigates.

A number of fishermen's houses have recently sprung up round the shore.

Proceeding S.E. one follows the green mountainous shores, often well-cultivated and with occasional beaches, until reaching

Cape Kastrosikiá, 12 miles southward, which provides an indifferent anchorage in 3 fathoms. Sheltered by some reefs from the west winds, it is, however, very rockbound, and is used only by a few small fishing craft which, during bad weather, haul out on the beach.

> *Remember the moment when Preveza fell*
> *The shrieks of the conquer'd, the conquerors' yell;*
> BYRON, *Childe Harold's Pilgrimage*

Préveza. A little commercial port now becoming touristy.

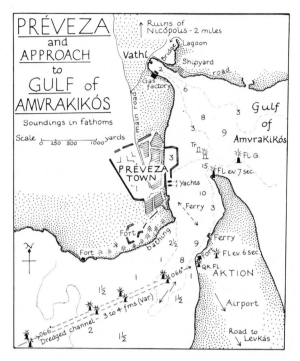

Approach. Chart 1609. This is interesting, and there should be no difficulty until nearing the end of the dredged channel when the tidal stream sets at about 40 degrees to the ship's course. The channel, claimed to be dredged to 29 ft, has sometimes silted in places to as little as 16 ft. It is seldom much more than 20 ft in places, depending upon previous weather conditions.

Berth. The most convenient place to berth near the town is at the northern end of the quay by the extremity of the harbour mole. Here the tide is slight and one can haul in one's stern to the quay in depths of $2\frac{1}{2}$ fathoms, but sometimes more convenient alongside.

Officials. A Port of Entry. Customs, Port Authority and Immigration.

Facilities. The water hydrant at the end of the quay has been removed. Market and provision shops are of good standard. There are three mediocre hotels, a new bank, and several tavernas. One can usually buy good fish which is caught in abundance inside the gulf. The meat, too, is usually good. Gas cylinders of all types can be filled while you wait at a gas factory on the road to Nicópolis about $1\frac{1}{2}$ miles out of town and beside Port Vathí. Ice can be bought at a fishmonger in the street S. of the market place.

A remote anchorage north of the town can be found at **Vathí.** This cove is flanked by a road on the E. side and a gas filling station opposite, but is quiet at night and well sheltered. It is on the fringe of a military area.

The quays along the waterfront have recently been improved and the town of

19

12,000 people has now acquired a modern look after many years of Turkish influence.

The hinterland is flat and extensively planted with olives. Much of the fish from the Gulf of Amvrakikós is brought to Préveza and then carried by lorry to Pátras and Athens.

Three miles to the northward are the extensive ruins of Nicópolis, built by Octavian (later styled Caesar Augustus) to commemorate his victory in 31 B.C. when he defeated Antony in the Battle of Actium.

History. The battle was the outcome of the Civil War which following the assassination of Julius Caesar in 44 B.C. had been resumed. The two contestants were Octavian, controlling the western part of the empire, and Antony the east. Each had large armies which together with the rival fleets finally came within striking distance of one another in the early spring of 31 B.C.

Octavian's fleet, mainly Liburnian galleys, had based themselves at Mítikas (where the blocks of the harbour mole can still be seen) and Antony's fleet, largely triremes, used the well-sheltered anchorages at the entrance to the Gulf of Amvrakikós close to Actium. Here the rival fleets, supported by their encamped armies, remained most of the summer months, Antony's men being far from content with this passive role.

According to Plutarch, Antony felt by the end of August that his chances of victory were waning and when he finally decided to put to sea he realized that morale was low. He first burnt his unmanned warships, embarked his treasury in merchant vessels, put aboard the triremes' sails – an unusual practice before battle – and embarked a large number of soldiers. One morning early in September the fleet put to sea in a flat calm and soon sighted the galleys of Octavian lying in wait at the mouth of the estuary. The two fleets remained in sight quite inactive until about midday when the prevailing wind began to set in freshly from north-west. Now more than 400 of Octavian's galleys plunged in to attack the 200 triremes of Antony which they soon began to overpower.

In mid-afternoon during the heat of the action a vessel was seen to hoist a purple sail and passing through the fighting was soon heading to pass north of Levkás. This was Cleopatra bound for Egypt closely followed by Antony (as Shakespeare wrote 'like a doting mallard') abandoning his men to continue the losing battle. They soon fared even worse due to the weather, for according to Plutarch, many triremes were sunk by heavy seas in the late afternoon.

A year later Antony and Cleopatra had committed suicide, and Octavian had restored the Roman Empire and celebrated his victory by building Nicópolis. Nicópolis grew to become a fine city, being enriched during Justinian's days with large public buildings. It continued as a centre of Christianity into Byzantine times, and flourished until the end of the 9th century when, after invasion by Slavonic tribes from Bulgaria, its destruction was completed by a severe earthquake. The theatre, city walls and a couple of churches still stand, and even though the city has largely subsided beneath the waters of the gulf a visit to the ruins is still worth while.

Sixteen centuries later the strategic importance of Préveza was realized by Suleiman's great pirate-admiral Barbarossa, who established a Turkish naval base there in 1538. The Venetian possessions in the Ionian Islands were protected by a modern fleet of galleons and galleys based on Corfu. When these vessels passed down the coast, protecting Venetian merchant ships trading to Zante, Ithaca, Santa Maura, etc., the Turkish galleys at Préveza would pounce upon them whenever they chose. This they did with such crippling effect that the Venetian forces were withdrawn and Barbarossa soon earned himself the title 'King of the Sea'. It was not until some thirty years later, long after Barbarossa was dead, that the Christian fleet finally defeated the Turks at the battle of Lepanto. (See p. 51.)

The Gulf of Amvrakikós (Artá) extends for nearly 20 miles inland, and although it has a number of anchorages on both sides it is of limited interest to the average yacht. The northern shores, especially, are low and swampy, and until recent years malaria was prevalent. Almost more alarming is the warning in *Sailing Directions* that 'these marshes are infested by snakes and reptiles, some of which are venomous'. Despite these objections, English shooting parties coming here early in the century used to make their headquarters at Salaóra, and came away with plentiful bags of woodcock, snipe and duck.

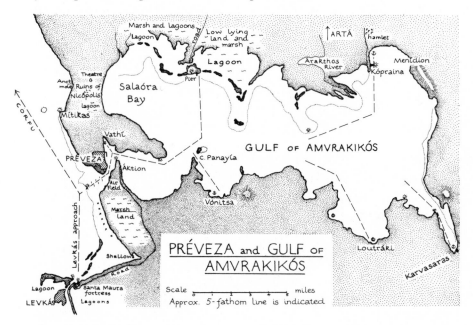

Vónitsa, lying on the southern shore, is a dull village in a pleasant setting beneath a large Venetian fort; it has a reasonably sheltered anchorage with quays off the village.

Anchorage. Chart 1609 shows the anchorage. The short pier with a lighthouse (Lt.Fl.R) has depths of 10 ft at its extremity. Although a few boulders extend under water the end of the pier can be useful for hauling in a small yacht's stern. Alternatively anchor one cable off. The day-breeze normally stirs up only a short sea of no consequence at the anchorage.

21

Officials. Harbour Master and Customs.

Facilities. Meagre supplies of fresh fruit, etc. at the shops. One or two poor tavernas. A freshwater tap 30 yds from the quay.

Vónitsa is dominated by an uninteresting, but extensive, Venetian castle and has behind it a cultivated plain. The completion of the new motor road may well improve its present low standard.

Kópraina Bay, lying in the N.E. corner of the gulf, is near the mouth of Arakthós River which, having flowed from the ancient town of Artá, now enters the sea. Shallow-draught fishing craft use this river which is claimed to be navigable for 4 miles, and even as far as Artá. Artá, which is of historical importance, is visited sometimes today on account of its medieval bridge and Byzantine churches, but the present village of 10,000 people has no attraction.

Both Árakthos River and a smaller stream enter the gulf side by side and have built up extensive sandbanks to seaward where fishing craft are often busy and many species of wild birds can be seen. The area requires careful exploration.

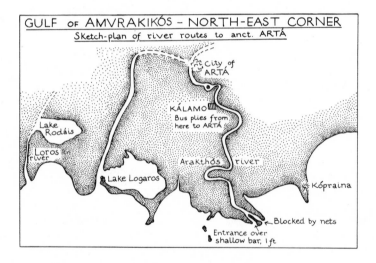

Directions. Enter Árakthos River by the southern entrance (1 ft on bar). The mouth of the northern stream is blocked by nets.

After the junction of the two river-mouths the depths in mid-stream are about 3–6 ft as far as the islet above Kalámia.

At Kalámia village there is a good bus service to Artá.

Alternatively, it is claimed that a more attractive venture is to enter the river Loúros and proceed by this river to Artá.

Anchorage. The easternmost sandspit, which is now overgrown with bush, extends southwards for a mile forming the western arm of Kópraina Bay. About 300 yds north of its extremity is a broad white tower (Lt.Fl.W.R.). When approaching, this should be kept fine on the port bow and the low-lying spit followed at a distance of a cable until arriving in the N.W. corner of the bay where there is anchorage in 5 fathoms, mud bottom, open to the south.

The place is flat and deserted; remains of an old harbour, quay and warehouses are the only shore objects; but there are a number of small fishing boats and a variety of wild birds. This corner of the gulf would be of interest only to those who enjoy exploring rivers by dinghy and bird-watching. There are pelicans, heron, pygmy cormorants, duck and a variety of cranes and waders.

On the eastern shore of the bay is the modern little resort of Menídi skirted by the new motor road which runs round the head of the gulf. Recently a small harbour has been built affording shelter from the westerly winds.

Karvasará Bay, lying in the S.E. corner of the gulf, has a loading quay, visited by small steamers, at the foot of Amfilohía village. At the head of the bay is a narrow spit with 10-ft depths, off which a yacht may anchor. *Sailing Directions* gives warning that near the end of this spit, during the last century, a small volcano erupted on two occasions, killing most of the fish in the gulf and covering the water with sulphur as far as Préveza.

Near Amfilohía village are remains of an ancient city with two walls ascending from the beach towards the hill on which are foundations of numerous square projecting towers.

Loutráki is a bay with a primitive hamlet. One can anchor conveniently off a sandspit, but the place has no particular interest.

Salaóra Bay is boarded by low sandy shores enclosing lagoons behind. Eastward of the light is a disused short stone pier with $2\frac{1}{2}$-fathom depths at its extremity; but other than a road there is nothing else.

ISLAND OF LEVKÁS
AND NEARBY ISLETS
  The Canal
  Port Levkás
  Port Dhrepáno
  Vathi Valí (mainland shore)
  Pálairos
  Spárti and Madhourí Islands
  Port Vlikhó Anchorages
    Nidrí hamlet
    'Tranquil Bay'
    Port Vlikhó
  Skorpió Island
  Sappho's Leap ⎤ see after islets
  Sívota Bay   ⎬ of Arkoúdi and
  Vasilikí Bay ⎦ Atokós

ISLAND OF MEGANISI
  Port Athéni
  Ambeláki Bay
  Port Vathí
  Port Spília

KÁLAMOS ISLAND
  Kálamos Village
  Port Leone

KÁSTOS ISLAND
  Port Kastós

ISLETS OF ARKÚDI
AND ÁTOKOS

ISLAND OF ITHACA (ITHÁKI)
  Port Vathí
  Dhexiá Bay
  Kióni
  Fríkes
  Pólis

Pis'Aetoú
Áyios Andréas
Péra Pigádhi
Sarakíniko Cove

ISLAND OF CEPHALONIA
  (KEFALLINÍA)
  Argostóli
  Lixoúrion
  Ássos
  Fiskárdho Bay
  Kakogito Bay
  Áyia Evfímia
  Sámi
  Póros
  Kateliós

ADJACENT MAINLAND COAST
WITH OFFLYING ISLETS
  Zaverdá
  Marathía Bay ⎤
  Astakós   ⎬ Dragamésti Bay
  Pandelémona ⎦
  Pogoniá
  Plateáli (Platea)
  Kómaros Bay
  Pláka
  Pétala
  Dragunára Islands
  Echinádes Islands
  Oxiá Island
  Skrófa

ISLAND OF ZANTE (ZÁKINTHOS)
  Port Zante
  Port Kerí
  Port Vrómi

PART II: The Islands of Levkás, Ithaca, Cephalonia, Zante and the Adjacent Mainland Coast and Offlying Islands

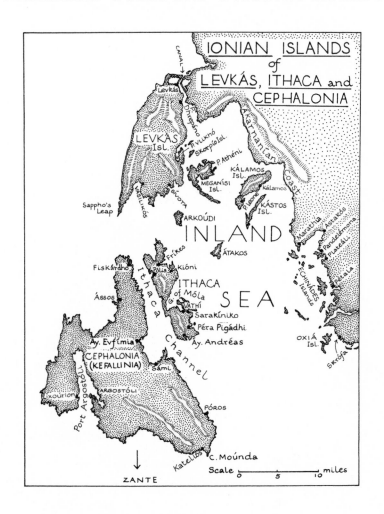

PART II: THE ISLANDS OF LEVKÁS, ITHACA, CEPHALONIA, ZANTE AND THE ADJACENT MAINLAND COAST AND OFFLYING ISLANDS

The Island of Levkás and nearby Islets

The Santa Maura of the Venetians, Levkás is only an island by virtue of the canal cut through the swamps which separate it from the Akarnanían coast. It is mountainous with a central ridge rising to 3,700 ft running from N.E. to S.W. The north and west coasts are bare and uninviting, but opposite the mainland the valleys open out towards the shore, the country is green and there are attractive villages with orange and olive groves. Although the main port has little attraction there are some delightful wooded inlets on the S.E. of the island as well as the circular, and almost enclosed, bay of Port Vlikhó. Edward Lear paid a number of visits to the island where he painted many attractive landscapes. The extensive oak forests to be seen inland in his day have largely disappeared, and so have the deer. In the villages few of the women still wear traditional dress or devote any time to weaving. Population is 24,600 today.

The Canal

Approach. Two plans on Chart 1609 show the canal approaches; they can be negotiated easily by day and, with care, by night.

(a) If coming from the north one can see the Venetian fortress of Santa Maura standing out over the flat country some miles off, but it has now been largely obscured by a large white factory with arched windows, lying close N.N.W. of the fort, which is visible a great distance to seaward. Only as one draws appreciably closer does the extremity of the northern entrance spit become clear. However, when a yacht is sailing towards this dead lee-shore – perhaps for the first time – one may become anxious at the delay in sighting the actual entrance, especially when being driven along by a Force 6 afternoon breeze. You cannot see the fortress of Santa Maura because the land all appears as one and the light tower on the extremity of the northern spit cannot be discerned.

Coming from the direction of Paxí a S.E. course leads one towards C. Tekkés (9 cables E.N.E. of Fort Santa Maura) which may be seen. When about one mile off turn south and head for the entrance leaving the light tower one cable off. A shoal has recently grown up south of the tower and one should continue southward until reaching a position 10 yds N. of a line of can buoys. (A dangerous rock, covered 3 ft, lies close south of the easternmost buoy.) Then turn westward towards the canal. (See plan.) The small cable-ferry, which plies frequently, shows by day two cones over a sphere, and by night a green, a white and a red light displayed vertically when the wire is up; it is usually lowered in response to a fog-horn signal.

(b) If coming from the south the large fort of St George makes a distant landmark. Three pairs of buoys mark the entrance, and there are well-placed perches marking the channel all the way to the port.

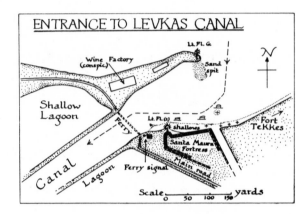

The canal is used by small steamers and caïques and is claimed to have a minimum depth of 17 ft. A pilot is neither compulsory nor necessary.

The canal and the long northern breakwater were built by the Anglo–Ionian Government in the middle of the last century. There had, however, been canals before; the early Corinthians dug one which subsequently silted, only to be re-dug by the Romans which in turn must have filled in during the Middle Ages.

The Port is merely a well-sheltered quay at the elbow of the canal, beside a growing village, almost become a town; much visited by yachts.

Berth. A yacht requiring fuel or water should berth as indicated in the plan, i.e. off the Yacht Station in 14-ft depths. The bottom is mud, good holding, and there is good shelter. The place is cooled by a seldom failing sea-breeze. There is considerable traffic at this quay, both yachts and caïques. If wishing to stay for more than a few hours, a yacht would probably be requested to berth alongside the quay, but with summer congestion they berth bows-to.

Officials. Harbour Master and Customs.

Facilities. Fuel and water at 'Garden Quay'; there are plenty of provision shops. Ice can be bought at a small factory, 10 min walk. Restaurants and tavernas are near by, and a small modern hotel has been built by the main square. Levkás produces a very good light Retsína wine.

4 Island of Cephalonia: Fiskárdho Bay, an attractive little anchorage

5 Island of Cephalonia: Ayía Evfímia, with yachts berthed off the quay

6 Levkás: looking southward showing the entrance to Port Vlikhó, on right

The village of 8,000 people has recovered from devastation of the last earthquake, and its economy is now fully restored. The church of Pantócrator, built by Morosini to commemorate the Venetian conquest of 1684, follows the classical Venetian style. There are three other churches built later, including the small St Demetrius with some holy paintings in oils. A small museum (with icons from damaged churches) and the library are close to the main square.

Anchorages close south of the Levkás Canal

See plan on next page

Winds. In the narrower channels a few miles south and east of the Levkás Canal the winds in summer are variable and often there are calms. Further south towards Ithaca, Cephalonia and Zante the day-breeze springs up towards midday and in the afternoon freshens to Force 3 or 4, dying away towards sunset. This weather may be expected on 80 per cent of the days. The appearance of cumulonimbus clouds accompanied by a marked fall in the barometer is sure indication of strong winds from the N.W. quadrant.

Port Dhrepáno, at the southern entrance to the canal, is no longer a port. The protecting mole lies submerged and unmarked, as shown on Chart 1609, i.e. it runs almost east and west between the projecting point of land and the port-hand entrance buoy – west of Vólios Island; its eastern extremity is about 20 yds S.W. of the buoy. The chart shows two temporary achorages: a shallow one north of the mole and a deeper one south of it. Both are good holding, but exposed completely to the southern quadrant, a direction to be feared only in event of thunderstorms or passing depressions. A primitive hamlet lines the shore, and a new short mole, one cable southwards, affords shelter to caïques which are frequent callers. Salt is shipped away from extensive salt pans on the lagoons.

There is no purpose in anchoring at Dhrepáno, and most yachts coming southward call at either Meganísi Island (see page 33) or at Port Vlikhó. The green wooded shores should be followed, where a new motor road has now been built to link Port Vlikhó with Port Levkás.

By crossing to the mainland shore one has the choice of two small anchorages:

Vathi Valí, which lies on the eastern, mainland shore. A long deserted inlet, open only through a narrow arc to the S.W., it provides suitable anchorage among foothills which rise reasonably gently and are covered with scrub.

Approach. Chart 1609. The 9-ft Miaoúli Reef lies 4 cables S.W. of the entrance; Cape Kefáli light and Áy. Nikólaos Islet (69 ft high) are useful marks.

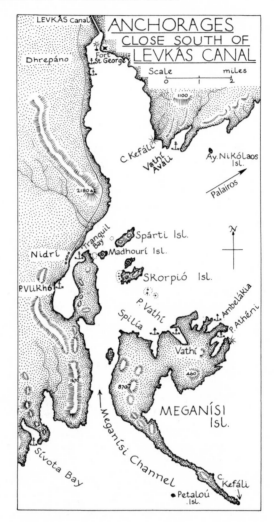

Anchorage. Anchor either towards the head of the inlet in 3–4 fathoms with room to swing, or off the mouth of a gully on the west side.

Pálairos (Zavérdha), a small, recently built fishing harbour, lies on the E. side of Zavérdha Bay (Chart 203).

Approach from the north following the shores of the bay. 14-ft depth near western extremity of mole (Lt.Fl.G). Beware of shallow patch close inside molehead.

Berth near S.W. corner of harbour in depths of 2 fathoms, or among fishing craft.

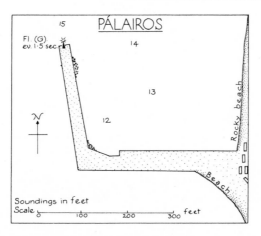

Facilities. Provisions and services in the village, but no water on the quay. Bus to Athens. The village is the centre of a cultivated area.

Continuing southwards towards Port Vlikhó one passes two small islands. The first is **Spárti**, uninhabited and without interest except for a pleasant open anchorage in a small cove on the north side. The second, much smaller, named **Madhourí** (or **Moúdra**), is thickly wooded, and on its western side standing out boldly against the pine trees, above the water's edge is a handsome baroque house. For many years it has belonged to the Valaorítis family, who have frequently played a prominent part among the intelligentsia of Greece. (See Plate 9.)

Port Vlikhó is an entirely enclosed spacious bay surrounded by mountainous slopes; part of it is shown in Plate 6.

Anchorages (see plan overleaf)

Chart 1620. On the western side of the entrance channel is **Nidrí**, a market garden and holiday village, which is the base for a dinghy sailing school and a main port of call for yacht flotillas. It has a long quay at which the Pátras ferry calls and to which a dozen or more yachts may secure temporarily. There are several well-stocked shops and tavernas and a tourist office at which money and travellers' cheques may be exchanged. There is a water tap on the quay.

'Tranquil Bay' lies across the narrows on the eastern side of the entrance channel; unnamed on the chart, it was given this title by Germain Gerard, a keen French yachtsman, and is a delightful anchorage where usually one may lie in relatively peaceful surroundings away from the noise of Nidrí. The shore is green; there are no dwellings but there may be a dozen charter yachts at anchor.

Port Vlikhó. There are a number of suitable anchorages all round the bay, including the N.W.

31

corner where there is a small shipyard, the S.W. corner off the village of Vlikhó, or off the hamlet on the eastern shore. Shopping is better at Nidrí than at Vlikhó. A charter fleet of small yachts has recently been based here.

Near the eastern shore of the bay, a small museum occupies the villa built by the distinguished German archaeologist, Dörpfeldt; early in the 20th century he discovered Mycenaean remains on the island which led him to believe that here and not Ithaca was the home of Ulysses. (*See also* pages 40 and 42.)

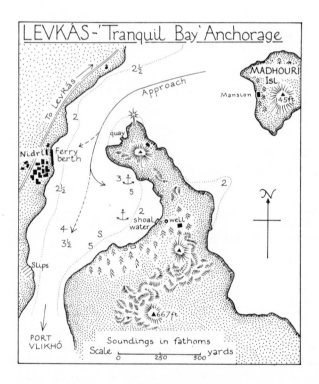

Lying 1½ miles S.E. of the entrance to Port Vlikhó is **Skorpío Island.** It was owned by the late Mr Aristotle Onassis and seen from seaward appears as a beautiful parkland estate. A road now encircles the island and one can see the small houses for the employees, generating plants and storehouses. One should beware of a dangerous rocky patch almost submerged which lies one cable west of Skorpió Island; Chart 1620 also shows the rocky shoal between Skorpió Island and the northern shore of Meganísi Island.

OTHER ISLANDS IN THIS AREA

Island of Meganísi

Chart 1620. This island is indented on the north side with some suitable inlets, each forming a pleasant night-anchorage for a yacht; see plan opposite.

Port Athéni. A long attractive inlet with almost all-round shelter. For solitude, anchor near the head of the northern cove. For better shelter, but unfortunately marred by a sunken wreck, anchor near the head of the longer southern cove, where there are a few open fishing boats and a rough track leading to a hamlet with shops and a good baker. (Avoid the reef which extends from the point between the two coves.)

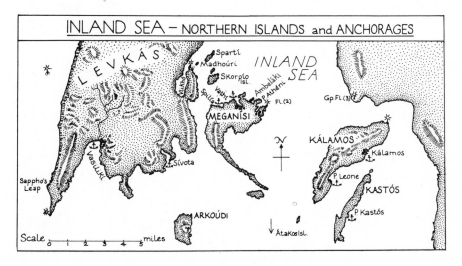

Ambeláki Bay has a number of coves in which a yacht can anchor on a sandy bottom in appropriate depths with room to swing, but it is a favourite location for flotilla barbecue parties in summer and some of these are noisy and last until the small hours. The next bay, not named on the chart but immediately east of Makriá Point, also contains several pleasant and sheltered coves and is more likely to offer peace and solitude.

Port Vathí consists of a little hamlet with its houses lining the waterfront of a very small port, lying at the head of the inlet. Open to N.W. The small houses show clearly in the distance. There are 2-fathom depths inside the extremity of the mole which should be given a wide berth. Ferry to Nidrí. A small cove to N.E. marked 'tannery' on the chart is a useful anchorage – 4 fathoms.

Port Spília, an inlet lying W. of Vathí, is the ferry station for the village of Spartokóri standing on the hill above the quays. The sea-bed falls away steeply off the quay (10-ft depths) and it would be difficult to berth stern-to; shelter with a wind E. of N.E. is poor. The ferry runs to Nidrí. The inlet is less interesting than those already described. (*See also* Spartokóri.)

East of Meganísi are the two uninteresting islands of Kálamos and Kastós each of which has anchorage suitable for a yacht:

Kálamos Island (see plan on page 33) is relatively large and tall with a farming population who mostly live in the hamlet beside the small harbour on the S.E. coast. It has two possible anchorages:

> **Village anchorage.** Chart 3496. A mole 150 yds long extends in a northerly direction, curving towards N.N.E. near its extremity. It protects the harbour from normal summer winds, but it is entirely open to N.E. Depths close to the mole being too shallow and irregular to permit a yacht to moor close off, anchorage in the middle, open to traffic, has 3-fathom depths on sand and short weed. In 1981 the mole was lengthened to 200 yds but the light (Fl.R) was still in its original position. A freshwater tap is at the root of the mole; there is a taverna, and bread and vegetables can be bought in the village.

> **Port Leóne,** though rather deep is sometimes more comfortable than the main port, especially in strong N. winds when gusts come off the mountains. The small hamlet appears abandoned.

Kastós Island (Chart 3496) is narrow and tall, with occasional patches of cultivation. The small hamlet on the east coast stands above a cove which can be distinguished by a mill on the ridge above.

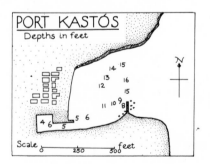

PORT KASTÓS
Depths in feet

> **Anchorage.** The mole on the south side of the cove has about 8-ft depths along the outer half of its inner side, shoaling to rocks at its root; it provides shelter for a small yacht in all but sirocco winds when waves are reflected from the cliffs on the north side of the cove. A narrow channel

with at least a depth of 5 ft leads to a boat harbour with depths of 4–6 ft which provides complete shelter, but only for the smallest yachts. A taverna close by is open in summer.

The population of Kastós Islet is about 100, and only the most rudimentary provisions are available. A weekly ferry runs to Astakós on the mainland.

Southward of these island groups are the two small but very prominent tall islets of Arkoúdi and Átokos.

Arkoúdi (Arkudi) Islet (Chart 203) is uninhabited and without an anchorage.

Átokos Islet (Chart 3496) is high and steep-to; temporary anchorage can be obtained in the open sandy bay on the east side of the islet, but it is liable to strong gusts from the tall hills above.

Returning to the hilly shores of Levkás one comes to two interesting ports and the dramatic white cliff where the famous 6th-century B.C. poet is said to have ended her life.

> *The very spot where Sappho sung*
> *Her swan-like music, ere she sprung*
> *(Still holding in that fearful leap,*
> *By her lov'd Lyre) into the deep.*
> THOMAS MOORE, *Evenings in Greece*

Sappho's Leap lies on the open west coast of Levkás, two miles north of Cape Dhoukáton, the island's most southerly point. The place is marked on Chart 203. There is no anchorage.

From the top of this perpendicular white cliff (200 ft above the sea) and sloping precipitously into the landward side is the 'ancient mount' beneath whose shadow Childe Harold 'saw the evening star above Leucadia's far projecting rock of woe'.

Apart from the well-known legend of Sappho, the leap was used, according to Strabo, for other purposes: on the Festival of Apollo it was the custom to cast down criminals from this headland into the sea, but to break their fall birds were attached to them. If a criminal reached the sea uninjured, boats were used to recover him.

On the S.E. coast are two anchorages well worth a visit:

Vasilikí Bay (Chart 720), though somewhat open, has three moles behind one of which a small yacht may berth off a small hamlet. (See plan overleaf.)

Approach. The plan on Admiralty chart is misleading, for the outer and inner moles are destroyed and largely under water; it could be dangerous at night. The second mole with a light at its extremity is becoming unusable owing to the silting. Its north side can now be used only by shallow-draught yachts and depths of barely 8 ft have recently been reported in the vicinity. The day-breeze causes gusts to sweep down the hillside from the N.W. broadside-on to yachts berthed at the quay. Deeper-draught yachts should anchor off; but during the afternoon, owing to the strong gusts, they may find boat-work difficult. In 1981 dredging was reported.

Facilities. Water and fuel are available at the quay. The hamlet has a few small houses built of timbered frames with brick or stone typical of Levkás. There are three tavernas and a number of small shops where supplies may be obtained.

Sívota Bay lies at the head of a narrow wooded inlet with natural all-round shelter in most attractive surroundings. Three tavernas, a number of farmsteads and a few new houses line the shore and a hamlet approached by a rough road is a mile and a half inland. The anchorage has good holding in 3–6 fathoms, but may be crowded during yacht flotilla visits. Water can be obtained from the tavernas.

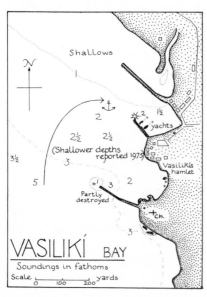

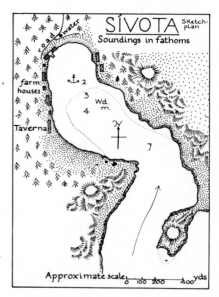

Island of Ithaca (Itháki)

When the brightest of all the stars came up,
the star which often ushers in the tender
light of Dawn, the ship's voyage was done
and she drew near to Ithaca.

Homer, *Odyssey*

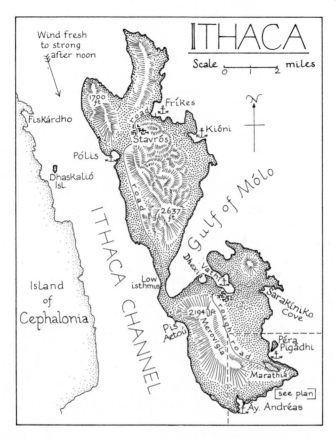

The two parts of this mountainous island are joined by a low-lying isthmus. A number of indentations provide sheltered and interesting anchorages for a yacht.

Port Vathí, the capital of the island, is a delightful little port in a charming mountainous setting. (See Plate 8.)

Approach. Chart 1620. There is no difficulty, day or night. A war memorial has taken the place of the fort marked by the chart on Hill 254. A yacht must pass north and east of the islet with the small white chapel, formerly a prison.

Berth

(a) Most yachts berth outside or inside the small inner basin the entrance to which is marked by yacht station colours. There are depths of 10–12 ft inside.

(b) It is also possible to use the former steamer quay. Ferry steamers now berth further north.

(c) In the event of a strong afternoon wind, it is pleasant to anchor for bathing under the lee of a

37

hill 5½ cables to the N.W.; here the bottom rises steeply 50 yds off shore and the holding is uncertain.

Officials. Harbour Master and Customs, but no Immigration.

Facilities. There is a water hydrant on the mole at the yacht station but the purity of the water has sometimes been questioned; the Shell office on the waterfront can arrange for good water to be brought in a tricycle tanker; it will also arrange for fuel to be supplied at the short but shallow jetty on the N.E. shore. Shops, restaurants, a small hotel and a bank are close at hand; the black wine of Ithaca is famous but in short supply. There is no ice. The Piraeus–Corfu and the Pátras–Cephalonia ferries call almost daily in summer.

After the serious earthquake of 1953 the port and buildings along the seafront were rebuilt and limited trade has been resumed with a small export of olives. Around the town are some terraces of vineyards and olives, but most of the countryside is barren.

A pleasant walk following the quay along the western side of the bay brings one to a small public garden with a plaque commemorating Byron's visit to the island in 1823. It is said that he used to row out to the islet with the chapel for his morning swim.

A steep road takes one up the slopes of Merovígla, above the town, to Perachóra, the site of the old Graeco-Roman settlement. From here the view is magnificent: beneath lie the fiords and Port Vathí, to the west the Ithaca Channel can be seen reaching out to Cephalonia (the home of some of Penelope's many suitors), and to the east are the 'summer isles of Eden lying in the dark purple spheres of sea'.

Dhexiá Bay lies in the Gulf of Mólo, close westward of the entrance to Port Vathí, and is largely protected by its two rocky headlands. Although of no particular interest today, it is commonly identified with Homer's Bay of Phorcys.

Anchorage. Chart 1620. There are depths of 7 fathoms in the middle decreasing gradually to 3 fathoms about 100 yds off the sandy shores. As the gusts usually come from the N.N.W., the best shelter is provided towards the cliff on the west side of the bay.

A description in the *Odyssey* (13: 96–112, Rieu's trans.) runs: 'In that island (Ithaca) is a cove named after Phorcys, "the old man of the sea", with two bold headlands squatting at its mouth so as to protect it from the heavy swell raised by rough weather in the open and allow large ships to ride inside without so much as tying up. . . . At the head of the cove grows a long-leafed olive tree and nearby is a cavern that offers welcome shade and is sacred to the Nymphs whom we call Naiads.' A cave answering this description lies on the hillside at the head of a valley 600 ft up 'away from the road' (13:123); it is still away from the present road.

On the N.E. coast of the island are two very pleasant anchorages.

Kióni. A delightful sheltered bay with a hamlet and summer villas tucked into the hillside. (See Plate 10.)

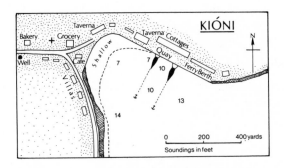

Approach. Plan on Chart 720. The three old windmills on the slope south of the entrance are easily distinguished.

Berth

(a) Stern to the quay on the N.E. side near the head of the creek.

(b) Let go in 5 fathoms at the head of the creek where shelter is good and holding fair. There is barely room for about four yachts to swing, but a warp can be taken to the sea-wall.

(c) Anchorage off the cemetery half-way along the south coast of the bay has also been found fairly satisfactory.

Facilities. A village store and a restaurant are on the quay and a local white wine can sometimes be bought. In summer a ferry plies to Port Vathí, much used by the Athenians who own most of the villas.

Fríkes lies at the head of an attractive inlet with a short mole and a growing hamlet.

Approach. Plan on Chart 720. A solitary windmill on Cape Akrotíri indicates the south side of the approach to the inlet.

Berth. The short mole has 2-fathom depths at its extremity and alongside; a light (Fl.R) is exhibited. Secure stern to the mole and lay out an anchor shorewards with plenty of cable because the holding is uncertain and strong gusts of wind may sweep down from the top of the valley. A slight swell enters the port when the afternoon breeze sets in.

Facilities. A road round the shore leads to a ramp for the car-ferry. Two tavernas and food shops in the port but up the valley at Stavros plentiful provisions may be obtained.

The port is used now and then for the export of agricultural produce grown on the fertile plain on the northern half of the island.

It seems that Fríkes can almost certainly be identified with Homer's 'Reithron below the wooded Neion' (*Odyssey* 1:186). The word Reithron means 'torrent' and it is significant that the longest stream in Ithaca reaches the sea in the Bay of Fríkes. Stavrós, the unsightly modern village of small shops and cafés bordered by clusters of small villas, stands on the top of the ridge separating Fríkes from the deep semicircular bay of Pólis on the west coast.

Pólis lies in the Ithaca Channel between Ithaca and Cephalonia. It is a wide bay open to the south-west.

> **Approach and Anchorage.** Plan on Chart 720. Anchor at the head of the bay, where the bottom rises sharply to 3 fathoms. Land by dinghy at the small boat camber in the N.E. corner.

> **Facilities.** There is nothing close at hand, but at Stavrós on the saddle of the hill, 30-min walk, limited fresh supplies may be bought.

It is generally accepted that this bay was used as the harbour for the ancient town of Pólis which stood on the ridge above. A few scattered Mycenaean 'finds' prove that there was a Bronze Age settlement here, and archaeologists believe that, despite the meagre evidence, Ulysses' palace lay northwards towards the Pilkata ridge, near the well by a stream which still runs today.

On the north side of the bay is the presumed 'Cave of the Nymphs'. Formerly standing close to the sea, its roof collapsed nearly two thousand years ago and there is nothing of interest there today, but during the last century archaeologists recovered Mycenaean pottery and a bronze sword and spear. Some of the finds may be seen in the small museum at Stavrós.

Pis' Aetoú has a plan on Chart 720, but it is of little or no interest to a yacht. It is an open bay with only a ruined house, near to which a yacht could find convenient depth to anchor, but the bottom is hard sand, giving uncertain holding, and it is fouled by several submarine cables from Cephalonia.

Áyios Andréas is a deserted bay in picturesque and mountainous surroundings.

> **Anchorage.** Plan on Chart 720. Let go in 5–7 fathoms off the shingle beach; there is very little room to swing and the holding on weed and boulders is uncertain.

There is no habitation or track running inland. One can land on the stony beach and passing two ruined cottages, each with a well, ascend the very rough torrent-bed, at the sides of which are long-neglected terraces with olives and

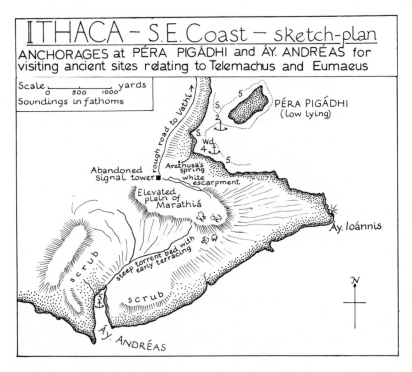

ITHACA – S.E. Coast – sKetch-plan

ANCHORAGES at PÉRA PIGÁDHI and ÁY. ANDRÉAS for
visiting ancient sites relating to Telemachus and Eumaeus

Scale ┐————┌ yards
0   500   1000'
Soundings in fathoms

PÉRA PIGÁDHI
(low lying)

rough road to Vathi

Abandoned
signal tower■

Arethusa's
spring

white
escarpment

Elevated
plain of
Marathiá

Áy. Ioánnis

scrub

steep torrent bed with
early terracing

scrub

Áy. ANDRÉAS

N

wild shrubs. A long climb brings one to the plateau of Marathiá, where it is
thought Eumaeus, the swineherd, had his stables. It is believed that Telemachus,
on his return from Pílos and Sparta, landed in this bay in order to avoid an
ambush laid by the suitors of Penelope. He too must have climbed this valley to
reach Marathiá, which is now a cultivated plain with olive groves.

Péra Pigádhi provides, in calm weather, a pleasant open summer anchorage
behind a low-lying islet.

> **Anchorage.** Plan on Chart 720. Let go in 2–5 fathoms on a sandy bottom on either side of the
> channel according to the wind.

There is no sign of habitation; one may land barely half a mile southward of
the anchorage at the mouth of a steep-to gully lying below a massive white
escarpment. Climbing up the gully with its running water one comes to
Arethusa's spring; it now flows far less abundantly than it did in Homer's day.
Above the great escarpment – called Korax (raven-rock) – where ravens still soar
today, one comes to the plateau of Marathiá. It was probably from here that

41

Ulysses challenged Eumaneus 'to throw him over the great rock if he finds that he is speaking false' (*Odyssey*, XIII: 407).

A yacht may anchor temporarily off the mouth of the gully in order to make a landing; the plateau and escarpment can also be reached either by a very rough road from Port Vathí or by Telemachus' route from Áy. Andréas.

Sarakíniko Cove provides an attractive deserted anchorage with reasonable shelter and good holding.

> **Approach.** Chart 203. The cove lies immediately south of Cape Sarakíniko.

> **Anchorage.** A yacht can anchor at the head of the bay, as convenient; a large yacht will need to anchor in 6 fathoms and run out a warp to an olive tree by the shore. The bay is open only to the S.E. normally a safe direction in summer.

One may land at the head of the bay, and climbing up a steep bank enjoy a delightful view across to Port Vathí, which can be reached by road; it is little more than a mile distant.

> **History.** Homer's observations on the island and the details of his story of Ulysses, King of Ithaca, appear to be borne out by today's evidence. Nevertheless in 1927, Professor Dörpfeldt, who had discovered Mycenaean remains on Levkás, propounded the theory that during the Middle Ages, when these islands were evacuated by the inhabitants, they lost their original identity, and that the Ithaca of Homer is the Levkás of today. There are, however, few people who uphold his belief, and the sites of antiquity to be visited by sea convince one that the Ithaca of Homer is the same Ithaca today.

> > *In Ithaca there are no wide courses, nor meadowland*
> > *at all. It is a pasture land of goats, and more pleasant*
> > *in my sight than one that pastureth horses . . .*
> > > Homer, *Odyssey*

Island of Cephalonia (Kefallinía)

This is the largest and most mountainous of the seven islands and, disposed over the four main villages, has a population of 137,000. Both Homer and Strabo refer to it as rugged and mountainous; it certainly lacks the soft beauty of Corfu. The lofty ridge which crosses the island from N.W. to S.E. rises to a largely bare summit called the Black Mountain (5,308 ft); it is easy to identify at a great distance to seaward. Pinewoods cover some of the lower slopes; on the foothills are the vineyards which grow the currants for export, and there are some cornfields; but the island generally lacks water.

The main port is Argostóli and, although a Port of Entry, it is not the most convenient one for a sailing yacht on account of tall mountains surrounding it.

Argostóli lies in the sheltered arm of a large natural harbour. It is the capital and largest place of the island, with about 7,000 inhabitants.

> **Berth.** Chart 1557. Either lay out an anchor and berth stern-to the quay, or secure alongside southward of the new quay which affords good shelter, even in N. winds. This part of the quay is inside the harbour gate, and therefore fairly private.
>
> Alternatively, one may anchor off according to draught, but this is somewhat exposed to the afternoon breeze which may reach Force 5 or even 6 in late summer.

> **Officials.** Police, Health and Harbour Officials. A Port of Entry where an unusual charge on foreign yachts may be demanded.

> **Facilities.** Provisions and ice are to be obtained in the main square near by; water at the quay. There is a bank, restaurants and a hotel.

The town, which formerly consisted of many three-storey houses with wrought-iron balconies, and was largely destroyed in the 1953 earthquake, has been subsequently rebuilt with modern shops and houses such as one might expect to find in other European countries. The large square with modern municipal buildings has also replaced earlier buildings set up during the governorship of Sir Charles Napier, whose statue is in Trafalgar Square,

43

London. In Argostóli there was a predominant influence inherited from Venice as well as something from Britain; many prominent lawyers, doctors, shipowners and local country families intermarried with Venetians and lived in the Cephalonian capital. Byron came here with his staff in 1823 and resided in the town during the autumn months before departing for Missolonghi to take a more active part in the War of Independence.

The Second World War was not a happy period for Argostóli. First occupied by the Italians who capitulated in 1943, the island was then invaded by German troops who, finding themselves lacking food, rounded up their late allies and, according to official records, shot a large number of the Italian garrison of more than 4,000 officers and men.

Lixoúrion, with 6,000 inhabitants, is of no particular interest; it has a small port with two breakwaters and 14-ft depths at the quays. Steamers load most of the currants there, but in strong south and east winds the quays are too exposed.

Lying on the opposite side of the gulf, Lixoúrion can be reached from Argostóli by ferry in half an hour. Following along the shore by the small promontory the ferry soon comes to a mill. This is only the reconstruction of the famous mill built by Mr Stevens, an Englishman, early in the last century. Its fame was due to the stream of water flowing from the sea which drove the corn-mill and then disappeared into a fissure in the rock, to emerge no one knew where. Many visitors came to see this phenomenon, and some American scientists, who tried to locate the eventual destination of the disappearing stream, met with no success. Then came the 1953 earthquake and all was destroyed. Recently the mill has again been set up, but this time worked by electric power to amuse tourists.

On the point of the promontory is Sir Charles Napier's lighthouse – a white rotunda supported by Ionic columns.

Ássos is a small inlet on the west coast which has been much publicized by Greek Tourist Offices. Although attractive, Ássos is hardly suitable as a summer anchorage; it is uncomfortably open to the north, whence a swell often rolls in.

Fiskárdho Bay. An attractive inlet with suitable sheltered anchorage and a small but growing village on the waterfront. Many charter yachts berth here.

> **Approach and Anchorage.** Chart 720. One may enter by day or night and anchor in the northern corner of the inlet in 4 fathoms where there is sufficient room for a number of yachts. Alternatively, a yacht may berth bows-to or stern-to in 1–2 fathoms at the southern or western quays among the fishing boats where there is excellent shelter.

7 Island of Ithaca: a general view

8 Looking towards Port Vathí

9   The mansion on Madhourí

10   Island of Ithaca: Port Kióni

Facilities. There are good provision shops, three tavernas and a post office. Water is difficult to obtain in summer, but one of the coffee-shops makes hot shower baths available to visiting yachtsmen. Daily bus to Argostóli.

This popular little anchorage has space for some 30–40 yachts but the quays are also used by caïques working their cargoes. It becomes overcrowded during yacht-flotilla visits.

The present name of the place is derived from Robert Guiscard, known to the Italians as Viscardo, the successful Norman chieftain who died here in 1085 while leading his second expedition against the Greek Empire. Had he survived it is thought that he might well have forestalled the Latins and established a Norman dynasty in Constantinople and on the shores of the Bosporus and Black Sea.

Kakogíto Bay (Chart 203), 3½ miles S. of Fiskárdho Bay, is one of several pleasant day anchorages in a small cove. Anchor close inshore and run out a warp.

Ayía Evfímia. A small village in a bay with a short, protecting pier; well-sheltered, except from the east.

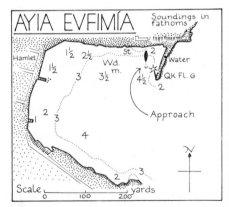

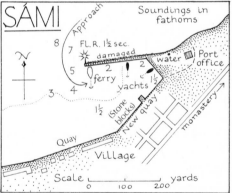

Approach and Berth. Chart 720. No officials. Anchor in 3 fathoms in the N.E. corner behind the mole, hauling in the yacht's stern to the quay where there are adequate depths for any size yacht, but caution is needed because the ballasting protrudes irregularly under water.

Facilities. Water from a tap in the centre of the quay. General store in the village. A small summer hotel-restaurant and two tavernas. Bus communication with Sámi and Argostóli. No sea communication.

45

It was from here that Byron, Trelawny and others made an excursion to Ithaca. On their return, according to Harold Nicolson, they visited the monastery of Moní Agríllion; it was an embarrassing occasion, for Byron, during an audience with the Abbot, had one of his convulsive fits. The old monastery survived until the recent earthquakes, but now only a ruined bell-tower remains and only one monk to care for the modern replacement of the monastery. The ascent from Sámi, with splendid views of the green mountainous country and other islands, is rewarding.

Sámi. A newly constructed harbour and village, and now the car-ferry port for the island.

> **Approach.** No difficulty by day or night. The harbour has been dredged to 3 fathoms and accommodates a car-ferry at the inner quay.
>
> **Berth.** Stern to quay close S.E. of ferry or alongside near ferry. Shelter, though good, attracts a swell due to the new quay which is being extended round the waterfront.
>
> **Officials.** Harbour, Customs and Immigration.
>
> **Facilities.** Fresh water can sometimes be obtained from a tap near the quay. Fuel and provisions can be bought nearby, and there are two small restaurants in the village on the water-front. A taxi to Argostóli takes 45 min, and the occasional bus $1\frac{1}{2}$ hrs. Ice must be brought from Argostóli, and water is often in short supply. There is no bank at Sámi.

Four steamers call each week connecting with Corfu, Pátras and Piraeus, and a car-ferry now plies twice daily connecting Sámi with both Pátras and Corfu. It berths at the extremity of the breakwater.

The whole village of Sámi (1,200 people) was destroyed by earthquake in 1953 and has been completely rebuilt with British funds. Although an important link for car-ferry communications it is disappointing to find so few amenities. This port has largely replaced Argostóli (the capital) as the major port of call for passengers and car-ferries, and the recently improved roads have now assured the importance of Sámi's commercial situation.

It was at Sámi that the Christian fleet under Don John of Austria assembled immediately before the Battle of Lepanto. A few miles inland, and west of Sámi, lies the recently discovered cave of Melissaní with its underground river now approached by a flight of steps. Here one may pay a small fee and explore the recesses of the lake and river by boat. An interesting discovery was recently made by two Austrian professors that when a strong dye is poured into the water at the sea-mills of Argostóli it may be expected to emerge in the river water at Melissaní some three weeks later.

If sailing northwards to pass through the Ithaca Channel, it should be borne in mind that a strong wind sets in from the north in the summer afternoons and is apt to come in gusts off the steep-to mountains.

Sailing southwards towards Cape Kápri one reaches the green Prónos Bay with the small and shallow port of Póros, adjoining some small hamlets and an impressive gorge leading to a green cultivated plain.

Póros. See Chart 720. This shallow cove is not recommended as a safe anchorage, nor is it of interest except for the gorge leading into the hinterland.

> **Approach and Berth.** The mole, which extends eastward for 120 yds, has a quay with 12-ft depths near its extremity (Lt.Fl.(G)). The shallow water at head of creek allows only just room for a medium-sized yacht to lay out an anchor and berth stern-to. Ferry takes up most of available space. N.E. winds are not safe for vessels in the port.
>
> **Facilities** are few. No water, a general store – a small summer hotel, two tavernas.

A loading tip on the eastern arm of the bay belonged to a former mining company, now liquidated.

Proceeding southwards with the intention of rounding the bold Cape Moúnda one should give a wide berth to the offlying Kákkava shoal as the bottom here has risen appreciably and soundings shown on the chart are no longer accurate.

Kateliós (Chart 203) is an open bay on the south coast 2 miles west of Cape Moúdra. The hamlet lies in a charming setting close under the nook formed on the eastern side of the bold Cape Kateliós – a green cultivated valley recedes into the mountain behind. The anchorage is recommended only to 'rock-dodgers' and even then in clear and settled weather.

> **Approach** to the anchorage is from the south heading east of the E. extremity of the hamlet and passing 150 yds E. of a large rock (about 15 ft) and a line of rocks awash, part of reef extending from shore. These lie about 2 cables E. of the cape which shows on its summit a Lt. Fl (2).
>
> **Anchorage** can be obtained about 150 yds from shore on a sandy patch in 3 fathoms.

The small local boats find shelter behind a rough mole by a few small houses, but the basin thus formed is shallow.

THE MAINLAND COAST AND SOUTHERN ISLETS OF THE 'INLAND SEA' – *see key map, page 25*

The sheltered 'Inland Sea' lies between the line of large islands, just described, and the mountainous mainland coast. Following this coast southwards from the

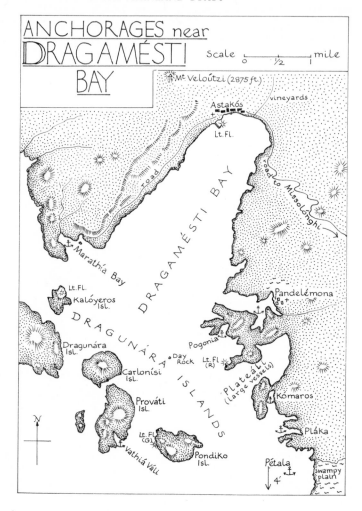

Levkás Canal only the new harbour at Zaverdá (see below) offers any shelter before reaching the vicinity of Dragamésti some 25 miles distant, but at one or two of the islands passed *en route* there are some pleasant inlets with good anchorages described on pages 33–4.

On the mainland coast are the following:

Zaverdá is reported as having a new small boat harbour with depths of 1–2 fathoms inside a mole which extends 100 yds westwards from the shore at the northern end of the village, then turns to continue northwards for a further 100 yds. The northern extremity of this mole is submerged and should be approached with caution particularly at night; the light shown on chart 203 was no longer operating in mid-1981. There is a taverna and limited provisions may be obtained in the village.

Marathía Bay (Chart 1919) lies at the northern entrance to Dragamésti Bay and is quite deserted. Here in mountainous green surroundings one may anchor in 3-fathom depths on a bottom of firm sand with plenty of room to swing.

Astakós (Chart 1939), lying at the head of the large Dragamésti Bay, is a large village overshadowed by Mt. Veloútzi (3,000 ft). A protecting mole extending 200 yds in a S.E. direction has 3-fathom depths at the outer part of the quay. Berth off second and third bollards. Ballasting protrudes underwater. The place is usually packed with yachts all summer.

The village has a number of shops where provisions can be bought, also fuel and ice, but there is no water on the quay. A ferry runs to Kálamos and a bus to Athens. A new road cutting prominently into the mountainside links up near-by villages.

Following the coast southwards one comes to a number of deserted coves with rockbound sides, but suitable as yacht anchorages under most conditions. The mountains gradually give way to more gentle hilly country, uncultivated and occasionally scrub and scattered olive trees. Chart 203.

Pandelémona, an inlet with two arms, one with two small creeks. The northern creek of the N. arm is suitable only for small, shallow-draught yachts. Anchor off some ruined houses, behind which is a farm, and on the hill a ruined building, once a substantial home.

Pogoniá is an inlet of 300 yds facing S.S.W. Level bottom of mud, good holding in 3–4 fathoms and plenty of room to swing.

Plateáli (Chart 3485) is a large sheltered bay suitable as a fleet anchorage.

Kómaros is a 600-yd inlet open only through a narrow arc to S. Anchor 100 yds from the head of inlet in 3 fathoms on a bottom of sand or mud. W. side of inlet is shallower than E. side. A warp ashore might be helpful to restrict swinging space. At the head of the creek are some ruined buildings.

49

Pláka is a small inlet facing W. Anchor near its head in 3 fathoms on a sandy bottom.

South of Pláka the hills run down to a large area of swampy country with the Áspro River and some irrigation.

The near-by **Island of Próvati** has a sandy cove called Vathiá Vali facing S.E. but this is suitable only for a small yacht or catamaran.

Pétala, the most southerly anchorage, is close to the entrance to the Gulf of Pátras. There are depths here of 2–3 fathoms on a mud bottom with fine weed – good shelter and holding. At the head of the inlet, by the shallows, is a fishing settlement with many stakes and small boats.

Of the near-by islets, the Dragunára Group, which is largely uninhabited, and the Echinádes (named after the sea-urchin, because of their prickly outline) serve no useful purpose other than contributing to the beauty of the seascape.

Immediately south of the Echinádes, and forming a turning-point for the Gulf of Pátras, is Oxiá Island; but when crossing the mouth of the Áspro River one must keep considerably further off shore than the chart implies, on account of the continued silting (Chart 3496).

Oxiá Island. Mountainous, steep-to and uninhabited, this relatively small island affords an anchorage which might be useful to a yacht. This is in the north and is suitable in settled weather.

> **Anchorage.** Let go at the head of the cove in 3–4 fathoms with sufficient room to swing. The holding is good and the fetch to the north is about $1\frac{1}{4}$ miles.
>
> On the west side of Oxiá is another cove with precipitous sides, but the depths are rather great for anchoring.

Skrófa, on the mainland opposite Oxiá Island, is an isolated shallow inlet among the lagoons. Entrance is north of the islet, but very shallow, and no longer suitable even for a small yacht. It is, however, of interest that on New Year's Day 1824, Byron's *Mistico* (a fast lateen-rigged vessel with tall poop) bound for Missolonghi was glad to put into this secluded little inlet to evade the pursuing Turkish gunboats.

Proceeding southwards one turns into the Gulf of Pátras (see Chapter 2), where the shallows now extend almost a mile off shore.

It was here that in 1571 the hitherto invincible Turkish fleet suffered an overwhelming defeat by that of the Christian states of Europe at the Battle of Lepanto.

History. The Christian fleet of 208 galleys and six galleasses commanded by Don John of Austria had previously concentrated at Corfu. This mighty fleet with its 80,000 men – more than the whole peacetime strength of the British Navy – sailed south to seek and destroy the Turks, and on the early morning of 7 October found them unexpectedly with their 230 galleys at the entrance to the Gulf of Pátras – known at that time as Lepanto. Meanwhile before engaging the enemy some French and British historians state that the Christian galleys, in order to lower the trajectory of their forward guns, had removed their iron battering rams (*espolones*) – a story which nautical research experts find difficult to believe.

The galleys that fought this action were about 137 ft overall, their beam being one-eighth the overall length. There were 25 oars a side, each nearly 50 ft in length and handled by 5 men who stood up to their work, some pulling, others pushing to immerse the blades in the water; they then fell back on their benches pulling the blade through the water with a very short stroke. The armament was formidable; 5 guns were mounted on the bows, also 10-pounders and lighter guns on either side as well as crossbows and arquebuses. Each galley had a complement of 250 oarsmen and 150 officers, soldiers and sailors. The lateen sail was set only when cruising and was furled in action.

The Turkish galleys though greater in number were smaller and less well armed, with their bows and poisoned arrows, scimitars and swords.

By far the most powerful warships present were the six galleasses provided by Venice. They were large and heavy vessels with a deck above the oarsmen to carry a broadside armament of small guns as well as the well-armed soldiers. The battle began with the galleasses, disposed in pairs, being rowed into action leading the galley squadrons to plough their way into the heart of the Turkish fleet. Sinking many galleys by gunfire, the arquebuses and crossbows created havoc with their crews before the Turks could make effective use of their close-combat weapons. The Christian fleet soon established its superiority and continued to overwhelm the Turks who, after fierce fighting throughout the day, had only 30 galleys still afloat. The Christian fleet lost only 17 galleys, but the casualties on each side were enormous, estimated at 30,000 killed and half this number wounded. But 12,000 Christian galley-slaves were liberated and 3,500 Muslim captives became galley-slaves; the myth of Turkish invincibility was exploded for ever.

[The life of a galley slave was later described by John Evelyn who, on a visit to Marseilles, was taken for a short trip in a galley. He wrote: 'Their rising forward and back at their oars is a miserable spectacle, and the noise of their chains with the roaring of the beaten water has something strange and fearful in it to one unaccustomed. . . . They are ruled and chastised – without the least humanity: yet for all this they are cheerful and full of knavery.']

News of the great victory reached Venice ten days later, when a galley arrived trailing Turkish ensigns in the water and the crew in Turkish dress and waving captured weapons. Even in London, whose countrymen had taken no part in the action, 'bells were rung and there was great jubilation'. Newspapers still remind us of the anniversary of this great battle fought more than 400 years ago.

Under the cloudy water and the silting mud where this action took place undoubtedly lie pieces of armament and fittings of sunken galleys. Peter Throckmorton, leading American sea-archaeologist, having recently examined the area with modern sonar equipment was not optimistic about the prospects of an archaeological expedition. In some Yugoslav museums can be seen magnificent figureheads recovered from sunken Turkish galleys; the flag flown by Don John is preserved in the cathedral at Gaeta, while the Ottoman standard captured in battle can be seen in the Doges Palace at Venice. A contemporary painting of Gianandrea Doria's own galley painted by Vecellio, probably a brother of Titian, hangs in the National Maritime Museum at Greenwich.

Though the galleys had fought their last major action they continued in the Mediterranean for another two centuries, their activity being limited to piracy. Their crews came mostly from Livorno, Algiers, Sicily and Malta; only in France were the galleys taken over by the Navy, and it was not until the Revolution that the remaining galley-slaves were at last freed.

> And above the ships are palaces of brown
> black-bearded chiefs,
> And below the ships are prisons, where with
> multitudinous griefs
> Christian captives, sick and sunless, all a labouring
> race repines
> Like a race in sunken cities, like a nation in the mines.
>
> G. K. CHESTERTON, *Lepanto*

Island of Zante (Zákinthos)

This island comes third in importance among the Ionian Islands after Corfu and Cephalonia. In ancient times it was praised by Strabo for the richness of its woods and harvests and more recently was known by the Italians as the 'Flower of the Levant'. From seaward the countryside seems hardly deserving of such praise, but when standing on the high ground looking down upon the great central plain one appreciates the rich green cultivation. There are splendid views across the plain towards the tall mountains beyond. Population 39,000.

Port Zante. A spacious port with an attractive modern town surrounded by partially bare hills. (Map on page 54.)

Approach and Berth. Chart 720. If following the rhumb line between Port Zante and Killíni care should be taken to avoid the unmarked rocky shoal where H.M.S. *Montague* was wrecked in 1800. During the summer afternoons a fresh northerly breeze may be expected in the southern part of the Zante Channel. Proceed to the north mole and berth beyond the projecting jetty, stern-to quay and bows to the S.W.; anchor in $2\frac{1}{2}$ fathoms. The bottom is soft mud, but the holding appears adequate. Good shelter except in sirocco (S.E.) winds when the harbour is very disturbed and a yacht must shift berth into the southern corner where getting ashore can be difficult.

Officials. A Port of Entry. Port Authority and Customs.

Facilities. Fresh water at the quay can be arranged by the Harbour Master. Diesel fuel is available at the quay and petrol at a garage in the town near by. Good provision shops and a very palatable Zante wine (dry) is available on draught. Some good tavernas near the quay and on the waterfront a new hotel and restaurants. An excellent bathing area close N. of the harbour.

In the summer, a car-ferry runs three times a day from Killíni (Glarenza) on the mainland ($1\frac{1}{2}$ hrs); there is also a daily air connection with Athens and hydrofoil to Pátras.

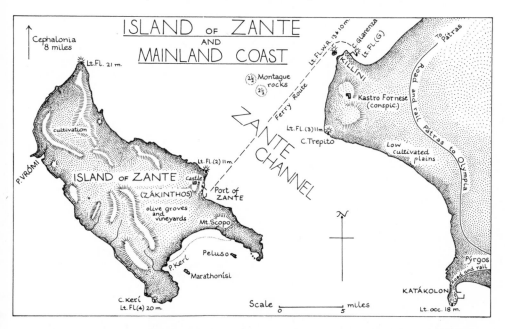

In the great earthquake of 1953 most of the old Venetian town was destroyed including the English Church of St John. The Venetian church of St Nicolas, however, survived as did many of the tombstones in the English cemetery. This is entered through the old wrought-iron gates beside the Royal Arms of Queen Victoria. There is almost nothing surviving today to mark the Venetian–British culture which had once happily blended with that of the well-to-do families of Zante. The modern town, reconstructed after the plan of the former Venetian one, accommodates about 13,000 people; its main square and public buildings especially are attractive. A museum houses some altar screens, frescoes and minor treasures from the wrecked churches.

Recently, extensive harbour improvements were made, including the dredging of the western side of the port and the rebuilding of the inner quays. The extension of the south mole provides additional berthing space for small steamers, which lift considerable quantities of currants, gypsum, olive oil and lemons, upon which the island's prosperity depends.

53

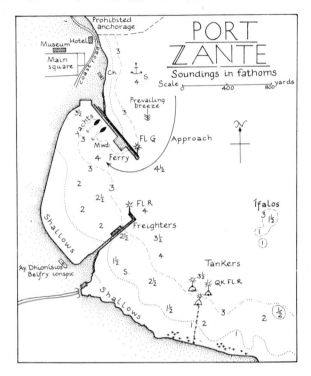

The currants, mostly grown in the great plain, are produced from the dwarf vine. When the fruit is fully ripe it is gathered about August and spread out on levelled areas to dry for three weeks under the hot sun. Each estate has its own drying area, and often these colourful patches may be seen, especially on the high ground, a long way from seaward. Currants from Zante have been shipped to England since the 16th century, at which time they were also made into wine, and these currants were known in England long before the kitchen-garden shrub was introduced; the latter is unknown in Greece. The word currant is a corruption from the French *Raisins de Corinthe*.

Near the southern tip of the island one may anchor in

Port Kerí (Chart 207), a cove, open between N.E. and S.S.E. lying on the west side of Kerí Bay.

> **Anchorage** is near the end of a destroyed stone pier in the S.W. corner of the cove. The depths slowly decrease from 3 to 2 fathoms. Let go 70 yds S.E. of the pier's extremity, towards the high southern shore. Bottom is sand.

Facilities are very limited. Only a bar, open in the tourist season, when bathing parties come out for the day. Possibly a little fruit and vegetables can be bought, and sometimes a locally produced Rosé wine.

There is no longer anything of interest to be seen. A pitch pool by the shore is no longer used, and there are others further inland shown on the chart. They were described by Herodotus (IV.195), but today the pitch is rarely used even on local boats. The land is cultivated; cattle are to be seen grazing and olive groves are maintained.

The whole west coast of Zante is inhospitable with steep-to white cliffs. The only possible shelter is at

Port Vrómi, a very small creek with steep-to sides, open over a narrow arc to S.W. Local boats and very occasionally a small yacht has put in for the night during calms or offshore winds. There is only limited room to anchor, for the creek narrows and a warp must be run ashore. The place is entirely deserted. One would not like to be caught here in unsettled weather.

On the extreme N.E. end of the island is an islet **Áyios Nikólaos** (Chart 203). Temporary anchorage may be obtained in the creek between the islet and the shore, but it is poor holding on hard sand and subject to gusts down the valley. Ashore are two small houses but no road.

History. Zante, like most of the Ionian Islands, suffered only a brief Turkish occupation, and when the Venetians came in the 15th century the island soon began to prosper. The growing of olives and the currant trade began to thrive, and also the commercial port which, on account of the loss of Modon to the Turks, now became the main provisioning and watering base for the Venetian merchant ships trading with the East. The Pilgrim galleasses and naval escorts also had to make use of Zante as a base. In Queen Elizabeth's reign, with the founding of the English Levant Company, merchant ships came here to load with currants, and also called here when routed to Levant ports. Many English merchants began to congregate in the town in pursuit of commercial interests, and their descendants continued to reside here until very recent years. The Royal Navy has frequently been associated with Zante. After the Battle of the Nile, the inhabitants presented Nelson with a sword and cane; Codrington came here to provision his allied squadron immediately before the Battle of Navarino in 1827; and Abney Hastings, that great exponent of iron-ships and red-hot shell so successfully used against the Turks in the War of Independence, came here a year later, badly wounded on board *Karteria* where he died a few days later.

2
The Gulfs of Pátras and Corinth

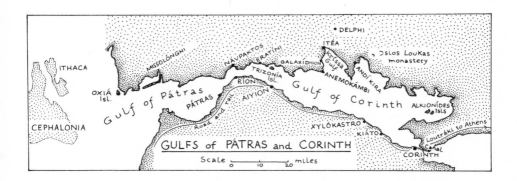

GULF OF PÁTRAS
  Missolonghi (Mesolóngion)
  Pátras (Pátrai)

GULF OF CORINTH
Northern Shores
  Narrows of Ríon
  Návpaktos
  Eratiní
  Trizonía Island
  Anemokámbi ⎫
  Galaxídhion ⎬ Gulf of Kríssa
  Itéa ⎪
  Sálona Bay ⎭
  Andíkira (Áspra Spítia)
  Alkionídes Islands
  Loutráki
  Corinth and the Canal
Southern Shores
  Áiyion and minor anchorages

2

The Gulfs of Pátras and Corinth

THE GULF OF PÁTRAS

The Gulf of Pátras is 13 miles wide at its mouth, where the shores are low; the northern side is shallow, with swamp water from the Áspro River. From the tall, rocky Oxiá Island at the northern entrance it is 30 miles to Pátras, a relatively large port, lying among green mountains near the head of the gulf.

Along the northern shores of the gulf suitable anchorage can be found in accordance with the fathom contours on the chart, and there is complete shelter at the small port of Missolonghi approached by a 3-mile canal. On the south coast there is nowhere suitable, moreover a Prohibited area extends off the coast for $5\frac{1}{2}$ miles from C. Pápas.

In the summer months it is usually calm at night and in the forenoon, but towards midday a sea-breeze sets in from the westward which can excite a small sea at the port of Pátras. As one enters further into the gulf towards the Narrows of Ríon the mountainous scenery becomes magnificent.

A number of fishing craft are based at the low-lying creeks and at night their lamps create a dazzling impression over the waters of the gulf. In addition to usual sea fish, mullet, bream, sardines, there are turtles which may often be seen in early summer making their way into the lagoons.

In early spring and September, woodcock, snipe, duck and quail are shot both here and on the marshes near Lepanto and Dhrepáno. In the country behind Pátras there are a number of unfrequented ravines where plenty of redleg partridges may be found.

Missolonghi (Mesolóngion). A historic little town and port approached by a 3-mile canal.

> **Approach.** Chart 1676. Though the low swampy coast is difficult to discern, the buoys marking the southern end of the canal are large and well lit.
>
> The canal is marked by four pairs of beacons and is nearly 3 miles in length. The beacons are lit and sited 50 yds apart on the sides of the canal; but it is noted that the sides are very irregular and sometimes narrow from the official width of 50 yds to only 30 yds or less. Although the banks are marked by large beacons, the actual line of the bank may often be discerned by its

discoloured water. There are depths of 15 ft in the channel all the way, except at the entrance which sometimes silts to 2 fathoms and even less.

Berth. In the basin forming the port, there are 3-fathom depths with sufficient room to ride at anchor or haul in the stern to one of the quays. The port has been rebuilt with modern quays, and further swampland has been reclaimed. There is perfect shelter. To obviate a recurrence of malaria, the basin and lagoons are frequently sprayed from aircraft.

Several small coasters use the port, and it is claimed that vessels of 600 ft and 17-ft draught may be accommodated, although they would not always clear the bar.

Facilities. The town, with a population of 15,000, has been considerably improved in recent years, and on summer evenings people may be seen dining at tables around the main square, while a colourful fountain plays in the middle. A small summer hotel and taverna are near the port; there are no shops close to the port, but it is only a 10-min walk to the town. There is a water-tap at the N.E. corner of the basin. Beyond is a 'Garden of Heroes' with Byron's statue in the centre and that of Captain Abney Hastings in a prominent position. In the town square is a museum with a few relics of Byron.

Mesolóngion is famous for its gallantry during the early twenties of the last century when its defences against the invading Turkish army excited world interest in the Greek cause. It was also here, just before this event, that Byron had tried to rally the various Greek factions but died shortly after his thirty-seventh birthday.

Byron's original house on the shore of the lagoon was destroyed with the rest of the village when the Turks overran Mesolóngion in 1826. A year or so later, this and other dwellings were reconstructed on the same foundations, and so now an unattractive two-storey house reputed to be that of 'Veeron' is possibly much the same as the original building. It was here that Byron spent his last three unhappy months in the cause of Greece.

His mission had ended disastrously, most of his tasks being unfulfilled; moreover, his staff had failed him. The long chain of disappointments had taken a toll of his health; he wrote almost no poetry, although on his thirty-seventh birthday, with sudden inspiration, he composed 'The Sword, the Banner and the Shield'. Byron's few happy moments were on the occasions when he tore himself away from the frustration of office work. Paddling across the lagoon in his canoe, he would find a horse awaiting him and would then spend a few hours riding over the flat country, at that period clear of marauding Turks. Returning from one of those expeditions, a heavy rainstorm overtook him; soaked to the skin and chilled by the cold April wind he was soon seized with rheumatic pains. Already he had suffered from a 'stroke' and became delirious.

The four doctors, in whom he had little faith, resorted to bleeding, but his strength quickly waned and he died on 19 April 1824. After an autopsy the body was embalmed, placed inside a tin-lined case, with 180 gallons of spirit in a large barrel. A small vessel took three days to sail it to Zante; as she sailed out into the lagoons, thirty-seven mourning guns were fired at minute intervals as a last tribute from the Greeks, who proclaimed national mourning for twenty-one days. The brig *Florida* then sailed with the body to London, where the English judged Byron differently: not only was an Abbey burial denied but neither bust nor plaque were placed in Poets' Corner until 145 years had passed. On 8 May 1969, a stone memorial was dedicated.

Pátras (Pátrai). A medium-sized commercial port, capital of the Peloponnesus: the third largest city in Greece.

Approach and Berth. Chart 1676. This is easy day or night, but there is no convenient berth. The best place is near the southern end of the centre mole which is sheltered from N.E. winds which are often fresh in summer. Westerly winds, which are more frequent, can also cause inconvenience at this berth, in which case a yacht should shift to the north side of the mole. It is not a safe port in which to leave a yacht unattended, except in the early part of the day when it is usually calm, but in 1971 the detached mole was extended by 100 yds in a N.N.E. direction which improved the shelter.

The centre mole with a broad quay was recently rebuilt but berthing space for a yacht can still be difficult to find.

Local officials. As necessary for a Port of Entry. A British Consul resides in the port.

Facilities. Provisions and limited yacht stores are available close at hand. There is a good freshwater tap on the jetty. Three or four hotels and some good restaurants are near by. Two or three banks. Engine repairs can be undertaken. A ferry port for Corfu–Brindisi car-ferry, Ancona and Genoa car-ferries and for Cephalonia ferries. A motorway and railway connects with Athens. Fuel can be obtained but only expensively by tanker.

Entering Pátras harbour, the beautiful view of the surrounding green mountains is obscured by the larger buildings of the town.

The port developed as a result of the currant trade before the last century. Usually one or two large freighters are working cargoes at the quays. The town of 95,000 people is uninspiring, but it lies conveniently on the Athens railroad, whose diesel trains also reach Olympia in $3\frac{1}{2}$ hrs. The country around is beautiful and partly wooded, its rising slopes growing vines and oranges; the Claus wine factory is worth a visit. There are magnificent views from the Venetian castle above the town.

Built during the height of its commercial prosperity early in the last century on the grid system, the arcaded buildings on the waterfront provide welcome shade from the hot sun. This, however, is the more agreeable part of the city; a wide main artery, leading inland, comes to a long flight of broad steps. Avenued by oleander shrubs in red and white, this stairway leads up to the only historical monument now remaining – the castle, almost entirely Venetian and mainly in good repair, standing on the spur of the hill.

The interest is not so much in the castle itself but in the view from the top which is the grandest in Greece. In the evening light it looks its best: the distant peaks of Zante and Cephalonia can be seen to the westward; on the northern side of the gulf is the tall Oxiá Island; sweeping further towards the east are the lagoons of Mesolóngion and the two nearer mountains of Kerásovo and Marakínthos; finally one sees the two fortresses guarding the Narrows of Ríon and the walls of the ancient city of Lepanto climbing the slopes behind.

11 Delphi: the Thólos

12 Levkás: Santa Maura fortress – view from inside; *not* visible from the northern approach

13 Návpaktos: fortified entrance to the medieval port

History. Pátras was the scene of the crucifixion of St Andrew, and many Greeks still believe that his remains lie beneath the high altar of their principal church. There is, however, certain interest to Scotsmen in the story of a Greek monk who during the 4th century, fearing a Barbarian invasion, carried off the remains of the saint to Fife, where subsequently a fine cathedral was built at St Andrews to perpetuate his memory. The Italians also claim to have at least some portions of the saint, for at the annual fiesta at Amalfi a large and colourful procession emerges from the cathedral of St Andrea bearing the treasured casket they believe to contain the bones of St Andrew.

In modern times the Greek Church played a prominent part here, for in 1821 the Bishop of Pátras raised the flag of independence, an event of such patriotic significance that the incident was for many years portrayed in old-fashioned engravings in holy places until superseded by more recent pictures of Greek patriots repelling German parachutists, and other warlike scenes.

THE GULF OF CORINTH

Coming to the **Narrows of Ríon**, once known as the 'Little Dardanelles', one leaves the Gulf of Pátras and enters the **Gulf of Corinth**. At the Narrows the width is a couple of miles and on either side lie the ruins of a low fortress, Turkish structures imposed upon military works of Venetians, Crusaders and earlier intruders. At the elbow-bend north of the port of Pátras an appreciable current is sometimes whipped up suddenly by the wind, thus making progress through the Strait difficult without using power.

The well-sheltered ramps on each side of the Strait enables an efficient car-ferry service to operate across the Narrows.

The Gulf is 65 miles in length, with the Corinth Canal at its eastern end. The scenery on either side is mountainous: green slopes flanking the northern shores ascend Mount Parnassus – 'Mother of surging streams' – and on the south are the tall ranges of the Peloponnesus. Whereas the northern shores are indented and provide shelter at a number of places, the southern coast is mostly straight and without protection.

The wind in summer usually springs up freshly from the west about midday and dies away towards sunset. At night there is often a gentle breeze from the east which may continue until the forenoon. In unsettled conditions squalls may come off the mountains with considerable strength; but the more dangerous symptoms occur with humid easterly weather when the wind may do a volte-face and blow with great strength from the west. This may last a few hours or more and then suddenly cease:

> *Gone like a bird, like a blowing flame*
> *In one swift gust when all things are forgotten.*
> EURIPIDES

THE NORTHERN SHORES

Návpaktos (Lepanto). A minute fishing port, rich in history, and worth a visit for the satisfaction of entering such an interesting old walled-in port. In summer almost a dozen small yachts crowd into this small basin.

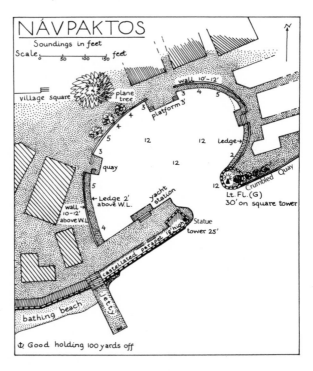

Approach and Berth. Chart 1676. The medieval fortifications on the hillside may be seen some miles off. The opening in the old wall of the port is easy to discern. (See Plate 13.) Outside, the quay on E. side of entrance now crumbled away. The E. side of harbour now lacks mooring rings and bollards; on W. side, the ledge above the quay is sometimes covered. The best shelter is close off W. quay with anchor to E.

The circular harbour is very small being only 80 yds across.

Officials. The Harbour Master's office is above the berth mentioned.

Facilities. Fresh water, fuel and provisions are available. A modern restaurant is by the port. Of the medieval town only the walls remain. By walking along the top towards the clock tower a wonderful view may be had of the whole Gulf of Corinth.

It was at Lepanto that the Turkish fleet sought shelter before setting forth for the famous battle against the Christian states of Europe. (See page 51.)

Eratiní is a small hamlet lining the waterfront of a cove which affords good protection from the west winds.

>**Anchorage** is about 70 yds off the beach in 5–7 fathoms with good holding; a slight swell rolls in during strong winds.

>**Facilities.** Bread and vegetables can be bought. A bus runs daily to Amphissa and a car-ferry crosses to Áiyion on the Peloponnesus. A new coast road to Athens is now completed.

Trizonía Island

A very pleasant sheltered anchorage with a small hamlet of 100 people.

>**Approach.** Chart 1676. It is easy by day or night, but once inside the entrance of the bay, its northern shore should be given a berth of 80 yds.

>**Anchorage.** There are convenient depths off the hamlet. The bottom is mud with a thin carpet of weed and the holding good. Being open to east, it is sometimes practical to anchor in this southern portion of the bay to gain better shelter.
>
>The main village of Trizonía is on the mainland, half a mile across the strait; but the island has a small yacht club and two shops selling a variety of provisions, also a simple meal. The peasants cultivate corn, vines and olives. Fresh water, piped from the mainland, is available.

Looking northwards towards the mainland village is the fine view of the valley with cypresses, vines and red oleanders ascending to the high Parnassus above. The new zigzag road ascending the mountainside somewhat mars its beauty.

Kríssa Gulf (Krissaíos Kólpos)

Chart 221. On the western shores at the entrance lies the 'developed' cove of Anemokámbi, then comes the pleasant little port of Galaxídhion; towards the head of the gulf, the commercial port of Itéa (a necessary call for visiting Delphi). Salona, the former name for the bay at the head of this gulf, is of interest only on account of a spirited naval action which took place during the War of Independence. (See pages 66–7.)

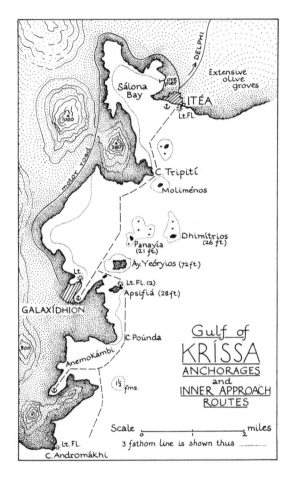

Anemokámbi (or sometimes **Andromáki**). A creek with all-round shelter recently lined with villas. A convenient night anchorage half-way along the Gulf of Corinth.

Approach. Charts 1600 and 221. Easy by day, but the position of the offlying shoal (10 ft) four cables east of Cape Tráklos should be kept in mind.

Anchorage. About 100 yds from the head of the creek is a depth of $2\frac{1}{2}$ fathoms with a bottom of soft mud.

The country around grows some crops and there are one or two peasant cottages in the distance. The new Athens road passes by.

Galaxídhion. A pleasant, sheltered cove suitable for yachts visiting Delphi. The village lines the waterfront of the S.E. cove.

Approach. Charts 1600 and 221: By day the islands are easy to discern and there is no difficulty in entering the inlet with an attractive pine-wood on its S.E. side. For those without the large-scale chart the following direction may be useful:

It is unnecessary for a medium-sized yacht to follow *Sailing Directions* for the deep-water route.

On leaving Anemokámbi steer north-eastwards to round Cape Poúnda, and then lay a course towards the islets of Apsifiá and Áyios Yeóryios (which first appear as one island). After passing between them head N.W. to pass northward of the low islet of Pétales (surmounted by a white stone beacon). It marks the end of the spit extending N.E. of the eastern headland of the port; from here one may safely steer into the entrance.

Anchorage. The quays were rebuilt in 1971, but when berthing stern-to one should beware of the under-water ballasting which protrudes irregularly. There are depths of 10–12 ft close beyond the former ferry-pier; this provides protection from the mountain squalls which often blow suddenly from the north. It is sometimes recommended to moor head and stern in the middle of the cove. Under certain unusual weather conditions phenomenal tidal waves, similar to those in certain Sicilian and Spanish bays, have been experienced here; the safety of a yacht when moored to the quay under these conditions is precarious.

Facilities. Limited provisions to be bought. Water by lorry. Two or three restaurants and small summer hotels. A bus service, which has replaced the ferry, runs to Itéa, to Delphi and to Athens.

The village, now of little significance, lies opposite a pinewood on the other side of the bay. In a modest little museum are exhibited some relics from ships, and a few paintings which illustrate the importance of the place during its prosperity as a maritime centre more than a century ago.

History. When the War of Independence started, Galaxídhion, like Ídhra and Spétsai, had a useful trading fleet of its own. In 1821, when the Turkish squadron set out to plunder Greek shipping there were sixty vessels at Galaxídhion. The Turkish admiral returned to Constantinople with thirty-five of them in tow and thirty prisoners hanging from the yard-arms of his flagship.

Itéa. An unattractive town with an unsheltered roadstead used by steamers for embarking iron ore and olive oil. It may be worth a call if visiting Delphi, though in this case Galaxídhion as an alternative port is a pleasanter place to berth.

Approach. Chart 221 and *Sailing Directions* make the approach instructions clear for entry by day or night. In May 1977, the extension of the pier by about 100 yds to seaward was almost complete; it is intended to accommodate all but the largest cruise ships which previously landed their passengers by boat. When this is complete it is intended to build a marina for 200 yachts close east of the pier.

Berth. Secure the stern to the west side of the pier with anchor to the westward, north of the point where the new extension projects from the older, narrow portion. The holding is good. The day-breeze can make either side of the pier uncomfortable.

Officials. A Port of Entry, with Harbour, Customs and Immigration authorities.

Facilities. Water and diesel fuel are available on the quay; apply to Apostoles Poulos, whose office is opposite the root of the pier. There are modern hotels, mediocre restaurants and adequate shops. The town has 2,000 inhabitants employed in mining, at small factories, especially olive oil, and dealing with exports by sea and land.

Ancient Delphi is 20 kilometres along a good, well-graded road at an altitude of 2,000 ft. Perhaps the finest classical site in all Greece, Delphi, described in detail in many books, has several good hotels and can be reached in 40 min by taxi, or by bus in an hour.

The hinterland of Itéa, the mouth of the gorge of Pleistós, is a mass of olive-groves. The ubiquitous culture of olives in the eastern Mediterranean, although perhaps no longer a matter of life and death, is still the most important factor in the nourishment of the people. It takes the place of butter and fats, and is the means of cooking – its ill-effect on the stomachs of newcomers from the west is often apparent.

The trees, usually cultivated in large groves of about twenty trees to the acre, are often seen from seaward standing well above sea-level yet comfortably sheltered below the top of the ridge. They are said to prefer calcareous soil, and according to Pliny a rich soil often causes disease and a poorer quality of oil. Normally each tree may yield a quart of oil, which a robust man often consumes in little more than a week.

Beyond the town of Itéa the industrialized shores continue to the head of the bay. Formerly known as the Bay of Sálona it was once the scene of a spirited naval action during the Greek War of Independence.

On 29 September 1826, the iron corvette paddle-steamer *Karteria* commanded by Captain Abney Hastings, led a small Greek squadron consisting of a brig and two gunboats into the bay. Here at anchor was a Turkish force consisting of an Algerine schooner, six brigs and two transports. Hastings anchored 500 yds off the nearest enemy ship which then opened fire. Hastings did the same, but with deliberate ranging shots, followed by hot shell from the long guns and 'carcass-shells' from the carronades. (His preference for hot shell rather than shot was because it was feared the solid shot might penetrate both sides of the enemy ships without doing much damage within.)

The effect of *Karteria*'s fire was terrific. The magazine of the Commodore's ship blew up; another carcass-shell exploded in the bows of a brig which began to sink; the Algerine was so damaged between-decks that she had to be abandoned; and more hot-shell set on fire two of the other brigs.

This successful action was considered to be the earliest effective proof of the superiority of an iron-ship, steam propulsion, and hot projectiles fired from large guns. Nevertheless, it was nearly 30 years before the British Admiralty began building iron ships propelled by the steam engine. As early as 1803 Nelson had written to the Admiralty: 'If you do not adopt Mr Bell's* Scheme other nations will, and in the end wax every vein of this Empire.'

Continuing eastward a number of sheltered anchorages are found with rather deep water and therefore more suitable for larger vessels. The chart reveals an occasional projection of sand or mud brought down by mountain torrents and suitable in emergency as a yacht anchorage. For the most part these bays have no interest. One place is worthy of mention:

Andíkira (Áspra Spítia). Two anchorages on the shores of a deep mountain gulf can be useful for visiting Ósios Loúkas.

> **Approach and Anchorage.** Chart 1600. There are quays around the S.W. corner, but it is very shallow. Anchor off the S.W. corner of the bay, beyond the mooring buoys off the church and large tree.

> **Facilities.** There are adequate shops, and taxis are available. In Isidhóros Cove, there is a taverna on the rocky spur on its western shore.

The surrounding mountain scenery is impressive – the Monastery of Ósios Loúkas is 20 km by taxi from Andíkira; it is one of the most important Byzantine monuments in Greece, the church, decorated with mosaics and the crypt with frescoes, both date from the 11th century. In 1977 there were ten monks in the monastery, but responsibility for the valuable church decorations has been assumed by the Ministry of Ancient Monuments.

Alkionídhes Islands, lying 8 miles N.E. of Melagávi Point, consist of four islands, largely barren, with two partially occupied monasteries and a few private holiday houses.

> **Approach.** Chart 1600. The islands can be recognized from afar by the conspicuous white monastery on the hillside. It would appear from the chart, when approaching from the north, that one would find suitable anchorage between Dhaskalió and Zoödhókhos Piyí, the N.E. pair. This is not so, for the channel shelves suddenly to a depth of only 3 ft in the narrows, and the holding here is poor.

* Mr Bell was a prominent marine engineer.

Anchorage. Make for the southern shore of Zoödhókhos Piyí, the most easterly island, where a cove will be found near a small monastery surrounded by eucalyptus trees. In the centre of the cove are depths of 4 fathoms on a bottom of thin weed on mud. Although open between S.S.E. and S.W. (a 2-mile fetch) the cove is sheltered from the N.E. day-breeze.

The monasteries appear to be occupied only during the summer months when some work on cultivation is carried out. Formerly called Kalá Nisiá (the Beautiful Isles) they apparently had many visitors some years ago.

Loutráki. A modern watering-place with a short mole affording limited protection from west. Loutráki is a convenient place to bring up for the night in calm weather when waiting to pass through the Corinth Canal.

Berth. Anchor towards east and stern to the mole – holding uncertain with large boulders. In fresh westerly winds a yacht should seek shelter at Corinth. A weak red light is sometimes exhibited at the extremity of the mole.

Facilities. Plenty of shops, provisions, hotels and restaurants. Bus service to Athens and tours to the Peloponnesus.

Certain historical sites can be conveniently visited from Loutráki:

Mycenae may be reached by bus, via Corinth, in about 2 hrs. Buses leave for Corinth every hour.

Perakhóra, a mountain village N.W. of Loutráki, may be reached by car in 20 min (or by the bus); it is an attractive drive through green hilly country. The Heraion excavations lie towards Melagávi Point, where there is a shallow bay approachable by small caïque only.

Athens is about 2 hrs distant by train or bus.

> *Many a vanish'd year and age,*
> *And tempest's breath, and battle rage,*
> *Have swept o'er Corinth.*
> BYRON, *The Siege of Corinth*

Corinth. Chart 1600. The new harbour protected by a breakwater from westerly winds lies beside the uninteresting modern town.

Berth. In fine weather berth stern to the quay off the yacht station. If the wind should reach Force 6, it is best to cast off from the quay and ride to an anchor; the holding is good, firm mud. With strong westerly winds the seas surmount the breakwater and one should not anchor too close to it. In event of the wind veering to N.E. and becoming fresh to strong it is advisable to seek shelter off the shore S.E. of Loutráki. On S. side of new harbour beware of stone projections 2 to 3 ft above water.

Facilities. Water and fuel are available. Ice can be bought near the harbour (1976). Shops are a few minutes' walk, also some restaurants and tavernas. Expeditions to Akrocorinth, the ruins at old Corinth and many ancient sites on the Peloponnesus. Fast bus service to Athens.

Of the famous ancient Greek city of Corinth, little now remains. According to Thucydides, the Peloponnesian war of 431 B.C. was brought about largely by the jealousy between Corinth and Athens. Later destroyed by the Romans, Corinth was then rebuilt as their own city, becoming rich and luxurious at the time of Julius Caesar; it is mostly the ruins of this city which may be seen today. American archaeologists began to excavate at the end of the last century and one of their more spectacular achievements is the restoration of the theatre. Originally built in the 5th century B.C. to seat 18,000 people, it was rebuilt in marble by the Romans. In it they incorporated a special box for the emperor Nero. Nearby an inscription was found substantiating the famous story of the gladiator Androcles and the lion; it describes the occasion when Androcles' life had been spared due to the lion's timely recognition of the benefactor who had once extracted a thorn from his paw. The theatre is only one of many Roman remains excavated by the Americans; this ancient city is well worth a visit.

The ancient port of Lechaeum lies 3 miles west of the present port and was connected by high walls protecting a road leading directly up to the city. The largely silted entrance, difficult to discern from seawards, lies near the recently restored basilica; but it is disappointing to find that the inner port has become an area of black, reedy lagoons where only two quays and the canal can now be traced. Corinth's port on the Saronic Gulf at Kenchreai was recently excavated.

St Paul, who spent more than eighteen months here, was, on one occasion, brought for trial before the Roman consul; but 'Gallio cared for none of these things.' He subsequently wrote of the need for charity among the citizens of this wealthy commercial city and contrasted their materialism with a better world to come.

On Ákrocorinth is perched the ruined medieval castle with extensive 17th-century Venetian walls surrounding the summit of the rock. Standing 1,800 ft above the sea, it affords a fine view across the Gulf of Corinth, and over the Saronic Gulf to Cape Soúnion. Traces of walls date from the 6th century B.C., but most of those standing today are of medieval construction. Once occupied by Roger II, Norman King of Sicily, the citadel has changed hands many times, and on one occasion it was unsuccessfully attacked by the Knights of St John.

History. John d'Hérédia, a French knight, became Grand Master of the Order of St John in Rhodes in 1376. A year later he set out with a squadron of nine galleys to attack the Turks, accompanied by the Priors of England (Robert Hales), St Gilles and Rome. After joining a Venetian fleet off Crete they made for Pátras which they captured; but their attack on Corinth was an utter failure and d'Hérédia was taken prisoner.

The three priors promptly offered themselves as hostages to the Turks for the ransom of the Grand Master if they would release him. But d'Hérédia refused to allow the sacrifice to be made because he thought the Order 'could more easily spare an old man like himself than three young and vigorous knights'.

At the entrance to the Corinth Canal can be seen the two curved breakwaters which form a very small harbour for the purpose of protecting the mouth of the canal. It is not allowed to be used for berthing a yacht and may only be used by pilot boats and canal craft. Details for passing through the canal are given in *Sailing Directions* and *The Aegean*. In 1980, yachts were charged a minimum rate of 1331 drs. Payments are collected at the S.E. end of the canal. Photography is forbidden.

The Corinth Canal, little over 3 miles in length, was cut by a French company towards the end of the last century. The saving in distance by vessels proceeding to Piraeus from, say, the direction of Brindisi is almost 130 miles, and the canal is used by many small steamers and caïques. Since vessels cannot pass one another in the canal they may have to wait outside until the blue burgee is hoisted to signify that the canal is clear and they may then enter.

The soft stone surface of the canal's vertical sides crumbles away and is continually under repair which necessitates the canal being closed to traffic one day a week, recently on Tuesdays.

History. Before the construction of the canal, the Austro-Lloyd Steamship Company, which at the end of the last century had the monopoly of the Aegean and Levant trade, had to land its passengers at Loutraki, and then transport them by road to a steamer awaiting them on the Aegean side of the isthmus. However, the need for a canal was realized nineteen centuries before when the Emperor Caligula caused surveys to be made, and Nero actually initiated the diggings; but troublesome times brought the undertaking to nothing.

Meanwhile, although heavy ships could not be transported across the isthmus, the more easily handled galleys could, and for many centuries were hauled across on rollers. Only very recently was unearthed a section of this *diólkos* or limestone-paved roadway; it is 14 ft wide and the two ruts which bore the rollers are 5 feet apart. History records that Augustus after the Battle of Actium had his ships dragged across the isthmus when in pursuit of Antony. In A.D. 883 the Greek admiral also had his fleet dragged across when he was preparing to repel the Saracens.

THE GULF OF CORINTH – SOUTHERN SHORES

Following the Peloponnesian coast westward from Corinth one notices that it is well populated with a number of villages, large and small. The coastline is comparatively straight and the few minor indentations afford little shelter for a yacht.

One or two places with sandy beaches have recently become summer resorts, and in some cases a short mole has been built to allow local ferry boats to call; at Vrakháti and Kiáto a yacht may find protection from the short sea or swell; at other places small trading stations have sprung up where caïques call for shipments of grapes, olives and lemons.

The coastal road and railway from Athens to Pátras follow close to the shore, frequently crossing the torrent-beds which, after the rains, convey the flood water into the gulf. The new motorway cuts mostly inland.

The mountain of Spíra (with its monastery) 3 miles west of Xylókastro is easy to discern, and further westward is the steep Vouraikós gorge leading from Dhiakoptó to Kalávryta, a picturesque site with a shrine marking the spot where Bishop Germanus raised the standard of revolt at the beginning of the War of Independence. A railway and track have been made to encourage tourists to visit not only the revered site of the bishop's patriotic stand but the famous monastery of Megaspíleion, best visited by road from Pátras. This is a remarkable pile of white buildings standing one above the other let into the steep-to face of a huge limestone cliff. Above all stands the monastery church recessed into a large cavern. There is nothing special to be seen within, as the whole place was last burnt down in 1949 and rebuilt; the main interest lies in the history of the monastery's successful defence in 1826 against a large force of Turks under Ibrahim Pasha.

Apart from Corinth and the Canal the only port on the south shore is **Aiyion** (Chart 1676 with plan), an industrial town of 15,000 people. The Itéa ferry berths behind its breakwater and in the autumn months small steamers, that lift the currants grown in the hinterland, berth here too. The only reason for a yacht to call here would be for the good fresh water (once praised by Pausanius) available at the jetty.

Killíni (Glarenza)
Katákolon
Kiparissía
Próti Island
Navarin Bay (Navarino)
Pílos
Methóni
Sapiénza Island
  Port Lóngos
Stróvathi Islands
Gulf of Kalamáta (Messinía)
  Koróni
  Petalídhi
  Kalamáta (Kalamon)
The Máni
  Port Liméni
  Mézapos
  Yerolimín
Cape Matapan (Ténaron)

Gulf of Lakonía
  Asamáto Cove
  Port Vathí
  Port Kaío
Kolokíthia Bay Anchorages
  Meligáni
  Solotéri
  Nýmphi
  Kótronas
  Skutari Bay
    Fisherman's Cove
  Yíthion
  Eláia
  Xíli
  Plítra
Elafónisos Island anchorages and
  Vátika Bay
  Poríki Islet anchorage
  Sarakíniko Bay
  Elafónisos Village anchorage
    (Petri Isl.)
  Neápolis
Cape Maléa

3
The Western Shores of the Peloponnesus

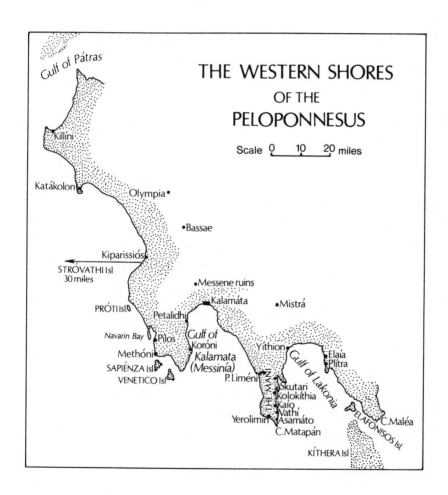

THE WESTERN SHORES
OF THE
PELOPONNESUS

Scale 0   10   20 miles

Gulf of Pátras

Killíni

Katákolon

Olympia•

•Bassae

Kiparissiós

STROVATHI Isl
30 miles

Messene ruins•

•Kalamáta

•Mistrá

PRÓTI Isl

Petalidhi

Navarin Bay

Pilos

Gulf of
Koróni

Methóni

Kalamáta
(Messinía)

Yithion

Elaia
Plítra

SAPIÉNZA Isl

VENETICO Isl

P. Liméni

Gulf of Lakonia

Skutari
Kolokíthia
Kaló
Vathí
Asamáto

THE MANI

Yerolimín

C.Matapán

ELAFÓNISOS Isl

C.Maléa

KÍTHERA Isl

3

The Western Shores of the Peloponnesus

Twenty miles from the entrance of the Gulf of Pátras along a dull, low sandy coast is the small shallow port of Killíni. Twenty-seven miles southward is the better protected port of Katákolon, while 50 miles further still is Navarin Bay, well protected and interesting to visit. On the south-west coast, the only secure port is Kalamáta in the Gulf of Messinia. Most of the places described provide temporary shelter during fine weather in the summer months.

Killíni or **Glarenza,** a former Venetian port, was silted for many decades, but has recently been rebuilt as the car-ferry port for Zante. The hamlet, formerly of shanty-like appearance is beginning to assume an air of modernity to conform to its status as a communication centre.

> **Approach.** See *Sailing Instructions* and Chart 1676. A buoy marks the extremity of the sunken mole, the last 80 yds of which has not yet been reconstructed. From its root the new breakwater extends for 500 yds and stands about 12 ft, being clearly visible from seaward. On rounding the buoy (Lt Fl. G.) one enters the newly dredged port where depths are 3 fathoms decreasing to $2\frac{1}{4}$ off the quay.
>
> **Berth.** Yachts should berth stern-to the quay near the curve towards its outer extremity. (Rings and bollards provided.) Note that at one or two places the ballasting of the old sunken mole may protrude from the quay. The inner portion of the port is occupied by ferry activity. A slight swell caused by the north wind may enter the port, but otherwise it affords excellent shelter. A few fishing craft also berth at the outer part of the quay.
>
> **Facilities** are limited. Two grocers' shops, a restaurant, tavernas, a hotel. Bus to Athens, $5\frac{1}{2}$ hrs. Trains to Pátras and Olympia. Car-ferry to Zante 5 times daily in summer. A car may be hired from a neighbouring village for the drive to Olympia, a journey of $1\frac{1}{2}$ hrs.

An outstanding landmark, the Castle of Klemútsi or Claimont (Kastro Tornese on the chart), is visible from the high land of Zante. It stands on the hill overlooking the harbour that was once the port of Genoese and Venetian trading vessels; it was then named Glarenza after the Duc de Clarence.

Begun in 1219, the castle was intended for protecting the coastal road from

Corinth to Kalamáta and Andrávida (the Frankish capital), and to ensure the safety of the port. Though smaller than some of the Syrian castles, this is considered the best example of a Frankish castle in the Morea. It was last used as a defence post during the War of Independence, when its Greek garrison was overcome by a Turco-Egyptian force under Ibrahim Pasha.

Katákolon (Chart 719, plan), a small, safe, commercial port, which is rapidly growing in importance.

> **Approach.** Plan on Chart 719 shows that entry is easy by day or night. Within the harbour improvements have recently been made in the S. W. corner: the existing quay has had the depths increased to accommodate small steamers, and a substantial stone pier extends for 220 yds towards the molehead with depths of $3\frac{1}{2}$ fathoms at its extremity and alongside.
>
> **Berth.** In strong winds a yacht should berth off the E. side of the main quay. In strong southerly winds a short swell of little consequence enters the harbour.
>
> **Port Facilities.** The village, with several supermarkets and fish restaurants, has much expanded. Fuel and water are available. The nearest town is Pýrgos, 12 min by car and half an hour by train. Occasional passenger ferries call here in summer.
>
> **Officials.** A Port of Entry. Customs and Harbour Authority at root of new jetty.
> The port receives over 200 small to medium-sized steamers in the year, mainly lifting currants growing in the interior. It is surprising to find such a wretched place where the port trade appears to be improving.
> A taxi may be obtained to drive to Olympia (45 min) or one can go by bus via Pýrgos in $1\frac{1}{2}$ hrs. The drive to the Doric temple at Bássae, passing through beautiful country, takes 3 hrs by taxi.

The Gulf of Arcadia or Kiparissía, a 30 miles sweep of open sandy coast, affords temporary shelter.

Kiparissía, an open anchorage protected by a 300-yd mole. Chart 719 gives a plan showing detail of the shallow anchorage.

Kiparissía, once the harbour for Messene, was known in the Middle Ages as Arcadia on account of the refugees who fled from Arcadia because of the Slav invasion. Although its harbour was a busy place in Byzantine days when the defences were strengthened, the present port is of no interest today. The upper village, however, is attractive; its winding streets, flights of steps and a Turkish fountain make a visit worth while.

Próti Channel has an indifferent anchorage under the island as shown on Chart 719. Navarino, so very much better, lies only 5 miles to the southward.
About 4 miles north of the entrance to Pílos is 'Port' **Voidhokoiliá**, shown on

a large scale on Chart 211. Weather permitting this can be used as temporary anchorage for visiting Nestor's Cave and the ruined fortress of Palaió Avarino, which are difficult of access by land. This is a perfect bay for bathing. It is open to winds between north and south but is partially sheltered by a small island. There are depths of 2 fathoms just behind the island, but there is certainly no port today.

Navarin Bay (Navarino), 50 miles south of Katákolon, is a large bay easy of access in bad weather; with its small sheltered port of **Pílos (Pýlos),** the place is also of wide historical interest.

> *Old man, go tell the wise Penelope*
> *That safe from Pylos I have sailed the deep.*
> *Odyssey,* XVI. 130–1

Approach and Berth. During reconstruction for accommodating large freighters and due to the many small tenders which bring crews ashore it would be unwise to anchor or berth off the

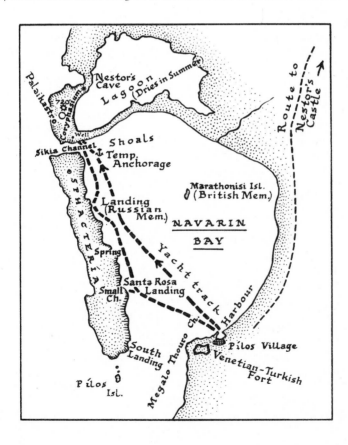

quay. The harbour is now very crowded and yachts are discouraged. The breakwater is being extended.

Facilities. A number of fresh provision shops, restaurants and modern hotels. Bus communication with Athens.

History. The earliest historical occasion recounted by Thucydides was the 'Sphactería incident' in 425 B.C., when a small Athenian naval contingent under Demosthenes eventually overwhelmed a besieging force of Spartans.

To investigate the scene of this early operation, one must proceed to the sandy shore close to the shallow Sikiá channel, and anchor off the ancient port of Coryphasium, whose mole can still be discerned disappearing among rushes into the sand. From here a mule track ascends the 700-foot hill to the fortress on Palaiókastro. This was where Demosthenes had detached himself from the Athenian expeditionary force bound for Syracuse, and having seized this peninsula with half a dozen triremes, set himself up for the summer months to defy the besieging Spartans. Standing on the top one now looks down on the shallow channel where Demosthenes had once sheltered his triremes.

The existing fortress is of medieval construction, with battlemented walls in good preservation, and from here there is a magnificent view across the large semicircular bay of Navarin towards the green undulating country beyond.

Descending the steep northern slope, one soon comes to the stalactite cave where Hermes was reputed to have hidden the cattle he had stolen from Apollo. It is known as Nestor's Cave. Inside, when the cloud of bats has scattered, the glistening sides become visible, lit by a shaft of light from a hole high up in the domed roof. From here the side of the dried-up salt lake must be followed to re-embark in the dinghy.

Crossing to the island, one realizes that the depths are too great for a yacht to anchor off the steep cliffs of Sphacteria; the only way is to land by dinghy at 'Russian Cove' while the yacht is anchored elsewhere. A rough track ascends to the most northerly of the three peaks, which had been the Spartan stronghold until the return of the Athenian fleet from Syracuse. Then the tables were turned and the besieger becomes the besieged. Demosthenes effected a landing, cut off Spartan supplies and eventually forced the surviving garrison to surrender. This dramatic and decisive conclusion to the campaign was never forgotten by the Athenians, and for six centuries the Spartan shields were exhibited at Athens. On the hilltop today is merely the ruin of a small fort; but it is the setting that brings to life the events of the narrative so vividly told by Thucydides. In 1827 an equally dramatic event took place which led to Greece obtaining her independence.

The Turkish-Egyptian army was occupying the Peloponnesus and a fleet of 82 warships, ranged in three lines, lay at anchor in Navarin Bay.

At 1.30 p.m. on 20 October Admiral Codrington led an allied fleet, including French and Russian squadrons, into the bay without any opposition from the Turkish batteries. Firing began when certain Turkish ships started shooting at British ships' boats. Immediately Codrington's fleet opened fire on the Turks and, fighting fiercely, they continued the action all day and during the night. During the darkness many Turkish ships could be seen bursting into flames, and when daylight came only 29 of the original 82 remained afloat. The damage and casualties among allied ships was extensive; although no ships were lost, considerable repairs had to be made good at Malta.

Britain and Turkey were not at war, nor did this 'untoward event' – an expression used in the

King's speech in Parliament – cause them to declare war. Although people in Britain celebrated this battle as a great and glorious victory, few realized how poor the efficiency of British gunnery had become – only twenty-two years after Trafalgar: H.M.S. *Genoa*'s first lieutenant, giving evidence at a subsequent court martial, stated that the enemy was so close that he could plainly see the whites of their eyes, yet *Genoa* battered her opponent for two hours without diverging from a parallel position, both ships being at anchor. It is perhaps significant that the Navy's first gunnery school, H.M.S. *Excellent*, was established five years later.

To the Greeks, whose liberation was achieved largely as a result of this far-reaching event, this bore out the philosophy expressed by Euripides:

> *There be many shapes of mystery*
> *And many things God makes to be,*
> > *Past hope or fear.*
> *And the end men looked for cometh not,*
> *And a path is there where no man thought;*
> > *So hath it fallen here.*

In the square of Pílos is an impressive memorial, with busts of Codrington and his allied Admirals; on the island of Sphactería, at Panagoúlas, and on the small islet of Marathonísi (Chelonaki) are small obelisks or modern plaques to commemorate the dead sailors of the French, Russian and British Fleets respectively.

Salvage of the Sunken Fleet. Much gold and valuable jewels were believed to have been sunk in the Egyptian flagship.

> *Wedges of gold, great anchors, heaps of pearl*
> *Inestimable stones, unvalued jewels,*
> *all scattered in the bottom of the sea;*
> > SHAKESPEARE, *King Richard III,*
> > Act I, Scene IV

Treasure-seekers have made repeated attempts to work on the sunken ships now lying in more than 20-fathom depths. The wrecks are largely buried in mud; in recent years Peter Throckmorton, the American archaeologist and diver, reported finding eight hulls with only their frames protruding above the soft mud. Further investigation is expected.

Apart from a well-preserved Turkish fort at the entrance to the bay, there is one further site that should not be missed. This is Nestor's Palace.

Vivid evidence of Pílos history dates back to the late Bronze Age. One should visit what Homer describes as the 'noble and notable building' standing on the hillside near the centre of the bay:

79

Nestor's Palace, discovered early in 1939 by Carl Blegen, stands in a commanding position overlooking the countryside; the area of the excavated palace is some 200 yds in length and about half this distance in breadth. As well as revealing the lavish arrangement and furnishing of the palace, Blegen discovered the linear B tablets; eventually deciphered these tablets disclosed much of the administration of the palace and also of the kingdom it ruled. Among the details of the defence organization were instructions for maintaining certain coastal watching stations and the provision of naval craft manned by 30 rowers at specified strategic points along the shore.

Methóni (until this century called Modon) has a shallow bay, inadequately protected by a breakwater, with a modern village close by. A massive Venetian fortress jutting into the sea dominates the port.

> **Approach and Berth.** Charts 207 and 719 show there are no difficulties day or night. After rounding the extremity of the breakwater the sea-bed rises very quickly. The most conspicuous object by day, not clear on the chart, is the large Turkish tower on the southern point of the fortress. In fair weather only, a yacht may berth to the small quay 20 yds inside the mole with

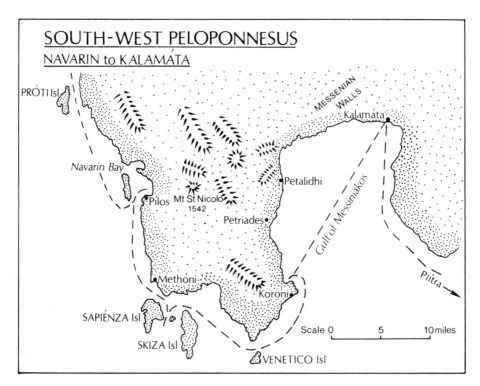

SOUTH-WEST PELOPONNESUS
NAVARIN to KALAMÁTA

PRÓTI Isl

Navarin Bay

Pílos Mt St Nicoló
1542

Petriades

Methóni

SAPIÉNZA Isl

SKIZA Isl

MESSENIAN WALLS

Kalamáta

Petalidhi

Gulf of Messiniakos

Koroni

Plitra

Scale 0   5   10 miles

VENETICO Isl

anchor laid out to the northward; the depths here are 10 ft – it may be preferable to anchor off, with the same shelter, in $2\frac{1}{2}$ fathoms where there is good holding and sufficient swinging room. The bottom is thin weed on sand and there are a few stones. A swell works round the end of the mole and in bad weather from the south the place is untenable.

In order to land at the castle or approach the village, one has to walk along the very rough 150-yard mole.

Facilities. Fresh water and fuel are laid on to a small quay near the molehead. The village has little character. A small hotel and a café are on the sea-front overlooking the sandy bay, which in summer attracts visitors. The road leads to Pílos and thence to Athens which can be reached by bus in 8 hrs. Very few vessels call here, and only three or four fishing craft are based on the port.

Early History. Methóni first played an important part in Roman times. During the Civil War in the spring of 31 B.C. Marcus Agrippa, Octavius' admiral, set off with his naval squadron to capture Methoni. From here he cut off Antony's corn supplies from Egypt. Now moving northwards towards the Ionian Islands he lured Antony's fleet at Corfu to move south to oppose him. This move left open the mastery of the Otranto Strait and thus allowed Octavius' army, based at Brindisi, to slip across to Albania unmolested. After landing at what is now Palermo they were soon marching southward to contribute towards the overwhelming defeat of Antony at Actium.

Some centuries later following the collapse of the Byzantine Empire the Venetian trading hegemony needed the use of Methóni (now called Modon) as the focal base for commerce. While Venice 'sat in state throned in her hundred isles' her 3,000 cargo vessels and forty-five war-galleys, largely in trade with Constantinople, Cyprus, Levant and Egypt, had to use Modon as their base for naval escorts, food, water, and resting point for crews. When they lost it to the Turks after 1500 it was more than a disaster for Venice.

The vast Venetian fortress is now of limited interest, for within the walls hardly a building remains. The last time it was effectively used was in 1770 when the Russian fleet had based itself at Navarin. The fortress, then garrisoned by a strong force of Turks, constituted a threat to Russian supplies arriving by land and the Russian navy decided to capture it. An expedition supported by eighteen 24-pounders manned by Russian sailors from the fleet, together with 2,000 Greeks, failed to dislodge the garrison which was eventually relieved by a force of 6,000 Turks. Modon continued as a thorn in the flesh to the Navarin base until finally the Russians were compelled to abandon it.

On the cape pointing S.S.E. towards Sapiénza Island is the prominent Venetian light tower:

Protecting Methóni is the **Island of Sapiénza**, which, in the sailing-ship days, provided a useful anchorage for vessels bound for the Aegean.

Port Lóngos provides anchorage for medium-sized vessels in southerly and westerly weather, but with S.E. winds a heavy swell makes the place untenable.

Approach and Anchorage. Approach can be made only by day using the southern entrance. The southern part of the inlet affords the best anchorage, but the bottom being soft mud the holding is unsure. Close by the western shore are three submerged wrecks, one of which is the 18-gun frigate, H.M.S. *Colombine*, sunk in 1834, another is an Austrian brig; but none of them fouls the anchorage. At the head of the inlet is a jetty and a beach where the lighthouse-keepers (the only inhabitants) haul up their boat in calm weather.

The rightful ownership of this insignificant, deserted island was contested by the British Government in the middle of the last century on the grounds that it was a former Venetian possession and therefore should have been surrendered to Britain. A British squadron was sent to Piraeus, and the threatened use of forceful measures was only averted by the intervention of that distinguished traveller and Hellenophile, Colonel Leake. The claim was finally dropped.

Stróvathi Islands, lying 30 miles west of the Peloponnesus coast, are seldom visited by a yacht, for it is scarcely worth the effort when there are more attractive places with better shelter on the mainland.

Anchorage. At the larger island the anchorage affords poor holding on a bottom with large boulders. The anchor should be buoyed and the weather must be settled. Off the smaller island the holding is said to be better.

On the main island is the monastery, which once put up a stout resistance against the infidel. It no longer shelters any monks. There is only a caretaker, and the building, though rather delapidated, still defies the violence of stormy weather and rain. It is occasionally inspected by a Pappas from Zante.

Anthony Butler visited the island in 1977 and found two lighthouse-keepers, a farmer cultivating 3 hectares, two horses and a spaniel. Bread and onions were offered. Shooting parties were expected for slaughtering the migrating doves. On the smaller, but unpopulated island, shearwaters were nesting.

Proceeding eastwards past the two deserted islands of Skíza and Veneticó into the wide Gulf of Kalamáta (Messinía) one then follows the coast in a northeasterly direction. Beyond the next headland is the other 'Eye of the Republic':

Koróni. This old walled city has become a small village with a sheltered anchorage protected by a breakwater.

> **Approach and Berth.** Chart 719 with recent plan of the anchorage elucidates the approach quite clearly by day or night. The fortress walls and bastions are visible a great distance off. 100 yds off the southern shore and up to 70 yds from the breakwater the bottom is short weed and sand. Further out, and west of the extremity of the mole there are some rock slabs.
>
> The anchorage is slightly exposed to the afternoon day-breeze from north-west, which may make boat landing rather a wet undertaking.
>
> In the event of sudden N.E. winds a yacht may find anchorage under the lee of Livadia Point.
>
> **Port Facilities.** Plenty of shops and tavernas have recently opened.

The Venetian fortress, standing on the hill overlooking the village and port, is interesting to explore. The convent, occupying part of the summit, is inhabited by a number of nuns, who take a great interest in maintaining a colourful flower garden.

An interesting excursion passing through beautiful country is a 20-min drive to Petriádes village. Here is the only place in Greece where in the summer months the large 'Ali Baba' jars (*amphorae*) are made without a wheel – a unique process practised apparently only by this one family in the village.

Continuing on past Koróni to the head of the Messínian Gulf you come to the relatively large commercial port of Kalamáta – *en route* is an anchorage:

Petalídhi. Chart 719 (plan). A convenient anchorage off an uninteresting hamlet, which is useful for shelter in southerly winds.

> **Approach.** The low-lying Cape of Petalídhi may be recognized by a white church. The ancient mole has recently been built up and extended to a distance of 150 yds in a N.E. direction from the cape; but during winter gales this has now been swept away and in 1976 only some concrete blocks remained.

Kalamáta (Kalamón) is a commercial port of considerable activity in the autumn months when many steamers call to load with figs and currants.

> **Approach and Berth.** Chart 719. The town is easily distinguished against the hinterland by day, and at night the harbour lights can be seen at only half the distance claimed.
>
> After entering the port, a yacht should make for the north-west corner and berth in the basin with stern to the quay near the Port Office. Mud bottom, and depths of 28 ft nearly everywhere

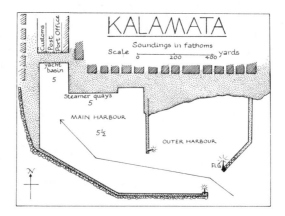

– good shelter. The outer breakwater has recently been extended and a new east mole is under construction.

Officials. As for a Port of Entry – Offices by the port.

Facilities. Fresh water is laid on at the quay and fuel is available close by. A good market, many shops, restaurants and hotels. Air and bus service to Athens (6 hrs), also the slower train.

The town of 50,000 inhabitants lies at the foot of a hill with a former acropolis. A frequent bus service connects it with the port. The surrounding country is cultivated, mostly with vineyards and olive groves.

Near the town is the ruined castle of Villehardouin, named after the Crusader Knight, whose heroism and chivalry (revealed in his chronicle) had the effect of stimulating the literary development during the 12th and 13th centuries and sending knights-errant to establish principalities and kingdoms throughout Europe and the Near East.

The walls of ancient Messíni set up in the 3rd century B.C. can be reached by car in 40 min. A lengthy section, which still remains intact despite the many earthquakes, is remarkably impressive for the perfection of the bonding of these huge masses of stone.

KALAMÁTA TO CAPE MALÉA

Leaving behind the cultivated plain at the head of the Kalamáta Gulf one follows the mountainous rocky eastern shores for 43 miles until reaching Cape Matapan. The coastal features are in marked contrast to the gentle cultivated shores on the west side of the gulf.

The massive Taygétos range with peaks ascending to nearly 8,000 ft

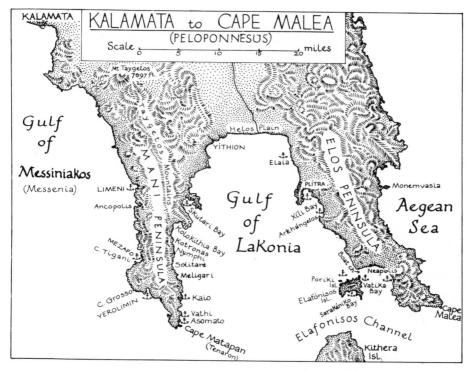

KALAMATA to CAPE MALEA
(PELOPONNESUS)
Scale 0 5 10 15 20 miles

dominates the countryside; it also influences the winds sometimes causing violent squalls which can worry a sailing yacht. There are only three inlets or small ports which can afford shelter to a yacht and these can be used only provided there are no strong winds between W. and S.W.

Some 13½ miles before reaching the inlet of Liméni is the only possible fine-weather anchorage off this rocky coast. This is close north of an islet (with a white church) lying close off the cliffs beneath the small hamlet of **Kardhaméni**. Here in depths of 3 fathoms one may anchor close north of the islet entirely exposed to westerly winds; in settled weather one may land in the dinghy at the small fishing-boat basin (Lt Fl. R. at N. entrance) close beneath the small hamlet with small modern hotels and one or two houses.

Liméni, although said to be the best-sheltered inlet on the eastern shore of the gulf, is entirely open to W. and claimed by local seamen to be unsafe.

Approach. There are no hazards, and one can proceed towards the hamlet on the southern shore about ½ mile inside the headland. The depth shelves slowly to 3 fathoms. On the S. headland is a LT. Fl. (g).

Facilities. Water and fuel are available.

85

Liméni is the port for Tsímova which commands the only pass through the Taygétos range to the small town of Yíthion at the head of the Gulf of Lakonía.

From Liméni southwards a number of unusual villages with prominent square towers can be seen from seaward on the hill slopes. This is the country of the *Deep Máni*, and these Nyklian towers were feudal strongholds built from about 1600 onwards by the descendants of the former Nyklian families who came to the underpopulated *Máni* country on the destruction of their own city. Some of these towers are still lived in, though in other places the villages are largely deserted. They appear more interesting than attractive.

The people nowadays are pleasant enough, but Captain Beaufort, writing 150 years ago, remarked: 'In the district of Maina, the southern province of the Morea, there is a regularly organized system of absolute and general piracy. The number of their vessels or armed row-boats fluctuates between twenty and thirty; they lurk behind the headlands and innumerable rocks of the archipelago; all flags are equally their prey, and the life or death of the captured crew is merely a matter of convenience.'

Following the rocky coast southwards one passes the Caves of Diros. These have now become a great tourist attraction and have been electrically lit. They are best visited by coach or car from Yíthion.

Mézapos is a small bay some 10 miles S. of Liméni protected from S.W. by the southern headland, the great rock of Tigani ('frying pan'). Sprawling on its peak are the ruins of the fortress of Maina, one of three great defensive works set up by Geoffroi de Villehardouin in the late 12th century to protect his S.E. domain of the Peloponnesus.

A partially deserted hamlet with a few shattered towers (the result of earthquake damage) is all that remains of the substantial village.

Berth in convenient depths near the small houses on the eastern shore.

After rounding the bold, steep-to Cape Grósso is

Yerolimín, a comparatively modern westernized village, having sea communications with Piraeus.

A short pier with a quay enables the mail steamer to berth in calm weather, but the place is very exposed to the westerly quarter, and the steamer has on occasions had to berth on the E. side of Cape Matapán at Vathí.

This little port has grown up since the middle of the last century and is a distributing centre for manufactured articles to the hill villages. Previously it had been a great haunt for pirates.

As one nears Cape Matapán the height of this mountain range has already begun to diminish and ultimately one sees the lighthouse standing upon what appears to be quite a low spit of land. So low is the Cape that in making a landfall from the southward one may expect to sight first the high land some miles northward, then when nearing the Cape the top of the lighthouse and lastly the Cape itself. This is the most southerly point of mainland Greece and very nearly the most southerly cape of Europe but Cape Tarífa at the entrance to the Gibraltar Strait wins by 14 miles.

Apart from a call at Koróni a visit by a sailing yacht into this gulf is hardly justified.

Rounding Cape Matapán and entering the **Gulf of Lakonía**, there are some attractive places on the mountainous steep-to *Máni* shores, but apart from one or two coves shown in the plans on Chart 712 there are hardly any safe places to leave a sailing yacht for more than an hour or two. This is largely on account of the squalls which may at any time descend with violence from the steep *Máni* ranges above.

Following northwards along the Western Shores the following coves are shown in plans on Chart 712:

Asamátos Cove, comfortable in settled weather when a small yacht should anchor in the north-west corner of the bay with a warp to the shore. The bottom here is inconveniently deep and shelves quickly. There is a fisherman's hut at the head of the creek and a tiny, disused chapel. This cove is less subject to squalls than some of the other places.

Vathí, known as Port Vathí, is a deep-cut inlet often claimed to be better than Asamáto though subject to violent squalls in westerly winds.

Port Kaío. This is the best shelter near Matapán. Though open to north-east, it is possible during adverse conditions to shelter in the northern creek close under the monastery. Usually a yacht anchors in the southern creek in 4–5 fathoms on a sandy bottom where holding is good and there is room to swing. One can, however, anchor closer inshore in $2\frac{1}{2}$ fathoms where a short quay and a still shorter 'mole' have been built (5-ft depth at its head). This can be used for the yacht's sternfast and can also provide shelter when landing by dinghy.

The 'towered' village is half an hour's walk up the hill, but hardly worth the effort, for most of the houses are deserted and only thirty people live there. The monastery standing on the hill on the north side of the bay is no longer inhabited.

One can walk to the lighthouse on Cape Matapán in an hour, following a goat track passing through the low scrub, which covers most of the hillside, and down to the cave of Ténaron, the entrance to Hades.

Entrance to the Underworld. In recent years during calm weather a few enterprising Hellenophiles have called here in yachts and caïques to make an examination of this legendary 'Entrance to the Underworld'. One learns that in earlier times Psyche was sent here by Aphrodite to fetch the mysterious casket which was to restore her beauty. Also the bereaved Orpheus when journeying in search for Euridice found his progress blocked by the evil three-headed watch-dog Cerberus, then guarding the cave. To overcome this obstruction Orpheus decided to rely upon his skill with the lute, and very soon Cerberus was lulled to sleep.

Modern explorers while swimming in the semi-darkness of this smooth-sided cave have reported the entire absence of any feeling of mystery. After an underwater examination into the furthest recess they found no sign of any further cave nor any sealed opening. The only inhabitants today are the bats and swallows.

Continuing into **Kolokíthia Bay**, which, though delightful with its green slopes and attractive valleys, provides very few places where one would care to anchor for more than an hour or two in a sailing yacht unless the weather was very settled:

Meligáni, a small bay, with a few houses, open to the east.

Solotéri, similar to the above, but more used by small caïques.

Nýmphi, a narrow rocky inlet 150 yds long with an open beach, and open only to the east.

Kótronas lies in a most delightful setting in a small bay with a quay (6 ft); anchorage is in 5 fathoms, close in there are stones on the bottom. Ashore there are a few houses and a taverna, a few fishing boats use the place. As this anchorage is so susceptible to the violent gusts from the hills, a small quay has been built into the rocks about 400 yds southward where caïques usually anchor for better shelter.

Skutari Bay (Chart 3351) has lovely scenery, but the anchorage is too deep for a yacht – it is liable to strong mountain gusts.In settled weather a yacht can anchor in one of the two coves on the east side of the bay. The better one is **Fisherman's Cove** which has good shelter in attractive surroundings from all directions except the West. Winds from this quarter give rise to mountain squalls which sweep across the bay with little warning other than unexplained turbulence of the sea. This precursory warning should be regarded as a signal to get out quickly on account of the 1½-mile fetch which very quickly makes the cove untenable.

Although strong and prolonged winds from the South and S.S.E. send in a heavy swell to

Skutari Bay there is no evidence of this in Fisherman's Cove. The anchorage is in 3 fathoms on firm sand.

Yíthion (Chart 712 plan) is a pleasant old port frequented by both trawlers and small steamers. The small town is useful for making excursions to Mistrá and the famous Díros caves. A modern suburb has grown up and as a result of tourism has recently expanded.

Approach and Berth. There are no difficulties day or night and a yacht should make for the inner harbour. The existing mole has been extended by a further 220 yds in a N.E. direction. The port has been dredged to a uniform $3\frac{1}{2}$ fathoms. Secure stern-to the quay with anchor to the eastward; the bottom is firm clay. Though the harbour appears to be reasonably sheltered, it can, in fact, be dangerous for a vessel to lie here in strong winds on account of the violent gusts from the Taygétos mountains. Easterly winds bring in a swell.

Officials. Harbour office in square near root of mole.

Facilities. Water and fuel are available at the extremity of the old mole. Petrol at the quay. Provision shops with excellent fruit and vegetables; hotels, pensions, restaurants and tavernas which provide good fish meals, especially those on the quay leading towards Kranái islet. There

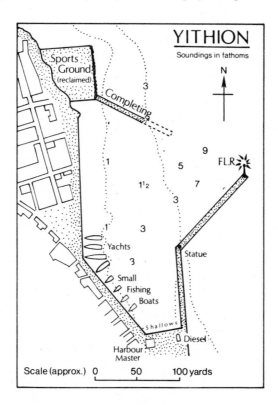

YITHION

Soundings in fathoms

Sports Ground (reclaimed)

N

Completing

9

1

5

FL.R

1^12

7

3

3

3

Yachts

Statue

3

Small Fishing Boats

Shallows

Diesel

Harbour Master

Scale (approx.) 0   50   100 yards

is a small museum. Steamers to Piraeus, Kíthera and Crete call twice a week. Buses to Athens, Sparta, Yerolimín, the Díros caves and Néapolis.

The town of 7,000 inhabitants is unspoilt and despite the influence of tourism it is one of the very few small Greek towns to have retained its old character. The elegant stone houses with their wooden balconies add to its attraction in making Yíthion a charming place to visit.

A good road passing N.W. over the mountains and through attractive green country, thick with citrus and olive trees, enables buses to reach Sparta in an hour. This is a modern town of little concern except for the famous Roman mosaic, but Mistrà, 15 min further, has the most interesting remains of a Byzantine town standing on a hill overlooking the magnificent country under the Taygétos ranges; several of its churches and monasteries are still in good order, and it is well worth a visit.

History. Although traces of ancient Yíthion, in the form of walls, are now visible underwater near the shoreline, the ruins of the Roman city extend some distance seawards. The town disappeared beneath the waves during the great earthquake of A.D. 374–5 and has only recently been professionally surveyed by skindiving archaeologists. Long before the Romans, however, Yíthion was the seaport of Sparta and a naval base; but once it obtained independence under Augustus its importance increased as a commercial port on the trade route between Rome and Athens, one of its assets being the quarries at Krokéai whose marble for lining Roman baths was much in demand.

Crossing to the E. side of the Gulf,

Eláia, a very small port with a short mole on its eastern side, lies at the foot of a prominent village, close N. of C. Moláon with a tower near by.

Xíli Bay with the port of Plítra is shown on Chart 712. Protected by a long breakwater, it is a dreary barren little place. In the event of southerly winds anchorage can be found under the lee of C. Arkhangelo.

Plítra

Approach and Berth. The depth of the breakwater in the approach channel is 12 ft and the bottom uneven rocks. By night a red light is exhibited on the molehead. Berth not more than 30 yds inside the molehead with stern to quay, bows northward. Bottom is broken rock, boulders and gravel. Above and below water rocks lie only 60 yds of the mole. It is not a safe harbour.

Facilities. Very limited provisions to be bought at the hamlet. No good fresh water available. Buses run daily to Sparta.

The port was constructed for the shipment of figs from the hinterland and is

colony, this noble cape was the last they were to see of their own country for many months to come. 'Round Maléa; forget your native country' was the saying attributed to them. Many centuries later, shortly after the heyday of Venice, from the 16th until the 19th centuries, trading vessels from the West, largely French and British, making voyages to the Aegean and Levant would often seek shelter west of this cape in Vátika Bay.

4
The Islands of Kíthera and Antí-Kithera with the Western Approaches to the Aegean

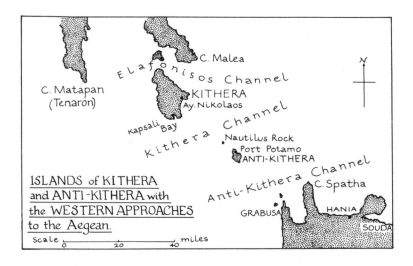

ISLAND OF KÍTHERA
  The anchorages of Panaghía and Makrí
  Kapsáli Bay
  Ayios Nikólaos (Avlémona)
ISLAND OF ANTÍ-KITHERA
  Port Pótamo
  Nautilus Rock

4
The Islands of Kíthera and Antí-Kithera with the Western Approaches to the Aegean

Weather. Vessels approaching the Aegean usually pass through the 5-mile wide Elafónisos Channel between Cape Maléa and Kíthera, although the other two channels, each 10 miles in navigable width, are also used by shipping.

The weather in the area of these straits can change quickly, especially in the spring and autumn when the wind may freshen to a strong blow from an unexpected direction. This occurs usually when a depression happens to be passing through the Mediterranean and the wind may spring up suddenly from the eastern quadrant.

Normally in the summer months a westerly wind of moderate strength may be expected, although on reaching Cape Maléa it may change and blow freshly from the north according to the strength of the Meltemi at the time. Under these conditions, if shelter is wanted, both the small ports of Kíthera are suitable for a yacht, or, in emergency, Grabúsa on the west coast of Crete. During the Meltémi season it usually blows from N.E.

The Western Approaches to the Aegean consist of three channels:

Elafónisos, between Elafónisos Island and Kíthera. It is nearly 5 miles wide and is used by most vessels approaching the Aegean.

Kíthera, between Kíthera Island and the groups of unmarked rocks N.W. of Antí-Kithera.

Antí-Kithera, between Antí-Kithera Island and the N.W. promontories of Crete.

> Forsaken isle! around thy barren shore
> Wild tempests howl – and wintry surges roar.
> WRIGHT, *Horar Ionicae* (1807)

The Island of Kíthera is mountainous and steep-to with a barren-looking coast. It has two harbours: on the S.E. coast is Ayios Nikólaos (Avlémona), and there is Kapsáli Bay in the south. Also two places of partial shelter on the N.E. coast, suitable for landing under favourable conditions: **Panaghía** (or Pelayía) with its 100-yd mole, and the sandy lagoon at **Makrí Islet**. It is formed in a cove sheltered by an islet affording protection from E. and N. winds.

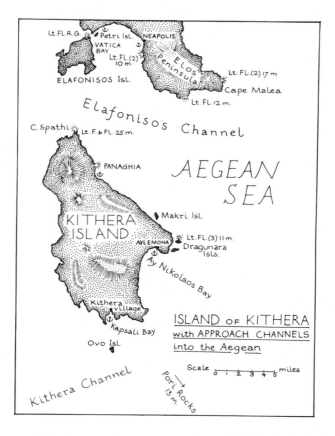

Anchorage at Makrí (plan overleaf)

(a) With easterly winds one should anchor west of the islet off the extremity of a stone pier in 2 fathoms on a sandy bottom with room to swing.

(b) With winds between N.W. through W. to S., one should anchor south of the islet in 4 fathoms on sand.

Caution. The obstruction shown between the E. extremity of the islet and the stone pier is the wreck of a 200-ft steamer lying about 15–20 ft under water, which is sometimes marked by a barrel-buoy.

The holding north of the breakwater is bad, being smooth rock with a thin layer of sand; but

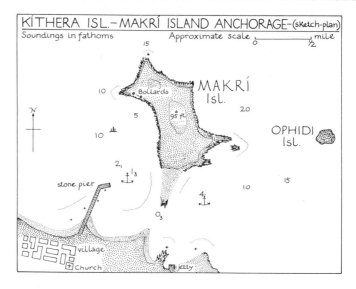

when anchoring closer to the pier one notices on the bottom an absence of sea-urchins; this is an indication of firm sand.

Facilities. Landing at the stone pier one comes to a primitive hamlet where very little is obtainable.

Kapsáli Bay, shown in a plan on Chart 712, lies in a mountainous setting with an anchorage open to the south. It is dominated by a massive Venetian castle. The *chora*, capital of the island, lies 600 ft up and is one of the most attractive little towns in Greece. (See Plate 14.)

Approach and Berth. Chart 712. Lying 2 miles south of the entrance is the conspicuous Avgó Islet, an egg-shaped rock standing at 650 ft. A yacht can either anchor in the bay in 4 fathoms or berth (with caution) behind the rocky spur on which the lighthouse stands, and where shelter is better. The new quay has a depth of only 8 ft, and is useful for securing a sternfast when the yacht has laid out an anchor to the westward. If laying out an anchor to the N.W. caution is needed to be sure of avoiding a reef lying off the beach. The sea bottom at the anchorage is sand, but near the quay among patches of sand are loose rock and stones, giving uncertain holding. The bay is susceptible to a swell, and untenable in sirocco winds. In the summer months westerly winds predominate, although northerly weather is frequent.

Facilities. Fresh water, which is good, is sometimes available from a tap near by, and has been piped to the quay, which has been improved; fuel oil also provided. Limited provisions can be bought and there is an attractive market at the *chora*.

The *chora*, a full half-hour's climb, lies on the hillside in a commanding position beyond the Venetian castle. It was the strength of the castle which so impressed travellers of the 16th and 17th centuries. Its one gate of entry was always guarded by twenty Italian soldiers and no one might enter without laying down their weapons outside. Six hundred people live in this little island capital; its winding, fascinating streets, with a modest hotel and restaurant and well-stocked shops, are remarkably clean and neat. Good fish and lobsters are often obtainable both here and in the port. People are everywhere friendly and tourists infrequent except in the height of summer. The country, although of no particular attraction, has motor roads to the other villages in the centre of the island.

A palatable *Retsína* wine – for which the island was once famous – is still exported from Kapsáli. The Piraeus steamer calls twice a week. For many years there has been a meteorological station here and one may obtain a useful forecast.

Ayios Nikólaos (Avlémona) is the little port of the hamlet of Avlémona. Though too small for a large yacht, *Sailing Directions* describes it as 'an excellent little basin with a depth of about $2\frac{3}{4}$ fathoms. Vessels can moor in safety, and the harbour is the best in Kíthera Island.' A swell enters the port in strong southerly winds.

Berth. A small quay with depths of 3 fathoms is sometimes occupied by caïques, otherwise it is the most suitable place for securing a yacht's sternfast, with her anchor laid out to the southward. The basins are small, but there is swinging room in the outer basin in depths of 3 fathoms, although one must avoid a number of small boat moorings.

Although the configuration of the port is attractive, the barrenness of the surrounding country and the poor decaying hamlet of little white houses makes only a limited appeal to visiting yacht.

History. The British will best remember Kíthera for the occasion when Nelson was Commander-in-Chief and the brig *Mentor*, carrying seventeen cases of the famous Elgin marbles, foundered in a gale off the harbour approach to Avlémona. It was two years before this valuable treasure could be recovered and conveyed to England.

Kíthera owes its early importance to its strategical position on the trade routes between Laconian ports and Phoenicia and Egypt. There is evidence here of the Minoans and later the Mycenaeans, but like many other Greek islands Kíthera has had its share of conquerors, yet no remarkable history. It was colonized first by the Phoenicians who introduced the worship of Aphrodite. The remains of her temple were seen as late as 1551 by the French Court Chamberlain and geographer, Nicholas Daulphinois, when his galley was delayed at Kíthera by bad weather. He spent a whole week exploring the island, and described the ruins of Aphrodite's temple 'on a high mountain'; there were two Ionic columns with others 'four-square' among which was a great portal with 'a statue of a woman clothed in Greek fashion of monstrous size'; the head had been removed and taken to Venice. Below the temple were the remains of the alleged castle of Menelaus, and on Mount St Nicholas were 'two chapels with mosaic pavements showing figures of mounted hunters, harts, lions, bears, dogs and diverse birds'. Today the Sanctuary of Aphrodite has survived in the form of the magnificent 14th-century church of Áyios Kosmas.

At that time the island was 'full of woods' and the population very small. It abounded in wild asses having in their heads 'a stone of great virtue'; it was used against 'falling sickness, pain in the flanks, and was laid upon a woman that cannot be delivered of child'.

The most important conquerors were the Venetians, some of whose architecture survives.

They regarded Kíthera as a watch-post for the gateway to the Aegean, and administered it as part of the Ionian Islands, and so did the British during the period of the Septinsular Republic at the end of the Napoleonic Wars in 1815. It was then garrisoned by a small detachment under a subaltern's command, the garrison being relieved every six months, as it was considered to be 'a very lonely station'. Some English cannon, a bridge and a few graves are the only remains of this British occupation. When restored to Greece in 1864, although still one of the 'Seven Islands', it became administered directly from Athens.

Kíthera's small population still grows enough to maintain itself, but many emigrate to Australia or go to sea.

Between Kíthera and Crete is the small island of Antí-Kithera. The 10-mile-wide navigable channels on either side of it are used by vessels proceeding in the direction of Crete.

Island of Antí-Kithera

This island has a rocky inlet with a hamlet on the north coast, supporting a very small population.

Port Potamós. Chart 712 (plan). It is seldom visited, largely because of the heavy swell which comes in during the prevailing fresh northerly winds and westerly winds, and on account of the poor holding on a rocky bottom.

The only time that Port Potamós came into the news was in the spring of 1900 when a Sými sponge-boat put in to shelter in a small cove S.S.E. of the port. To while away the time at their enforced anchorage, a diver descended to examine the bottom for sponges. He was astonished to find not sponges but statuary. This proved to be original Greek and Roman copies of figures lying on the wreck of an ancient ship which had been conveying them from Greece to Rome. Subsequently, a number were recovered and are now proudly displayed in the National Museum in Athens. The wreck was a vessel of about 300 tons probably built during the 1st or 2nd century B.C., and was copper fastened and lead sheathed.

Nautilus Rock, about 10 ft tall, lies about 5 miles N.W. of Anti-Kíthera and $2\frac{1}{4}$ miles S.W. of the conspicuous Pori Islet (410 ft). It is one of a group of rocky islets shown clearly on Chart 1685. This rock is named after the frigate H.M.S. *Nautilus*, wrecked here during the dark hours on the early morning of 3 January 1807, when homeward bound with urgent dispatches from C.-in-C. to Admiralty. Running southward down the Aegean before a strong northerly wind she had, in the darkness, mistaken the silhouette of the islets for part of Antí-Kithera Island. She altered course to the west and so ran hard up upon the rocks. She soon began to break up, and those of the crew who were able managed to get washed up on the bare rocks where, for five days during the gale without clothing, food or water, they suffered great privation and many perished. On the sixth day four fishing boats came out from Port Pótamo and rescued 64 survivors of the total crew of 122.

> *O God have mercy on this dreadful hour*
> *On the poor mariner! In comfort here*
> *Safe sheltered as I am, I almost fear*
> *The blast that rages with resistless power.*
> SOUTHEY, *A Silent Prayer*

At the subsequent court martial it was revealed that the rock which *Nautilus* had struck was not marked on the chart.

Before crossing the Kíthera channels to Crete a decision will have been reached as to whether to pass along the north or the south coast of this long island. A brief description is given in the following chapter in the hope that it may be helpful to the visiting yachtsman in planning his cruise.

Introduction to Crete

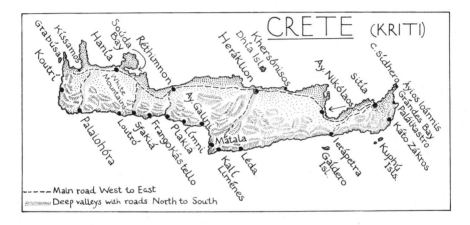

Known to the Greeks as *Kríti* this island was once the centre of the western world. It was also the home of the first European civilization.

With a length of 140 miles it is the longest island of the Aegean. It has also the highest peak – Mount Ída – more than 8,000 ft, at the apex of a great chain of mountains that form a spine through which half a dozen valleys provide the only communication between the north and south coasts.

Crete was the leading maritime power in the middle Bronze Age. According to Diódorus, it 'lay very favourably for voyages all over the world' (that is the Greek world of the eastern Mediterranean). Probably at about 1500 B.C. when the disastrous Santorini eruption took place, the eastern half of the island suddenly became depopulated, the Minoan hegemony declining almost overnight in consequence. Recent geological surveys have proved that the whole surface of eastern Crete became coated with a layer of pumice powder which had been blown from Santorini by the prevailing wind. The sterile dust compelled the population to abandon this part of the island for many years.

In Roman times a good account of a voyage off the S. coast survives in Chap. 19 of the Acts, and it was St Paul who referred to the Cretans as 'Liars, evil beasts, slow bellies'. After the Arabs and Byzantines came the Fourth Crusade followed by the Venetian capture of Crete which they ruled for four centuries under the name of Candia.

Venice has left behind much architecture – lions, fountains, columns, harbours, lighthouse, monastery and fortifications; it also attracted the best of Greek scholars – Theotokópoulos, known as El Greco, was one of them. It was, however, an unhappy time for the Cretans, who were constantly in a state of revolt against their oppressive masters.

The Turks finally overran the island after a twenty-two-year siege in 1669 and held it until the eve of the First World War when the Great Powers handed it over to Greece.

Today the half-million inhabitants live in the towns and small villages mainly on the north coast. Only in recent years have the men, and the women too, taken to wearing western clothes.

The country scenery is grand; although more than half the island is impossible to cultivate, the northern slopes of the mountains and the elevated plains are rich with vines, olives and farm produce.

Food and Drink: The type of food in Crete is no different from the rest of Greece, but it is usually rather better. Fish is more plentiful and fruit and bananas, not only better but in great abundance; oranges, bananas, figs, walnuts are excellent. *Wine:* Red, white, rosé and *Retsína* are all obtainable. According to the time of year they can nearly always be found in draught form. Beer is obtainable everywhere. The local drink is *Raki*, known as *Tsikoudiá;* it is not always appreciated by western Europeans, but it, too, can be bought from the barrel.

Pilotage. On the south coast there are no entirely secure harbours. In the summer, however, it is reasonably safe to make use of certain anchorages. The most troublesome enemy of the sailing yacht is the hard gusts which, with fresh north winds, blow strongly down from the mountains. So hard are these gusts off the S.E. coast that *Sailing Directions* warns sailing vessels to keep 5 miles off. This coast is, therefore, recommended only for yachts with power.

Prohibited Areas. Off both the north and south coasts of Crete there are large areas used for military purposes marked on the recent charts. Some of these are only firing or bombing ranges and when in action are referred to by their code-names in the Notices to Mariners broadcast daily at 15.30 on the radio national programme in Greek; and on the radio First Programme 728 kHz. Times and frequencies in 'Greece for the Yachtsman', E.O.T. booklet.

5
Southern Crete
(including the western and eastern shore)

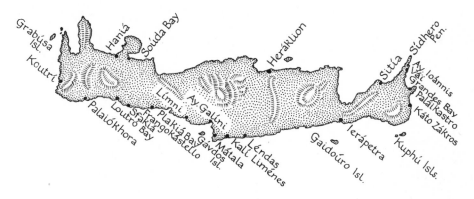

WEST COAST
   Grabúsa (Gramvoúsa)
   Koutrí

SOUTH COAST
   Palaiokhóra
   Loutró Bay
   Sfakiá
   Gávdos Island
   Frangokástello
   Plakiá Bay
   Límni
   Áyias Galínis
   Mátala
   Messará Bay
   Kalí Liménes (Fair Havens)
   Léndas
   Ierápetra
   Gaidoúro Island
   Kuphú Islands (Koufonísi)

EAST COAST
   Káto Zákros
   Grándes Bay
   Paláikastro
   Koureménos
   Váï
   Erimoúpolis
   Dhaskalió Bay
   Áyios Ioánnis

5
Southern Crete

Odysseus sailing in a Phoenician ship to Libya
passed under the lee of Crete, but 'when we had put
Crete astern the hostile Zeus brought on a storm'.

Odyssey

Those expecting to find this mountainous coast refreshingly green will be disappointed; but in the great valleys, cutting through the ranges, no finer or more diverse scenery could be found anywhere. There are a large number of olives and carob trees; often a rich red soil growing every kind of market-garden produce, and winding villages of little houses avenued with mulberry and eucalyptus.

The rivers, which once flowed continuously to the coast, have mostly become storm torrents and run only after the winter rains, because the forests were felled for the African timber trade in Minoan days and later, and the rainfall has declined. There are no forests surviving today, but there are still extensive chestnut woods at the western end, and the high mountains are lightly sprinkled with cypresses, firs and a few cedars. According to Pliny this island was the original home of the cypress, and in Hellenic days they could be seen among the snowfields of the White Mountains.

This is not the only change during the last three thousand years, for significant corrugations have appeared on the southern shores causing considerable changes in the character of the coast. Parts of the south-west coast have risen at least 20 ft while stretches of the southern shore have subsided some 15 ft. One may see today a former Hellenic port raised high above the cliffs, and elsewhere cave dwellings now deep under water.

From seaward one may sometimes see small villages standing on a hilly ledge surrounded by a small patch of cultivation. Beneath them on the coast were the small Minoan ports, some of which were revived by the Venetians and still survive today though they are mostly no longer of significance except for sheltering small local craft. A few terraces can also be seen climbing from the valleys up the mountain slopes, but their cultivation has been neglected for centuries. In the higher terrain are only sheep and goats.

Those who took part in the Battle of Crete will have nostalgic memories of these shores. It may be remembered that early in 1941 the ships of the Royal Navy had been severely damaged by the *Luftwaffe*, and bombed out of the Aegean. It was then realized that, no longer having naval support, the garrison of 32,000 must be evacuated from Crete. After suffering much damage and many casualties the Navy set forth once more from Alexandria for their final task with the Army. 'They started the evacuation overtired' wrote Lord Cunningham, '. . . and had to carry it through under savage air attack . . . it is perhaps even now not realized how nearly the breaking point was reached. But that these men struggled through is a measure of their achievement.' Making use of the beaches at Áyias Galínis (where there is now a small port), Sfakiá, and the beaches at Grándes Bay they rescued half the garrison, others being brought off from Heráklion. Though the best part of the troops were saved, the Navy lost heavily both in ships and men: altogether three cruisers and six destroyers were sunk as well as many damaged. Though Crete was occupied by the Germans for the next three years, the sites of the ancient Minoan ports were used continuously for landing liaison officers and stores to sustain the Cretan Resistance until the end of the war.

Grabúsa (or Gramvoúsa). A deserted anchorage off the E. coast in a dramatic setting by an offlying island among steep cliffs. (See plan overleaf.)

Approach (Chart 1631) may be made either east or south of Grabúsa Island, recognized by the Venetian fortress standing at 450 ft on the western cliffs.

Anchorage is on the south side of Grabúsa. The place is not safe in strong winds from the S.W., but it is, however, excellent shelter in northerly gales, and a number of small Greek vessels make good use of it today.

Facilities. There are none. Only a couple of shepherds are sometimes there to look after the sheep and goats brought round by caïque from Kastélli on the north coast.

Although the island is deserted today the anchorage is often used by local craft waiting for north winds to moderate.

The supporting walls and some of the gateways into the Venetian fortress are still in good preservation. There is no means of access from the opposite shore on the mainland of Crete.

History. At the time of the Greek War of Independence this place was a thorn in the flesh to the shipping of all countries entering the Aegean. In the two years before 1827 (when piracy was partly subdued) no less than 155 vessels were pirated and their cargoes brought in here for sale. Of these vessels, 28 were under the British flag. To protect shipping nine sloops of the Royal Navy were allocated to the archipelago, and in 1828 an Anglo-French expedition was organized to destroy the base at Grabúsa.* In February of the following year, while attempting to beat into the anchorage in pursuit of some pirates, H.M. brig *Cambria*, due to an accident, missed stays and was wrecked on the reef south of the islet.

When Grabúsa was captured, 6,000 people were found on the island with 3,000 muskets and captives both male and female – 'Such misery and wretchedness I never beheld,' wrote the Senior Naval Officer, 'many hundreds of them living in holes in the rocks.' The expedition destroyed all the pirate boats and found a certain amount of plundered property which was put on board the transport *Ann and Amelia* for conveyance to Malta. After this expedition there were only minor acts of piracy in the Aegean; these did not cease until the middle of the last century.

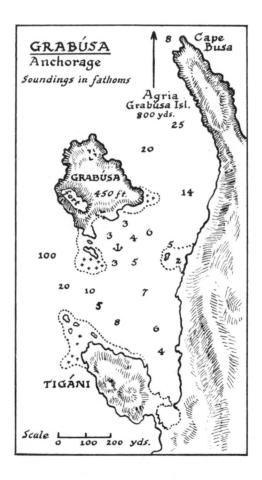

*This was probably the first organized expedition to stamp out piracy since that of Pompey eighteen centuries earlier. On that occasion he captured 846 vessels and took many captives, largely from the small Cilician ports.

14   Island of Kíthera: Kapsáli Bay

15   Methóni: the walls of Modon

16   Crete: Grabúsa, the solitary anchorage

17   Island of Kárpathos: Port Pigádhia

The Changing Coastline. Following the coast southwards for 6 miles you come to the headland of **Koutrí**. The few ruins now remaining are those of the ancient city of Phalásarna described by Strabo as possessing an artificial port and a temple sacred to Artemis. Captain Spratt, a surveyor, making some careful studies of Crete in the middle of the last century, proved that the coastline of S.W. Crete had risen considerably since the days of Greek and Roman geographers; in some places the shore, together with its ancient ports, lies as much as 26 ft above the present sea-level. The greatest upheaval was further east between Selino and Lissos (Áyios Kírikos) where certain ports, once the sea outlets for some Hellenic mountain towns, have entirely disappeared.

Phalásarna harbour resembles a Roman galley port, being hewn from the solid rock, *it now lies 20 ft up above the cliffs*. A recent examination of the coast by the Greek surveyors shows that considerable deposits of sand have filled in the small inlets and brought the fathom contours more than 100 yds away from the land.

This place is not an anchorage for a yacht, although in calm weather one may anchor temporarily in 3 fathoms and land by a rough track. Large vessels sometimes anchor under the lee of Petalídes Islet half a mile to the S.W.

South Coast

*These fierce flaws are beyond my knowledge. From all directions
the seas run at us, and amongst the hurly-burly the black ship
drives.*

ALCAEUS. 600 B.C.

There are no entirely secure harbours on the south coast of Crete, but in the summer it is reasonably safe to make use of anchorages in certain bays. The most troublesome enemy of the sailing yacht is the hard gusts which, with fresh north winds, blow strongly down from the mountains. So hard are these gusts off the S.E. coast that *Sailing Directions* warns sailing vessels to keep 5 miles off. This coast is, therefore, recommended only for yachts with power.

When visiting these ports it is sometimes interesting to bear in mind their earlier importance in Minoan days when they had a lively trade with Africa, and again in Roman times when this trade, especially with Egypt, was revived. When the Venetians came in the 13th century, sea trade was again revived though it had shifted mainly to the north coast. Four centuries later, when under Turkish rule, commerce fell to a low ebb and on the south coast, there were only

109

a few Cretan ship-owners with small schooners; the Turks, however, fearing raids by pirates, established a coastguard service, each headland having watchmen who could communicate by a system of fire signals.

With regard to the anchorages described in the following pages only two ports are considered to be undisturbed and safely sheltered: Loutró Bay traditionally considered to be safe all the year round, and the recently constructed Áyias Galínis. The latter is more suitable and convenient for a yacht.

Temporary anchorage at the western end of the coast can be found at:

Palaiókhora, a prominent headland with a small village affording sheltered anchorage either side of its isthmus according to the weather.

Approach and Anchorage. (Plan on Chart 1633.) The low walls of the Venetian fortress stand out clearly, and normally a vessel proceeds to the anchorage on the E. side of the promontory off the village. There are depths of $2\frac{1}{2}$ fathoms 200-300 yds east of a small stone pier. Here the bottom is sandy, but closer inshore are rocks. At the root of the small stone pier is a 2-ton crane, and from it a quay extends for 300 yds in a N.E. direction. This bay is completely open between E.N.E. and south, and in strong northerly winds the anchorage on the west side of the promontory is to be preferred off the sandy beach.

Towards the S.E. extremity of the promontory there is a very small horseshoe-shaped basin

used by local fishing craft. To afford better protection from S.E. a short mole has been built and high walls have been set up to provide shelter from the westerly quadrant.

Facilities. Plenty of fresh provisions can be bought; they come from Haniá three times a week during the summer. Tomatoes and cucumbers are grown in hot-houses west of the beach, oranges and tangerines in the hills above the village. A good wine can be bought. A large hotel has grown up on the bathing beach and there are many smaller ones, tavernas and cafés. Buses run to Haniá. Two ferry-services a week to the island of Gávdos, 20 miles distant.

The village, with nearly 2,000 inhabitants, is attractive. Its main street is avenued with mulberry trees and acacias; the kerb and the sills of the little houses are meticulously washed in white. Increasing tourism, mostly of the young and impecunious, has brought about a rash of ugly, cheaply built lodging houses under the E. side of the castle and in the village itself. Recently 200–300 tourists have stayed here all the winter. The local population of over a thousand (1978) are mainly occupied in fishing, and at the hot-house market gardens. The Venetian fortress has only its poorly fashioned retaining walls surviving, the rest having been quarried long ago. In the cool of the evening there is a delightful walk on the promontory by the small harbour with its golden sand, rocky pools, and often women gathering herbs.

Following the coast eastwards beyond Cape Flomés one comes to the wildest and most picturesque scenery on the coast: passing beneath the White Mountains one reaches Tripití, where two conspicuous crags meet at the entrance to the Gorge of Samariá – further inland are terraces on the side of a hill with vestiges of early habitation by the village of Ayía Rouméli. In very calm weather one may anchor off Tripití, but it is normally advisable to go to Loutró.

Loutró (Phoenix of the *Acts*) has traditionally been considered the most sheltered anchorage in southern Crete. The small hamlet lies at the foot of the bare steep mountains.

Approach. Plan on Chart 1633. Coming from the west a small white church stands conspicuously by the point and above it a buff-coloured Turkish watch-tower. There is deep water everywhere.

Anchorage. Anchor in convenient depths with ship's head pointing about E.S.E. and lay out a stern anchor. Both the holding and the shelter are good. In winter sirocco gales, the wind does not blow home, only a swell enters the bay; to guard against this eventuality vessels weight their cable. The anchorage is normally comfortable in a strong wind, although it suffers damage from a whirlwind during winter storms.

Facilities. Three small tavernas which get fish from Sfakiá. No water except that collected in private cisterns, and no easy land communication except by rough track to Sfakiá and Anópolis high up in the mountains.

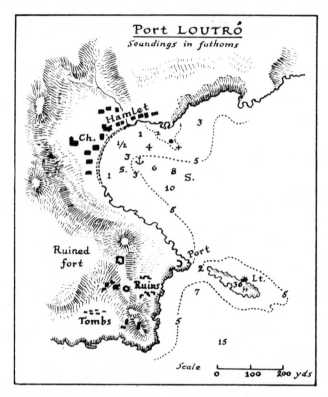

The hamlet of a dozen small white houses lies at the foot of steep, bare mountains; only one building known as 'The Chancery' stands out. A few tamarisks and a tall palm tree complete this peaceful setting. About seventy people live there, some being young seamen who are often away. Half a dozen small fishing craft provide the means of livelihood.

Local Roman inscriptions have proved that Loutró was a port frequented by Alexandrian shipping. According to St Luke's description in *Acts* (27:12) it was 'an haven of Crete that lieth towards south-west and north-west'. This would imply that he was describing the bay of Foinikiás lying on the west side of the promontory, and not the far better sheltered Loutró Bay on the east side, and facing east. However, some of the local people still refer to the ancient Phoenix as having been situated by the fragmentary remains at Foinikiás.

The port, mentioned by Strabo, was the outlet for Anópolis, now only a group of tiny villages on the hillside; but some columns and arches as well as remains show that it was once a place of importance.

The spectacular Gorge of Samariá can be reached by boat ferry or by land via

Anópolis to Ayía Rouméli, an exhausting walk often through steep hilly country. Ayía Rouméli village lies at the bottom of the gorge, and from here a rough shaded track ascends for 18 km to Xylóskalo where its tourist pavilion (with sleeping accommodation) is now reached by the Haniá bus.

After the Venetian epoch the place continued to operate a fleet of small square-riggers, fifteen or sixteen of which went on laying-up there until after the period of Napoleon. After this, trade began to decline, and by the middle of the last century the people were known for their 'lawless daring and deeds'. This was probably when the Turks built the small fort on the point and the castle on the hillslope, both of which still survive. Terraces and olive trees are still to be seen on the slopes above the hamlet, but cultivation has obviously been neglected for many decades.

Loutró used to be known as Katópolis (lower town) and the inhabitants of Anópolis (upper town) used to come down there in the winter.

Sfakiá, a small hamlet by the sea with the ruins of the former much larger village (1,200 inhabitants in 1821) straggling up the hill.

> **Anchorage.** Chart 1633. In settled weather anchor in 3 fathoms off the boat harbour where there is a landing place at a quay on the W. side. Little disturbance from the strong northerly gusts of wind.

> **Facilities.** Many small new hotels, lodging houses and villas which, from seaward have quite changed its appearance; provisions can be bought at the two main shops. Restaurants on the waterfront, a baker, a medical post. Six buses run daily in summer to Haniá ($2\frac{1}{2}$ hrs), two to Anópolis, 12 km up to the mountain by a rough road.

With a population of 400, Sfakiá is the provincial capital, whose people are famed throughout their history for their unremitting struggle for independence, also for their belief in vampires and the particular purity of their dialect. Until recently both poor and neglected, Sfakiá is now submerged under tourism and is no longer a pleasant place to visit in summer when as many as 1,500 people a day are said to be competing for accommodation. The sea is crowded with outboard motor boats. In settled weather small local boats can be hired at Sfakiá to take one to Loutró ($\frac{1}{2}$ hr) and Ayiá Rouméli (2 hrs), but not before early May. Alternatively the track over the mountains from Sfakiá to Ay. Rouméli is 27 km.

The ruined Venetian fortress on the S.E. promontory is said to have looked like a fortified palace. During the Second World War the beach was used as an evacuation point for those who managed to struggle across the mountains and ravines from the north coast. On the night of 22/23 May 1941 the King of Greece was embarked from here by a British cruiser and on 29/30 May 6,000 men, the last of the survivors of the original garrison of 32,000.

The offlying island of **Gávdos** (1,140 ft) is the Clauda of St Paul; it lies 20 miles south of Crete. Its few inhabitants are peasants, formerly from Sfakiá, but now their ties are with Palaiókhora. In the summer months one can land near a cluster of houses on the N.W. coast, a short distance from Kastrí. Landing can also be made on the east coast at Kaleryianá S.E. of Sarakíniko, at a shingle beach with a small pier, which is used by the mail caïque from Palaiókhora.

Apart from 'Calypso's vaulted cavern' and some arched rocks there is nothing to see. When Captain Spratt came here more than a century ago he described the local people, mostly from Sfakiá, as being 'a mixed and degenerate race' and expressed surprise when several of them swam out 'boarding his ship in a state of nudity'.

Frangokástello is an anchorage protected by a cape 6 miles east of Sfakiá. A substantial Venetian castle, entirely deserted and roofless, stands by the cape on the edge of an extensive plain, and extending in a S.E. direction 6 cables from the castle is a reef.

> **Anchorage** in 2 or 3 fathoms is in a small bay close northward but with strong north winds there are mountain gusts.

The castle was built at the end of the 14th century and although it is ruined one can still see the emblem of the Lion of St Mark above the door and coats of arms of the Querini and Dolfin families. During the uprising of 1828 Hadzí Miháli Daliána, an Epirot who had come to help the rebels, was killed there together with a thousand of his men. A nun subsequently collected his remains and buried them under the now ruined church of Ayios Harálambos. Every year towards the end of May or beginning of June just before sunrise a battalion of shadows comes out of the ruins and heads for the sea. Although scientists claim that this phenomenon is caused by a triangle of reflections from Africa when soldiers are training on a Libyan beach, the local people continue to believe in the shadows.

Continuing eastwards one comes to two coves, only one being of interest apart from the scenery;

Plakiá Bay, 8 miles east and 1½ miles north of the headland of Kakomoúri, is suitable in settled weather for temporary anchorage.

Límni, a small cove at the mouth of a ravine, lies 5 miles east of Plakiá. It may be recognized by the monastery of Préveli on the hill a mile westward; the place was used by the British for minor operations against the Germans between 1941 and 1943. Like the equally famous Arkádi near Réthimnon, the monastery took part in every resistance movement throughout its history. In 1941 it sheltered hundreds of British, Australian and New Zealand troops until they could be taken off to Egypt by submarine. It is well worth a visit.

Áyias Galínis (Erimoúpolis). The only artificial port on the south of Crete, and in the summer months the most sheltered port of call. (See plan overleaf.)

Approach. A tall substantial mole with a quay extends for 150 yds in a direction about 115° from the western side of the hamlet. At its extremity is a short tower sometimes lit, and above the root, about 60 ft high, is an obelisk. The mole, with tall protecting wall, is easily distinguished from seaward. There are depths of 30 ft off the molehead decreasing to 12 ft at its root by a broad quay (see plan on Chart 1633).

Berth. A yacht should berth either stern to the mole or off the broad quay by its root (12 ft) where there is a fresh-water tap. The port is well sheltered except in southerly winds, and the summer meltemi causes little concern. The bottom is sand.

Officials. Harbour Master and Customs. It is not a Port of Entry.

Facilities. Water from a small-bore tap against the outer wall of the mole near its root. Transit diesel fuel from a tank on the eastern extremity of the broad quay. Ice, brought from Heráklion, near the beginning of the first street up from the root of the mole. Diesel and petrol pumps at the beginning of the next street parallel. Hotels, pensions, restaurants and tavernas in abundance. Provisions of all kinds are available in the shops in summer, nearly all of them brought in from Heráklion. Daily buses to Heráklion, Réthimnon and Haniá. A taxi stand.

The port was built in 1953 for the purpose of shipping to Athens the fresh produce of the Messará plain, but this now goes by road to Heráklion in refrigerator lorries. Only one trawler now remains and she no longer fishes the waters off the African coast. With the decline in commercial activity, it seems unlikely that the red light on the molehead, destroyed in a S.E. gale, will ever be replaced.

The village, on the other hand, has expanded considerably with the advent of both summer and winter tourism, white hotels and villas now stretching conspicuously up the hillside. Áyias Galínis is said to have the warmest, driest winter climate in Greece. Though the population is still about 500, the young people now stay to work in the hotels and are no longer dependent on the oilcake factory for employment.

Westward of the mole are some remarkable caves set in the vertical cliffs by the water.

The usefulness of Áyias Galínis to a yacht is that she can usually be left here in safety while one goes off to visit the Minoan ruins at Phaestós and Ayía Triáda. A

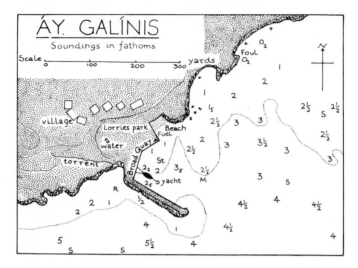

taxi can be hired. The ascent of Mount Ida (Psilorítis) can also be made from here by taking a bus to Kamáres where a bed and guide can be found before making an early start next morning. Kamáres is where the famous Minoan pottery – named after it – was recovered from a cave and sent to Heráklion museum. From here to the western summit of Mount Ida is a five-hour climb. On its summit is the little Stavrós church, where a night can be spent.

Messará Bay. The long beach extending southwards nearly to Mátala is of no interest from seawards. When viewed from the hinterland at Ayía Triáda (the famous Minoan summer palace standing on the hill), the valley leading towards the beach may be seen to open on a beautifully wooded and cultivated plain.

It seems apparent that with the drying up of the river, which many centuries ago flowed out of the great Messará Plain, the same process of nature has repeated itself as in Ionian Anatolia, i.e. the silt from the river no longer being carried swiftly to the sea has gradually been deposited in the river-bed and has built up a large flood plain; the sea and the waves have overcome the small outflow of water at the river-mouth and sealed the river exit with a beach.

In late medieval times there was a last attempt to maintain a port for shipments of produce from this plain: at Kókkinos Pýrgos at the northern end of the beach are remains of port buildings, but until the recent opening of a port at Ayía Galíni there has been no proper sea export of Messára produce for centuries. The area is now covered with plastic hot-houses and appears from seaward as a great lake.

Mátala. A horseshoe-shaped bay with a good bathing beach – suitable for temporary anchorage.

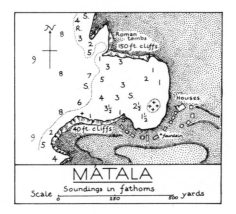

Approach and Anchorage. The bay may be recognized by the white cliffs on the northern side of the entrance. Anchor anywhere convenient off the sandy beach.

The bay is open to the westerly swell caused by the day breeze, and can attract mountain gusts in the event of strong north winds.

Facilities. Hotels, pensions, rooms, tavernas, restaurants and several well-stocked shops. Ice is brought daily from Heráklion. There are eight buses daily to Heráklion via either Phaestós or Pitsídia.

Mátala has been very much developed as a tourist centre, almost exclusively for the younger, much poorer tourists, numbers of whom took to living in the Roman tombs cut in the cliff on the north side or to sleeping on the beach in summer.

The port existed from early Roman until Byzantine times. What is believed to be a large wharf over which there is less than a metre of water can easily be detected by the breaking of the swell close to the shore and is very clearly seen by swimming over it. According to the *Odyssey* some of Menelaus' ships were wrecked here when returning from Troy. There is evidence of the port having been used as an outlet for Gortýna, the provincial capital, for communication and trade with African ports. At that time Mátala was probably a deep, sheltered inlet cut into the end of the valley: during the centuries the coast has changed. The cliffs have sunk an estimated 8ft and the inlet has subsequently been further restricted by the formation of a beach. Some of the houses cut in the cliff on the south side are now 10 to 15 ft under water. The top part of a galley-shed can be seen under the taverna on the south promontory. The presence of very eroded bollards hewn from the rock in the same area suggest that trading vessels used this port until much later times.

117

Kalí Liménes (Fair Havens) is a small bay open to the E. with a few fishermen's cottages round the beach and conspicuous white houses of the oil company on higher ground.

> **Approach and Anchorage.** See plan on chart 1633. The church of Áyios Pávlos has been rebuilt and is conspicuous. So are the four round white fuel-tanks on the islet which from a distance looks like a fort. Proceed into the bay and anchor in 2 fathoms in the S. corner close to the buoy where the tug lies. A stern line should be taken to the jetty on the N. side of the Áyios Pávlos promontory where a landing can be made. There are depths of $2\frac{1}{2}$ fathoms at its extremity. Strong gusts from the cliffs are less violent here than at many places.
>
> **Officials.** Harbour Master, Customs.
>
> **Facilities.** No provisions, no fuel for yachts: a small taverna which can do simple fish meals and has a telephone. Water from a well. Daily bus, two in summer, takes 2 hrs to do the 23 km over the mountains to Míres on a rough road. An even rougher road, usable only in dry weather leads to the Venetian monastery of Moní Odigìtrias and on to Síva where it joins the Míres-Mátala road.

The bay has been developed by an oil company as a bunkering station. Piers have been built to berth the tankers.

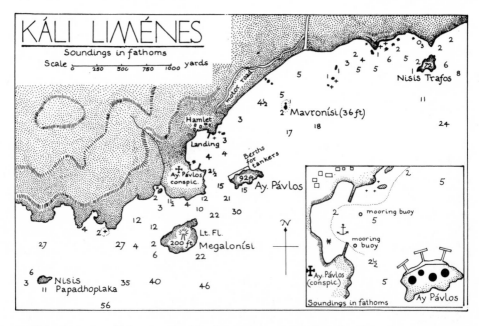

Fifty people still live in the hamlet and work on their land in the mountains growing tomatoes and olives. Half a dozen are fishermen but they haul out their boats from mid-November to the end of March because of the south-easterly gales. If caught by a gale in the harbour the trawlers lay out a warp to the W. side of the jetty on the S. promontory and secure stern warps to the E. shore.

To brighten the solitude of the lonely oilmen a number of peacocks have been established.

History. In A.D. 59 when St Paul was *en route* from Myra to Rome in a corn ship, they had been forced by the strong N.W. winds in the Aegean to pass under the S.E. of Crete. They reached Fair Havens. The question of wintering here arose; it was now after 5 October, and not considered safe to continue the voyage so late in the season. It would appear that they had a conference on board where, against Paul's advice, a decision was made to sail for the next port on the coast – Phoenix (almost certainly Loutró Bay) nearly 40 miles further. In *Acts* 27, the narrative continues: 'When a south wind sprang up they imagined that it answered their purpose and setting sail coasted along keeping close in to the shore. But before long a squally off-shore North-easter blew up and hit the ship, which was unable to head into it, so we let ourselves be carried along. We ran under the lee of the little island called Clauda [modern *Gávdos*] and managed with some difficulty to haul in the ship's boat.'

A fortnight later they were wrecked at Malta (See plan on p. 120.)

St Luke's description of the wind's direction as N.E. does not quite make sense in the narrative that follows. The controversial word is *Euroclydon*, whose exact meaning has been disputed. If N.E. was intended – an unusual wind off this coast – where the deep mountain valleys govern the direction – it would have suited the Roman corn-ship and given her an easy sail to Phoenix. Quite clearly it did not.

But having started with a southerly wind – 'which answered their purpose' – it

**Roman Merchant Vessel – about 2nd century A.D.
Sketch from a model in the Science Museum
(about 250 tons burden)**

seems likely that after reaching Cape Líthinos the wind headed them, coming in freshly from the north, that is from the Cretan mountains. A change of wind from this direction – a natural occurrence with a passing depression – would make nautical sense of the narrative, and explain how the vessel was headed off from the land by this strong wind, and, 'being unable to head into it', made for the lee of Clauda where they 'managed with some difficulty to haul in the ship's boat'.

An accurate record of a repetition of these weather conditions occurred almost exactly eighteen centuries later when the British Admiralty's auxiliary survey vessel *Spitfire* had put to sea from Fair Havens.

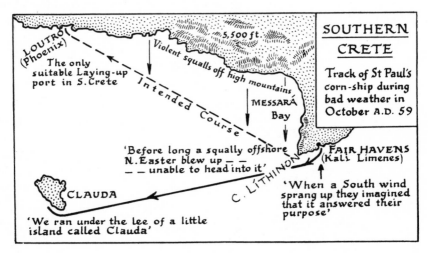

On this occasion, in October 1852, *Spitfire* experienced light flaws of wind from south and sometimes off the land. She accordingly raised steam to obtain some assistance from her paddles. On rounding Cape Lithinos the wind suddenly sprang up from the north, soon reaching gale strength. Only by raising a full pressure of steam did *Spitfire* eventually reach the head of Messará Bay and there obtain some shelter under the land while the gale continued.

Léndas (Léda) is a small open cove close under the prominent headland of Kefáles (Leon), which resembles a crouching lion. It lies 6 miles east of Káli Liménes. In 3-fathom depths there is shelter from the west, but the sea can be rather disturbed.

Formerly called Lebini, it was a port for Gortýna at the end of the Minoan period, and was also renowned for its medicinal spring waters which are still collected and bottled for sale in Crete. Some Minoan remains can be seen.

Southern Crete – The coast looking towards Káli Liménes (*after Captain Spratt*)

Ierápetra is the largest village on the south coast of Crete and is well worth a visit.

Approach. Chart 1633, plan and above plan. The village standing against a barren background is easily recognized from seaward. The oil factory chimney and minaret are both conspicuous, also the fort on the headland.

Berth. The anchorage is in the N.W. corner of the bay in convenient depths on a sandy bottom. Open between E. and S. from which quarter a swell often rolls in. There are steps on the north side of the jetty built on the ancient mole and a ramp at the root of it where a dinghy can be pulled up. Any attempt to enter the inner basin or the unfinished new harbour would for the present be unwise. A new harbour with approximate 2-fathom depths was under construction eastward of the village on the site of the ancient fort, but recent reports are lacking.

Facilities. Water from a tap by the S.W. corner of the fort. Petrol and diesel fuel in cans from the village. Increasing tourism has considerably expanded the village, and there are several hotels, pensions, lodging houses, tavernas and cafés. Very good restaurants on the waterfront towards the inner harbour. Adequate shops and very good fruit and vegetables in the market just off the main square past the post office. Eight buses daily to Heráklion, six to Áyios Nikólaos, two to Sitia and several to near-by villages. A good bathing beach.

This village with a population of 10,000, has been of importance throughout the centuries. During the Roman era it was quite a large town with three small harbours. Travellers in medieval times have described the ruined amphitheatre,

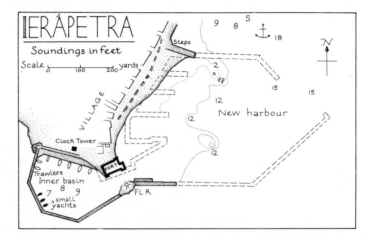

two theatres, temples, baths and aqueducts. At that time it was a village surrounded by walls, but in 1508 a severe earthquake destroyed everything and today the present village and the rebuilt Venetian fortress stand on the site of the original medieval architecture, embedded in the walls of some of the modern houses. The Turks walled the fortress in the 17th century: they also left a mosque and a small monument near by.

The small museum by the Town Hall has two exceptionally beautiful Minoan sarcophagi, one of which is the most remarkable ever found. Objects in the Ashmolean Museum at Oxford also testify to Ierápetra's importance in Minoan times. Two fine Parian marble sarcophagi of a much later period, brought off by H.M.S. *Medina* in 1860, are now in the British Museum.

Today Ierápetra has an international export trade in early produce, mostly tomatoes.

Gaidoúro is an uninhabited island of no interest, but in an emergency can provide anchorage under its lee from southerly gales. Fishing boats from Ierápetra sometimes fish in this area.

East Coast

Lying off the S.E. corner of Crete are the **Kuphú Islands** (Koufonísi) deserted and waterless, they are distinguished by their white cliffs. The largest of the group is low and flat. All are uninhabited but both in Roman and medieval times there was a small population. A few ruins of the Roman period remain and recently some Minoan remains have been discovered.

Proceeding north-eastwards for 6 miles one comes to Ampélos, with Kavállos Bay anchorage; but, on account of the violent squalls, during the meltemi season a yacht is recommended to give this part of the coast a wide berth. Four and a half miles further is the sandy Zákros Bay.

Káto Zákros, a tiny hamlet at the foot of a dramatic gorge.

> **Anchorage.** In the N. corner of the bay in convenient depths on sand. In front of the more northerly of the two tavernas, a rocky spit extends outwards for 100 yds with depths of only 3 ft over it. Other rocky patches are to be found in the S. half of the bay.
>
> **Officials.** A small Harbour Master's post, dependency of Sitía.
>
> **Facilities.** Two tavernas with rooms provide excellent fish meals. Basic provisions including fish can also be provided or ordered by telephone. Good water from wells. A rough road leads to Upper Zákros, 8 km away; a shorter track leads up through the gorge. From the village a twice daily bus to Sitía.

The interest in the place is the excavated Minoan site and the banana groves. Although examined by the British archaeologist Hogarth in 1901 when Zákros was then judged to have been an early trading port for Africa, recent excavations have revealed the remains of a large Minoan palace probably of the period about 1500 B.C. Many vases, storage jars, copper ingots, tools, ivory tusks etc. have been recovered from the ruins and sent to Heráklion Museum. Visitors who expect to see its restoration as grand and realistic as that at Knossós could be disappointed; but if they visit the museums of Greece, Britain or Germany, they will be astonished to see such a high standard in the delicate terracotta pottery and the exquisite ornamental jewellery recovered from these Minoan palaces and sea-ports.

Along the S. side of the harbour are a series of Minoan buildings which may have served ships using the harbour. Local fishermen claim that when the gorge floods a large ancient wall is temporarily revealed.

Grándes Bay. On Chart 1677, can be seen detailed plans of anchorages which, under certain conditions, are suitable for sheltering a yacht. The bay is entered after rounding the steep-to Cape Pláka which was, with little doubt, the Cape Salmone of the *Acts* where St Paul's ship made her landfall in late September A.D. 59 after leaving Cnidos bound for Rome.

The prevailing wind in the summer months is northerly, though during

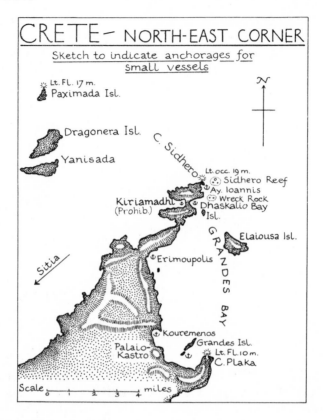

CRETE— NORTH-EAST CORNER
Sketch to indicate anchorages for small vessels

September the N.W. wind is prominent. Strong winds are usually preceded by haze and humidity.

In the southern part of this large bay, where the shore is often encumbered with rocks, are some small landing places with occasional anchorages where local caïques during summer collect farm produce and convey it to the north coast ports.

Palaíkastro, once two early Minoan sites, one on the prominent hilltop close to the shore, the other a town in the E. corner of the bay. This was excavated by the British School in 1962–3 and the finds are in the Heráklion Museum.

> **Anchorage.** There is no suitable place for a yacht to anchor in unsettled weather and the landing at a natural rock quay used by the fishing boats is very exposed. A pleasant bathing beach lies to the northward – nearly 2 miles from the village where there is much better shelter. (*See* Koureménos.)
>
> **Facilities.** A small restaurant at the root of this mole where ice can be bought from a factory in

18 Rhodes: Líndos, showing the harbour with the citadel beyond

19   Rhodes: entrance to Mandráki harbour

the village. Two other restaurants all kept by fishermen who serve excellent fish meals: the large white one in the centre of the bay has rooms and a telephone. From here a rough road runs up through the olive groves to the village, 35-min walk. Palaíkastro has just over a thousand inhabitants, mostly farmers or fishermen; a hotel and pension, two restaurants, good food shops, a taxi and a first-class blacksmith. Twice daily bus to Sitía and Upper Zákros, four in summer. Petrol from a pump. There is a pleasant bathing beach 3 km north from Paláikastro.

The fortified monastery of Toploú is only 5 miles from here and can be reached by a good road. The monastery, formerly defended by its own guns against pirates, was founded in the 14th century, but largely rebuilt in 1718; it has rather a gloomy appearance, but its little church contains some beautiful icons.

Kouremênos, little more than a mile northwards, has a 2-fathom anchorage off a sandy bay where there is shelter except in easterly weather. In northerly weather it provides winter shelter for the trawlers that work out of Paláikastro Bay. The local craft at both places, if overtaken by easterly weather, seek shelter under the lee of the S.W. extremity of Grándes Islet.

Váï. Incorrectly shown on Chart 2436, it is 2 miles north of Kouremênos.

Anchorage is off the sandy beach easily distinguished by thick groves of palm trees on the shore. The name comes from the old word for a palm tree. Now usually called Fínikos, the place appears on Greek charts as Finikódasos (palm grove). The trees were said to have been introduced by the Arabs in the 9th century, though local legend maintains that they grew from stones spat out by Saracen pirates or Egyptian sailors. They are probably indigenous.

Facilities. Two restaurants in the S. corner of the bay, made of wood and very inconspicuous among the trees, open from Greek Easter until the end of October. In those months provisions can be bought from them. A water pump in the car park. In the summer 4 buses daily to Sitía, none in winter. An asphalt road now running from Paláikastro to Erimoúpolis has a turning off to this beach. The village of Váï is on the main road 3 km away.

Erimoúpolis (Ítanos), 1½ miles north of Váï, has good sheltered anchorage close off shore on a sandy bottom at the northern end of the bay. Fragmentary remains of the Geometric to the Hellenistic periods on the acropolis, part of an Early Christian church can be seen close to the shore. Now, the place is utterly deserted, but it was once a sizeable Roman port where freighters sailing from Egypt would put in to shelter and perhaps await favourable weather to help them continue into the Aegean.

Following the coast, with its barren hills, northward and passing inside the uninhabited island of Elása you come to

Dhaskalió Bay, affording shelter in north and west winds and often used by local craft. Depths shoal gradually from 5 fathoms, the anchorage recommended being in the south corner. Landing is strictly prohibited.

The coast now continues towards the northern point of the Sídhero promontory, and after passing two small headlands one reaches the last little anchorage on the east coast. This sector of coast has a prohibited area extending from one mile S. of the narrow neck of land separating the E. coast from Órmos Ténda. It is expected that this prohibition may be extended southwards but is unlikely to include Erimoúpolis.

Áyios Ioánnis. This is a delightful little creek suitable for a small yacht in peaceful deserted surroundings.

> **Approach.** After leaving Dhaskalió Bay care should be taken to avoid a small group of rocks (mostly under water) lying 400 yds off shore. There is a safe passage inside. These rocks are referred to on the earlier English charts as 'Wreck Rock'.

> **Anchorage.** A yacht should enter the centre of this 2-fathom creek heading in the direction of the lighthouse and there is not room to swing. Moor head and stern. A rocky ledge with depths of only one fathom extends for about 50 yds from the shore. It is strictly forbidden to land.

Should a yacht be coming from the direction of Rhodes and wishing to enter Áy. Ioánnis, she is recommended to sight the offlying reefs usually awash.

Rounding Cape Sídhero. The land falls away towards the cape (with its tall, prominent lighthouse). There is a clear passage of 600 yds when passing inside the Sídhero Reef, some of whose rocks are awash or showing above water.

Sponge fishing off the east coast of Crete provides some of the best-quality sponges. Divers from Kálimnos and Sými in the middle of the last century dived here from sprit-rigged craft without apparatus, using a 20-lb marble slab at arm's length both to sink and steer them to the desired place on the sea-bed.

The 15-ton motor trehandíri some years ago replaced the early sponge fishing boats; at that time the divers were wearing rubber suits inflated by air from a pump in the boat.

Working in groups of half a dozen or more, the divers arrived on their station early in May and then prepared for their task. With a supply of compressed air they could remain in depths of more than 12–15 fathoms without suffering from a bleeding nose, and since the best sponges, as Aristotle observe, 'come from the greater depths', they grew to accustom themselves to working in 20–30 fathoms. Unassisted, a diver could stay down only $1\frac{1}{2}$ to 2 min., but with compressed air, wearing a rubber suit, they remained down gathering sponges until the net was

Sponge boats, after a sketch by Captain Spratt (mid-19th century)

filled. Accidents were rare although divers subconsciously feared attack by sharks, but it was seldom that one was made. In the days of Pliny it was the dogfish they feared, especially the prospect of attack during their ascent to the surface. It was in later life that the effects of deep-diving were felt.

In Roman days the best sponges were brought up from the shores of Cape Malea and Lycia. The Greek divers, who for at least two centuries have come mostly from the island of Kálimnos and some from Sými, have, until recently, exploited the North African shores, but sponge-fishing here has now been denied them and they are back in Greek waters. Off southern Crete, near Áyias Galínis, have been profitable areas as well as off the E. coast, but they have hopes of Libya again.

Further east, the Turkish divers, mostly from Bodrum, fish for sponges off the Turkish coast. Also, off the Levant shores poor-quality sponges are gathered; only in the area of Ruad is there good-quality to be found. The rubber suit has been largely superseded by free diving. The diver nowadays is towed by a line from the sponge-boat at a convenient depth close above the sea bed, and supplied with air through a tube from the boat.

6

Rhodes and Adjacent Islands

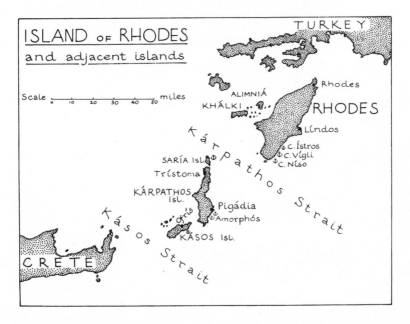

Eastern Gateway to the Aegean; the passage from N.E. Crete to Rhodes

6
Rhodes and Adjacent Islands

EASTERN GATEWAY TO THE AEGEAN

The passage from N.E. Crete to Rhodes

Both the Kásos and Kárpathos Straits have a navigable width of about 25 miles; the summer winds blow freshly from the north-westerly quarter.

During the summer, sailing vessels from Crete making for Rhodes are recommended to pass northward of Kásos (but within the protection of the rocky islets off the N.W. coast), thence under the lee of Kárpathos – keeping a couple of miles off an account of the strong gusts from the tall mountain range. Thence under the lee of Rhodes to Mandráki Harbour. Sheltered anchorages on this route are given in detail under the heading of each island. Motor yachts may prefer to pass the S.E. side of Kásos although it is not such an interesting route. Day passengers are recommended as the temporary anchorages are unlit.

The **Kásos Strait** is used by local traffic and a few larger vessels plying between Greece and Egyptian ports. It is 25 miles wide, but for 1½ miles off the Cretan

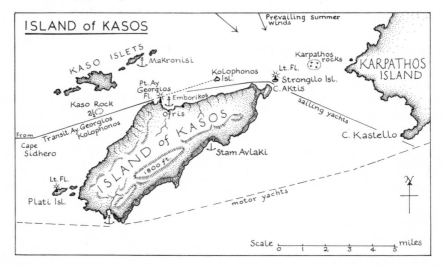

shore it is encumbered by rocks. The current is usually south-going but is much influenced by winds.

Approaching the north side of Kásos Island, a yacht should converge on the N.W. coast so as to clear the Kásos Rock (2½ fathoms) as shown on Chart 2824, i.e. Point St George in transit with Kolophónos Islet. After passing Point Áy. Geórgios the steep-to coast may be followed to the N.E. Thence pass between Strongiló Islet and Cape Áktis, head towards the southern tip of Kárpathos (Kastéllo Point).

> **Note.** The Kárpathos Rocks (6 ft under water) should be kept in mind. Emergency anchorages:
> (a) Under the lee of Kásos Island in an open bay close west of Stam Avláki.
> (b) On the S.E. side of Kárpathos, either at Makrí Yaló, or in the N.W. corner of Amorphós Bay.

When caught in bad weather north of Kásos caïques use an anchorage under the lee of the rocky islets where there is good shelter in convenient depths on a sandy bottom. The low-lying islet of Makronísi is claimed to be the best choice, though with Emborikós now becoming available doubtless some of the caïques would prefer to make use of this instead.

Island of Kásos

This small island, mountainous and barren, lying between Kárpathos and Crete, has half a dozen hamlets and, since 1962, a very small port at Emborikós. This serves the main village of Ofrís which has only a boat harbour.

The Port. Emborikós lies 1½ miles east of the village and is very small, protected by a mole, 150 yds in length, alongside the quay at which the mail steamer berths with difficulty in settled weather.

Approach and Berth. A large white church by the shore is easy to distinguish. The molehead is lit (Lt.Fl.G.). The mail steamer berths at the outer part of the quay and yachts near the steps at the bend in the mole in $2\frac{1}{2}$ fathoms. A road follows the shore to the village. In the event of a strong meltemi the steamer anchors on the lee of the island about 4 miles S.W. of Strongiló Islet (between Stam Avláki and Phíra Rocks) and communicates by boat with the shore.

The main village of Ofrís, built round the shores of the bay, accommodates most of the island's 1,350 inhabitants and today can boast of two small hotels, a bakery, a few shops and cafés. Little more than a hundred years ago the population was more than five times as large and, though then without its own harbour, Kásos shipping could be seen in many ports of the Mediterranean. Egypt attracted many of the young men, 5,000 of whom left the island and emigrated at the time of the construction of the Suez Canal. It is claimed that the pilot of the leading ship in the procession at the opening of the Canal was a sailor from Kásos.

Kásos now grows enough for its own consumption; it is primitive and unspoilt, and from seaward somewhat unattractive. Yet it is one of the few remaining places which still keeps the traditional, longitudinally divided rooms with raised sleeping quarters on one side; these have beautifully carved wooden balustrades and pillars. On the hill between Ofrís and Emborikós the date 1824 is picked out in white stones; this was the year the Egyptians ravaged the island, leaving it deserted.

Island of Kárpathos (Scarpanto)

This seldom-visited island is long, mountainous and narrow, lacking an adequately sheltered harbour suitable for a yacht in the summer months. There are some indentations, but strong gusts of wind off the mountains sweep down upon the S.E. coast during the meltemi season. Trístoma, the only well-sheltered harbour in Kárpathos lies on the north-west coast. It is closed all the summer and autumn months because of the dangerous sea breaking at its mouth. The port-of-call is Pigádia on the south-eastern shores.

The tall mountain range, rising to nearly 4,000 ft, forms the spine of the island; it runs from end to end and causes hard gusts to sweep down to the S.E. shores, thus limiting the places where landing is possible. In addition to Pigádia there are some small, well-sheltered sandy bays on the S.E. end of the island, where the land is lower and the valleys are more fertile, and there are signs of cultivation. At **Makrí Yaló** the adjoining cove, Amorphós, is the more suitable for temporary anchorage.

Pigádia, also known as Port Kárpathos, the principal village of the island, has a small inadequately sheltered port.

> **Approach and Anchorage.** Chart 2824 shows the anchorage. The mole, 100 yds long, runs in a N.W. direction from a small projection on the north side of the town; its extremity has a Lt. (Fl. R). It does not provide shelter against the prevailing mountain gusts which drive a vessel hard against the quay. It is advisable for a yacht to lay out an anchor and to make use of warps to hold her off. Depths of $2\frac{1}{2}$ fathoms until near the root of the mole, and the bottom is mud. Shelter is poor and there is often a swell. It is sometimes preferable to anchor in the northern corner of the bay, as suggested in *Sailing Directions*.
>
> A yacht should bear in mind that when the steamer calls she takes up most of the space alongside the quay.

> **Facilities.** There are a few provision shops, spring water in some of the houses, fuel at a garage, a restaurant, cafés, some small hotels and one or two tavernas. The mail boat calls four times a week in the summer months and continues to Diafáni, 14 miles further north where she lies off in the bay. There is a small airport providing communication with Rhodes.

Only a few hundred people live in the village around the port, but nearly 6,000 on the whole island, and although so close to Rhodes, life here is surprisingly primitive. A large number of the men receive remittances from England, the United States, Italy and elsewhere where they have worked for most of their lives.

British charts sometimes use the name Scarpanto, the Italian form of Kárpathos.

Trístoma on the N.W. coast is an attractive and out-of-the-way harbour with half a dozen houses, 3 hours by mule from the nearest village. It cannot be used during the meltémi season or during strong onshore winds.

> **Approach.** Chart 1666 illustrates the topography of the port. In fresh north winds such an alarming sea is whipped up at the entrance that the port is closed all the summer months.
> *Note.* The ruined church shown on the chart no longer exists.

> **Anchorage.** This should be chosen according to weather conditions.

> **Facilities.** One could formerly buy sufficient provisions for daily needs from the inhabitants, but in 1977 only one family remained.

Also on the west coast is the very small harbour of **Fíniki** in 35° 29.5 N, 27 08.5 E. The natural indentation in the shore is improved by the short breakwater, thus affording a better degree of protection from the prevailing north wind.

> **Approach.** Keep to the breakwater side of the entrance in order to avoid submerged rocks and a conspicuous rock pinnacle. Depths of 9 ft in the centre of the channel.

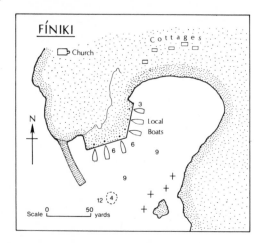

Berth. A quay where fishing boats berth affords only 6-ft. depth. Hence a medium-size yacht must anchor near the entrance and run a warp ashore.

There is only a poor little hamlet without amenities. The ruins of Palaió Kástro are one mile southward.

Up in the hills above Diafáni, in the northern end of the island, is the village of Olympós which is over 300 years behind the rest of the island. Here one can see the Karpathian dances in their purest form and many of the doors still have their remarkable wooden locks and keys of a pattern said to be Homeric.

One of the few reasons for visiting Kárpathos is to see the interesting national dress worn by women in the north of the island. They may be seen in the fields any day of the week wearing long boots and white breeches with a white skirt, looped up when working.

The little island of **Sariá** in the north is separated from the shore of Kárpathos by a very narrow, shallow channel. About 1¼ miles south of Alimúnti Point (its N.E. extremity) is anchorage in the very small sandy bay of Palátia. This, however, is barely practical for a medium-sized yacht which must anchor outside on a shelving sand and stone bottom, and run out a warp ashore.

From this desolate berth one has an impressive view of the extensive ruins of some ancient city. A few shepherds come here in the summer months, but few yachts ever call.

The Kárpathos Strait, separating Kárpathos from Rhodes, is without danger. Usually the current sets southward, but is influenced by the direction of the wind. The landfall at Rhodes should be made in daylight as the islets lying eastward of C. Prasonísi are unlit and off shore a current sets towards N.W. On the N. side of this cape it is well to keep in mind that with caution one can find anchorage with reasonable shelter towards the head of the bay. This is frequently used by local fishing craft.

The Island of Rhodes

The most beautiful is the free island of Rhodes.
PLINY XXXVI

The largest island and capital of the Dodecanese with green mountainous scenery; Rhodes has a long and interesting history.

In addition to the main port of Mandráki and the anchorage at Líndos, *Sailing Directions* refers to a number of places in open bays off the S.E. coast suitable as a lee nearly all the summer months. (Chart 1667).

ANCHORAGES OFF THE S.E. COAST

Cape Níso. The coves under this cape are sandy and there is good shelter.

Cape Vígli. A ruined tower is conspicuous standing on the cape. Yachts have found satisfactory anchorage N.E. of the point with the tower bearing 177°, good holding on sand, and with moderate N.W. winds there is no swell but no shelter from the wind. No sign of habitation.

Cape Ístros. Let go near a jetty on the S.W. shore where caïques are sometimes to be seen at anchor and where shelter from the wind is better.

Líndos, one of the three Hellenic cities, lies on the top of a high headland whose sides fall abruptly into the sea. Beneath it is **Port Líndos**, a sheltered summer anchorage from which one may conveniently land to visit the acropolis. (See Plate 18.)

> **Approach.** See plan on Chart 1666, which is not entirely accurate for depths or underwater delineation. There are no harbour lights, so that, except under a bright moon and with previous knowledge, entry by night would be difficult.

> **Anchorage.** Let go in about 2½ fathoms in the centre of the bay with Ayía Barbara chapel bearing S.E. A warp ashore is necessary. The nature of the bottom varies, being in some places mud or sand on flat rock and occasional ridges of weed which afford poor holding. There is a good shelter except between E. and S.E.

135

Facilities. A path leads up to the village which has several lodging houses, a restaurant, and a few provision shops, tavernas, cafés, post, telegraph and bank. There is bus communication with Rhodes.

This place is well worth a visit, and it makes a pleasant day's sail from the town of Rhodes and back during the meltémi season when there should be a broad reach and smooth water both ways. The acropolis of Líndos, set on a rock high above the sea, is one of the most spectacular sites in Greece. Here is evidence of the whole history of the island, dramatically and lucidly displayed; there is the classical Greek colonnade which caps the high platform of the acropolis with the temple of Athéna Líndos, the ruined Byzantine church, and the castle of the Knights. Even the Turks have left a fortification to round off this long tale.

The citadel opens on weekdays 0800 to sundown (Sundays and holidays 1000 to sundown). Coaches bring tourists from Rhodes who overrun the place most of the day. If landing from a yacht it is therefore advisable to land early or late.

Beneath the citadel is the modern village formerly celebrated for its pottery and its weaving. There are still two houses with working looms and four which exhibit the old plates, together with the poor modern copies which are for sale. The church should be visited because of the frescoes; though of a late period they are complete and traditional, and give an impression of how the Byzantine churches must once have looked. It is pleasant to wander among the little white houses which, unlike most Greek villages, are all still lived in and well preserved. Many of them incorporate Venetian windows and masonry, many have the Arabic dirt roofs and all have the black and white pebbled courtyards. The square has a beautiful fountain and shading trees.

Note: By night a restaurant on the beach at Port Líndos dispenses loud music, and to avoid this inconvenience yachts have reported a preference for the small bay south of the citadel inside the Cape – suitable in calm weather.

THE HARBOURS OF RHODES

The three harbours flanking the eastern seaboard of the city are shown on the plan taken from Chart 1666. The new Port Akándia is hardly used; its long breakwater is largely the extension of a far earlier mole.

The yacht harbour of Mandráki, originally an ancient port modernized by the Italians, formerly accommodated the caïques; but now that they have been moved out there is more space for the ever-increasing number of yachts.

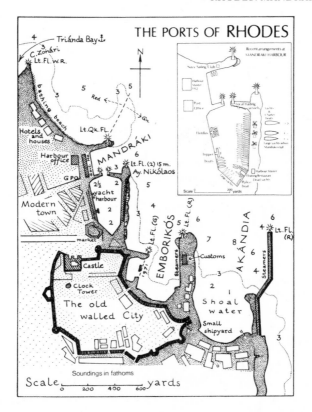

THE PORTS OF RHODES

Soundings in fathoms

Scale 0 200 400 600 yards

Mandráki Yacht Harbour

Approach. Entering Mandráki Harbour the extensive medieval walls of the old city come into view as well as the modern pseudo-Venetian buildings close to the quayside.

By day there is no difficulty in the approach. By night, however, if coming from southward along the coast, caution is necessary to ensure clearing offlying shoals.

The light on Fort St Nicholas can be clearly distinguished from afar; but the weaker light marking the extremity of the dangerous rocky point on the north side of the approach has, on a number of occasions, been washed away by winter gales and subsequently replaced. The last time it was washed away was before the loss of the yacht *Trenchemer* (Robert Somerset) in a S.E. gale during darkness on the night of 27 February 1965. The light was eventually set up on a safer site a few yards further inshore and was still in position in 1976. Its present characteristics: Qk.Fl.(G). shows over the arc of the approach and red through an arc towards west. Characteristics of the other lights can be found in *The Light List*.

In strong E. or S.E. winds a yacht is strongly advised against trying to enter Mandráki; she should make for Triánda Bay instead. (See *The Aegean*.)

Berth. Large yachts berth at the head of the harbour. Other yachts and charter flotillas usually berth at the eastern quay. The bottom is mud and the water rather foul. Although the harbour is completely enclosed, during winter gales from the S.E., heavy seas sometimes come over the breakwater.

Recently the harbour has been dredged and the southern quay much improved. The eastern quay rebuilt in 1976.

Officials. Health, Customs, Immigration and Harbour Master (office on the harbour front), this being the Port of Entry. Customs office for yachts on S. quay.

Facilities. Water, telephone and electricity at the yacht quays. Fuel at Fina station. A large Turkish-style market with a raised octagonal fish pavilion is on the harbour front and all provisions can be bought in or around it. Fruit and vegetables are in greater abundance than anywhere else except Crete, but they are also more expensive. There is a soft drinks and mineral water factory. A large selection of deep-frozen food. Draught wine is obtainable outside the market on the S. side. Other shops of every kind in the streets behind the market. Several banks, a casino, over 200 hotels, many pensions and rooms. Some good restaurants and tavernas, museums and a library. Steamers from Piraeus run five times a week (about 20 hrs) and berth at the Emborikós harbour. Ferries ply to the other islands. A caïque service to Marmarís. Five flights a day to Athens, one a week direct to London. Buses to all the villages.

A special Customs agreement with the Greek Government enables certain supplies, among which are British spirits and tinned provisions, to be bought cheaply.

Repairs and Laying-up. The busy boat-yard Nereus has been established to undertake slipping of yachts, but since repairs by mechanics and skilled artisans are hard to come by, except in the old city, owners are encouraged to undertake their own work. Travel-lift (capacity 60 tons) has been installed and storage space provided for more than 100 yachts. There is an all-in price for slipping, the first 7 days on the slip being free and after that a nominal charge. Gardienage can also be provided for yachts berthed in Mandráki Harbour. (Nereus, Odos Australis 19, Rhodes. Tel: 22.717.) For laying up in winter a concrete yard has been built, but bearing in mind the climate of Rhodes it is recommended that wooden yachts should lay up afloat at the yacht moorings at Mandráki. **The Commercial Port** has recently been enlarged, and the new port of Akándia, completed in 1971, has 500 yds of quay space.

The town of today was much restored and newly built during the 30-year Italian domination between the two World Wars, and for years it has been a large, flourishing, summer resort with numerous hotels, pensions and a port of call for many cruise ships. The medieval architecture of the Knights of St John is to be seen everywhere in the old city, which is well worth visiting. There are some Turkish mosques and Byzantine churches, and one should walk round the walls.

On leaving the town, the sight of the country with its pleasant villages soon restores the feeling of being in Greece. On the N.W. coast there are the other two Hellenic cities of Kámiros and Iálysos and castles of the Knights of St John.

Westwards are two unimportant small islands lying close off Rhodes – Alímnia and Halkí – both have sheltered bays but are rather deep for anchoring.

History. Earlier history of Rhodes tells of the tremendous sieges, first in the 3rd century B.C. and again in the 16th century from both of which there is evidence today. Following the earlier sieges Rhodes became one of the most prosperous centres of the Hellenistic world, and its city was nearly five times the size of the Old City of today. Its acropolis built on Mount Smith (named after Admiral Sir Sidney Smith of Napoleonic times) has been excavated and the foundations of a stadium, theatre and two temples unearthed. But the medieval architecture, standing nearly intact, is that set up by the Knights during their two centuries of ruling the island from 1309 to 1522, when their navy was continually destroying Arab shipping.

The famous Colossus, a wonder of the world, probably stood where Fort St Nicholas now is, and rose to a height of slightly more than 100 ft. It was a statue to Helion, the sun god, standing erect and not as the postcards show, astride the harbour. The skin of the statue was formed by bronze made from the captured siege engines of the Syrian king, Poliorcetes; it was probably fastened by dowels to an inner core of iron and limestone blocks. It stood for only half a century having been toppled into the sea by a destructive earthquake in 227 B.C. The broken metal lay in the shallow water of the harbour for 900 years, when it was bought for scrap by a Levantine Jew who took it back to Tyre in Syria where the metal was first moulded.

Rhodes, now one of the most popular tourist resorts in Greece, owes its prominent part in early history to its strategic position at the gateway to the Aegean: from Hellenistic days to early Roman times maritime supremacy gave Rhodes prosperity and culture. Its strategic position was belatedly recognized by the British in the Second World War when, in the autumn of 1943, their foothold in the Aegean islands had to be abandoned, losing six destroyers, two submarines, more than 100 aircraft and nearly 5,000 men.

139

Bozuk Bükü	Antalya
Marmaris	Selimiye
Ekinçik	Alanya
Skopea Limani	C. Anamur
Kastellórizo Isl. (Gk.)	Soğuksu
Kaş	Ovacık
Kekova Demiryeri	Taşucu
Finike	Kızkalesi
Taşlık Burnu	Mersin
Çavuş	Iskenderun
Tekirova	

20 Marmaris: a growing tourist resort in a mountainous setting

21 Kastellórizo: an aerial view of the port, which offers good protection for yachts

22 Kekova: with its sprinkling of small boat harbours

23 Kekova: the Lycian tombs often lie half-submerged, as a result of coastline subsidence

24 Myra, near Andraki Bay: a Lycian rockface necropolis

7
Turkey

Introduction to Southern Anatolia

The southern coast of Anatolia is by far the least-known part of the Mediterranean seaboard, yet the scenery is unsurpassed.

The main feature is the magnificent coastline. The heavy rainfall induces a lush green vegetation which ascends the valleys to the mountain ridges above. Here is a skyline whose sharpness of form transcends anything elsewhere in the Mediterranean.

The archaeological interest is also considerable, ranging from substantial remains of Lycian, Greek and Roman periods to surprisingly well-preserved Armenian and Lusignan castles. (It is strongly recommended to take George Bean's two standard works: *Lycian Turkey* and *Turkey's Southern Shore*.)

Ports of Entry. Marmaris, Fethiye, Kaş, Finike, Antalya, Alanya, Anamur, Taşucu, Mersin and Iskenderun.

Formalities. On arriving at Turkish ports, you will find that formalities have recently been simplified. Officials should be visited as follows:

(a) On arrival from foreign waters: Medical Officer; Passport Police; Customs office.

(b) On departure to foreign waters: Harbour Master; Passport Police; Customs office.

(c) On arrival from Turkish waters: Customs office.

(d) On departure to Turkish waters: Harbour Master; Customs office.

On arrival in Turkey it is advisable to get a Transit Log taking you to the furthest port you are likely to visit in Turkey, and then most of the port officials in between should not or do not seem to worry about any formalities.

A circular letter dated 23 June 1981, written only in Turkish, states that yachts are permitted to embark friends and relations in a Turkish port, but chartering is not allowed. Previously, one has had to cross to Greece to pick up a new crew.

During the period of military government a yacht on entering or leaving a Turkish port may be required to obtain clearance by visiting the military authorities also. At some of the smaller bays may be stationed a minor detachment of soldiers or Customs guards, and one of their duties is to ascertain the nature of any foreign craft or persons arriving on the coast. They are, however, usually pacified when presented with a crew list, preferably embellished with a rubber stamp which they can show to their officer in due course. The Turkish army, though not necessarily very military in appearance, is the pride of the country and a foreigner should comply with reasonable requests. Half a million of Turkey's 55 million population are under arms.

Changing crew: while each Customs' area may take a different view of regulations, it is possible that yachtsmen may be prevented from picking up crew in Turkish ports (under cabotage rules). It is strongly advised to check on this situation before planning any crew change in Turkey. Crew may, however, be legally embarked if the yacht is immediately clearing from Turkey.

Yachts' Mail are best sent poste restante.

People and Conditions. Until after the First World War most of the lesser ports had small colonies of Greeks and Armenians. Some of them formed the nucleus of the artisan population and others contributed in some way towards the prosperity of the port. These minorities have now vanished and with them the sparkle of life which formerly animated these small communities, and gave them more importance than they have today.

The standard of education has recently improved, since school is now compulsory between the ages of seven and twelve.

Conditions ashore are no longer primitive: often fresh water and fuel can be obtained and one may expect to buy fresh vegetables, fruit and fish. Usually a modest meal can be obtained. The recent completion of the new coastal road has rapidly transformed the coast and one must now expect to find villas and hotels in what were once deserted bays. Museums close on Mondays, banks on Saturdays and Sundays. Taxis must be bargained with; self-drive cars are to be found only in Istanbul, Ankara, Izmir, Antalya, Marmaris and Kusadasi. (The figures on the road signs at the entrance to towns and large villages refer to population and altitude.) Road accidents are considerable, but mostly due to defective material rather than driving.

Medical Treatment may be obtained free in national hospitals. There are said to be good doctors and dentists at Marmaris and Datcha. Medical and car insurance can be purchased from Europa Assistance, 252 High Street, Croydon.

Changing Names. Very recently the Turks have given their own titles to places known for centuries by names which reflected the nationality of an earlier conqueror —many were of Venetian or Genoese origin; others French, such as Cavalière and Provençal, which was so called by the Knights of St John during their settlement in Rhodes.

Fuel. With the general shortage of fuel, it is very difficult to obtain in Turkey.

Pilotage. Glossary of Turkish words often found on the chart and their equivalent English meanings:

Turkish	English	Turkish	English
Ada	island	Kale, Kalesi	Castle
Ak	white	Kara	Black
Boğaz	Strait, channel, estuary	Kırmızı, Kızıl	Red
Bucak	Creek	Köprü	Bridge
Burun, Burnu	Point, cape, headland	Körfez	Bay, Gulf
Bük	Creek, bay	Koy	Bight, cove, creek
Büyük	Great	Köy	Village
Dağ	Mountain	Kücük	Small
Demir yeri	Anchorage, Roads	Liman, Limanı	Bay, harbour, port
Deniz	Sea	Nehir, Nehri	River
Dere	Valley, stream	Sancak	District
Dogu, Şark	East	Şark	East
Hisar	Castle, fort	Şehir	City, town
Iç	Inner	Şımal	North
Irmak, Irmağı	River	Su	Water, stream, river
		Tepe	Hill, tumulus, peak

Local Craft. In Turkish waters there is very little coastal traffic. One sees the Turkish type of Aegean lugger called a *çektieme*. They were usually larger and with a more pronounced sheer than their Greek contemporaries. Sails have been discarded and the canvas weather screens replaced by built-up bulwarks. The sponge fishermen mostly come from Bodrum and use *trehandíries* similar to those of the Greeks, often making use of their sails when on passage. The Turks refer to their small wooden coastal craft as *takahs*.

Sponge Fishing methods have recently changed. Until a few years ago one often saw the familiar rubber suit triced up to dry; but now the diver no longer wears the rubber suit. He is supplied direct by a power-driven air-pump and towed by a light line over the sea-bed. The boat's propeller is fitted with a guard and the diver has a small emergency oxygen supply harnessed to his shoulders.

Turkish trading schooner now being superseded by modern vessels without sail

Turkish Sea-Terms may be traced back through the centuries, and it is interesting to note that so few words stem from the Ottoman tongue. The majority of terms and expressions have come in via the Greeks and betray their Venetian origin. This is hardly surprising when one remembers that since the time of the Turkish occupation of Anatolia (i.e. about the period of the Norman conquest of England), the Ionian Greeks have both built and manned the Turkish trading craft and their warships. Moreover, for at least two centuries the Venetians controlled a number of Anatolian ports.

The following summary of terms may be of use to a yacht:

pruva, bas	bow	*flok*	jib
kiç	stern	*mezzana*	mizzen
güverte	deck	*tandilisa*	halyard
direk	mast	*laşka*	'pay out'
bumba	boom	*vire, çek*	'haul in'
karina, omurga	keel	*iskele*	port
mayistra, yelken	mainsail	*sancak*	starboard

Food and Drink

Fresh food is available at most places (meat is often tough so fish for choice, although this is not always obtainable). It is sometimes difficult to shop when away from the towns, although with a few words of Turkish one can forage in the village and find eggs and tomatoes, an assortment of fruit and the local flat brown bread eaten by the peasants. In the towns food is abundant, good and cheap. Market-day is usually Friday.

Some food terms:

ekmek	bread	*meyve*	fruit
et	meat	*portakal*	orange
dana	veal	*elma*	apple
sebse	vegetables	*visne, kiraz*	cherry
su	water	*kayısı*	apricot
serbet	fruit drink	*incir*	figs
süt	milk	*fındık*	nuts
şarap	wine	*buz*	ice

iyi pismirmis	well-done steak
orta ,,	medium ,,
az ,,	rare ,,
şekerli	very sweet coffee
orta	medium ,,
az şekerli	little sugar
sade	no sugar

Wine, which is largely a State monopoly, can be obtained at most places and is often palatable.

Red (kırmızı): *Yakut, Buzbağ, Dikmeni, Adabağ, Kalebağ.*

Dry white (beyaz sek): *Doluca, Çubuk, Güzel, Marmara, Tekel, Misbağ, Izmir, Kulup.*

Sparkling wine: several brands of which *Inci Damlası* is probably the best. (*Kavaklidere* champagne is not recommended.)

As a liqueur local people drink *Raki*, also *Kanyak*, a distant relation to brandy. Mersin specializes in an orange liqueur.

Vodka with fresh orange or lemon juice is worth a trial.

Bonded Stores. In 1980 at certain ports one could buy wines, spirits, etc. at the government depots on the quay providing payment was made in foreign currency.

Fish (Balık). On the Turkish seaboard fish is greatly to be preferred to meat. Some of the more popular fish are:

hamsi	anchovy	*dil*	sole
levrek, lüfer	bass	*sinarit*	(small species)

palamut	bonito	*tekir*	red mullet
mandagöz mercan	sea bream	*sardelya*	sardines
böcek, istakoz	crawfish	*kalkar*	turbot
çipura	gilthead bream	*manda göz*	sea bream
kefal	grey mullet	*mürekkep, baliği*	squid
uskumru	mackerel	*kiliç*	swordfish
iskariot	parrot fish	*orkinos*	tunny, tuna
karides	prawns	*gümüs*	whitebait
		orfoz	grouper

Red mullet and sometimes bream are caught by trawling, and also by offshore nets: parrot-fish are also caught by this means. Grouper and bream are often hooked on long lines; grouper, as well as the parrot-fish, are also caught by basket-fishing. Dogfish seem to survive in polluted waters, the details of which especially around Mersin and Iskenderun were unobtainable at the time of writing.

Weather

Temperature. This coast is slightly hotter in summer than the Aegean: in May and early June close under the land the weather has been described as delightful, with temperatures up to 70°F. In the latter part of June and July, the temperature rises to between 80°F and 90°F. In August the climate can be oppressive, with the thermometer well above 90°F; in September and October it begins to fall.

Winds. Though the prevailing day breeze in the summer months is from S.W. the high Taurus ranges sometimes have a pronounced effect on the winds off this coast. As the ordinary Admiralty chart cannot show such an expanse of land, the diagram on p. 147 illustrates the proximity of these tall mountains to the coast.

Breaks in the mountain chains where cultivated plains have developed are by the rivers at Antalya in the western Taurus and eastward of Silifke in the main range where the mountains attain heights up to 12,000 ft and are intersected by substantial rivers.

There is normally a pleasant day breeze off this coast followed by a calm, and then a light night breeze; but, especially in the autumn months, there is sometimes a fresh to strong offshore wind at night coming from the Taurus ranges; it can have a disturbing effect as far off as Cyprus.

Although in pleasant summer conditions when sea breezes and gentle westerly winds are almost unbroken, there occur at the beginning and end of the sailing season occasional interruptions from passing depressions; most of these originate in the Mediterranean, and are far smaller than those from the Atlantic, though no

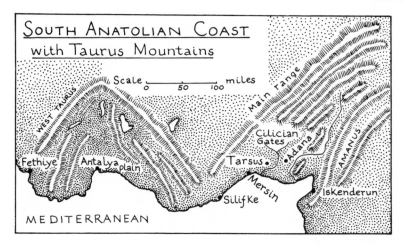

less intense. Thus the period of bad weather is of shorter duration, though it can be equally disturbing.

Current. A normal flow to the westward is often perceptible close off the coast. Only off certain headlands does the current exceed 1 knot and show inconsistency in its direction after strong adverse winds.

The Coastline. Harbours and anchorages are described in two parts:

PART I – Rhodes Channel to Anamur
This is the more appealing section of the coast. There are some good sheltered inlets and primitive places with sites of great archaeological interest. The Carian coast, green and indented with foothills rising gently towards the western Taurus, reaches as far as Fethiye. Here begins the steep mountainous Lycian (Cape Gelidonya) coast with ancient remains of great interest, especially the tombs. Beyond is the Gulf of Antalya with the rich Pamphylian Plain on the eastern side of the gulf. After only 50 miles it gives way to another great massif, that of Western Cilicia with the main Taurus ranges rising abruptly from the sea as far as Anamur. This is where a sailing yacht should make a decision as to whether or not she wishes to visit Cyprus.

PART II – Anamur to the Syrian Frontier
The steep wooded coast stretches for some 70 miles to beyond Taşucu, until reaching the rich fertile Plain of Cilicia; this is watered by several rivers, and the agricultural produce is shipped away through the spacious commercial port of

147

Mersin. The Gulf of Iskenderun lies beyond, between the Taurus and Amanus ranges.

This section of the coast has less attraction than the western part described in Part I: the anchorages are more open and often rather restricted even for a medium-sized yacht.

The following characteristics should be noted by a visiting yacht:

(a) *Petrified beaches* consisting of gravel or coarse sand calcified by a cement paste brought down by the local stream were prevalent early in the last century. Although a few petrified beaches remain, recent observations have shown that in most cases sand has been blown up and altered the character of the beach.

(b) *Sea Level.* In 1973 the Colston Research Society concluded that the sea-level relative to the land had not changed more than 3 ft either way in the last 3,000 years. The ecstatic change in the eastern area described in this chapter appears to show that the sea level relative to the land has risen a few feet. Certain steps and quays have subsided under water during the centuries, but possibly in some cases the weight of masonry could have had some influence.

PART I
RHODES CHANNEL TO ANAMUR

CARIAN COAST	LYCIA	PAMPHYLIA
Bozuk Bükü	Fethiye	Antalya
Arap Adası	Gemile & Karaca Ören	Laara
Çiftlik Bükü	Yorgun Köyü	Selimiye
Amos	Patara	Fiğla
Turunc Bükü	Kalkan	Alanya
Marmaris	Kastellorizo Isl. (Greek)	Aydap
Karaağaç	Buçak Denizi (Vathí)	Gazı Paşa
Yörük Cove	Longos	Yakacik
Ekinçik	Kaş	Karataş
Dalyan Isl. (Caunus)	Bayındır (Sevedo)	Anamur Burnu
Skopea Bay	Kekova Demiryeri	
Köcek	Gökkaya	
Tersane Adası	Ucağız Köyü	
'Four-Fathom Cove'	(Tristomos)	
'Twenty-two	Xera Cove	
Fathom Cove'	Castle Anchorage	
	St Stephanos	
	Andraki (Kokas)	
	Finike	
	Karaöz	
	Taşlık Burnu	
	(Gelidonya)	
	Su Ada	
	Çavuş	
	Cineviz Limani	
	Deliktaş	
	Tekirova	
	Kemer	

PART I

RHODES CHANNEL TO ANAMUR

Carian Coast

Leaving the N.E. of Rhodes one crosses the Rhodes Channel and heads for the tall rocky shores of the Turkish coast.

Near the tip of the peninsula is the port of Bozuk Bükü (ancient Loryma) recognized by its imposing Hellenic fortress still guarding the entrance.

Bozuk Bükü (Arsenal Bay). Chart 1604. The first of four anchorages, 36° 35′ N. 28° 5.4′ E., *en route* to Marmaris.

> **Anchorage:** In the inner part of the bay with good holding on hand; or if too gusty, move to the S.W. corner beyond the fortress and if necessary run out a warp to the shore.
>
> Except for a couple of small dwellings the place was almost deserted when recently visited, and the fact that no buildings have been set up in the last few centuries may account for the excellent condition of the Hellenic fortress. This is of oblong shape, about 350 yds long by 30 yds wide, built of huge stone blocks, some 15 ft long. Only the crumbling towers seem to have suffered the effects of time.

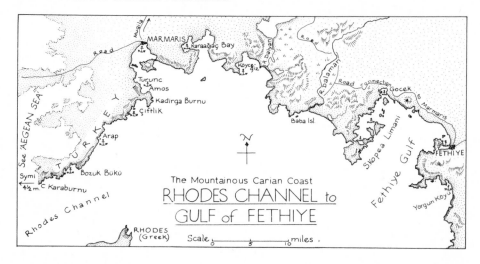

The Mountainous Carian Coast
RHODES CHANNEL to
GULF of FETHIYE

History. This sheltered port is known to have been used by Athenian ships in the Peloponnese war; again at the Battle of Cnidus and in A.D. 305 by Demetrius during his attack on Rhodes when it served as a naval base.

Some 8 miles further to the N.N.E another cove:

Arap Adası. Chart 1604 (36° 35.0′ N. 28° 5.4′ E.). Open to S.E.; anchor behind the island in 3 fathoms, choosing a sandy patch. This place is less interesting than

Çiftlik Bükü. Chart 1545 (36° 42.8′ N. 28° 14.2′ E.). Open to E. and S.E.; anchor in 2½ fathoms, sand, near head of the bay. No houses in sight; some cultivation and fine scenery. Day breeze gusts not uncomfortable.

Amos is a temporary anchorage close north of Cape Hisar. (Not named on English charts.) The only purpose of calling here is to land and make a steep climb up the hill to see something of the Hellenistic ruins of which perhaps the small theatre is the most interesting. The trip can also be made by a local ferry boat from Marmaris in little more than an hour.

Turunc Bükü. Chart 1545. Lies 1½ miles south of entrance to Marmaris Bay.

    Anchorage on a sandy bottom at the entrance to the southern cove of the bay. Excellent shelter.

Marmaris (Marmarice). This small port – now become a popular tourist resort – lies in a delightful green mountainous setting.

Approach. If entering by the W. Channel watch for the rock visible above water.

Berth. Although a new quay has been built, yachts report that it affords only limited shelter. Many berth here or stern to the quay during settled weather, but squalls sometimes sweep down from the mountains, when it may be advisable to anchor in the N.E. corner off the castle. A marina is planned in the area between the stone pier and the incense trees, having been planned to start in September 1981.

Officials. A Port of Entry with Immigration, Health, Customs and Harbour officials.

Facilities. Water at the quay, fuel at garage, market, provision shops, restaurants, hotels etc. Port of call for mail steamers and cruise ships, daily ferry for tourists to and from Rhodes all the summer months. Daily bus to Izmir, Istanbul, and to Fethiye.

Marmaris, a growing small town of 6,500 inhabitants, is still attracting foreigners to build summer villas, which now spread along the coast line. The winding streets at the back of the town and the old castle of Suleiman (1522) are interesting to visit, but no archaeological remains are to be seen. Roads have recently been improved and there are spectacular drives to Muğla and Daça; also to Dalyan continuing by more hazardous connections of coastal road to Fethiye and Antalya.

History. In sailing-ship days the British Admiralty recommended Marmaris and the larger bays of Karaağac and Vathí for 'the many snug coves contained in them; these are suited to the various purposes of airing stores, stretching rigging, repairing boats, erecting tents for carpenters, armourers and coopers, and for unloading and carrying transports and prizes'. At the beginning of this century the British and Austrian fleets visited the place most years each enjoying the other's good company.

Karaağac, ancient Cresse, another inlet with Yörük Cove in the northern corner and though recommended in *Sailing Directions*, better shelter has been found in the southern corner off Kuraca in about 8 fathoms. The place appears to be deserted, surrounded by bare mountainous slopes. (See Chart 1545.) In the N.E. corner near Easter Islet small steamers call occasionally to embark ore.

The Turkish Navy was making use of this inlet in 1981 and yachts have been asked to leave.

Ekinçik affords almost perfect shelter in deserted surroundings and can be very useful as a temporary base for a yacht whose crew might wish to visit the fascinating ruins of ancient Caunus.

Approach. Note that the dangerous rock west of the entrance to the bay has a depth of only 6 ft over it.

Berth. There is a choice of two:

153

(a) The cove on the E. side below a ruined fountain: run out a warp to a rock; (b) north of a jetty in the N.W. corner with a warp ashore to a pine-tree.

Two miles further eastward, is the small islet of **Dalyan**, whose limited lee provides anchorage for those wishing to proceed by boat up-river to visit the ruins. A local motor-boat may appear and offer to take one to visit the ruins of Caunus.

Anchorage. See Chart 1886 and *Sailing Directions*. In order to derive shelter from the prevailing S.W. swell a yacht should anchor off the N.E. end of the islet where depths of 2½ fathoms extend from the islet towards the shore for 150 yds. The width of the islet however, being so narrow and thus presenting a limited barrier against the swell, compels a yacht to anchor as close to it as possible and run out a warp to the rocks. Not suitable for a large yacht.

The word Dalyan means 'a fishing net with fixed poles' and this method is still to be seen in use on the river.

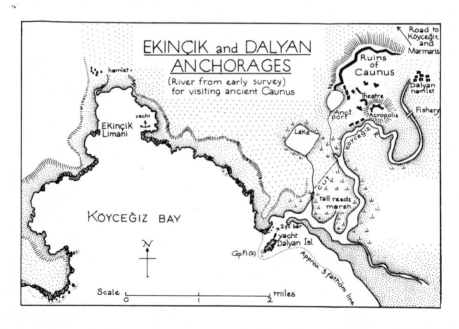

The river leading to Caunus has a shallow entrance (2 ft on the bar) with its approach channel, difficult to discern, passing between the red-faced cliff and a white hut by the beach. The river then meanders among reeds and bamboos to Caunus (2¼ miles) and to the modern village, 1¼ miles further. In Strabo's time ships used to berth at the port of Caunus which can still be seen, overlooked by the ruins, today. There are a number of fish-traps across the stream, gilthead and white bream being caught, some sent by lorry to Izmir and much sent abroad. Small fishing craft are continually entering and leaving the river; it is sometimes convenient when wishing to visit the ruins to hail one of these boats and take advantage of their local knowledge – a bargain can be made, the trip taking about three to four hours.

The ruins are well worth a visit, more for the actual site of Caunus and the wonderful view, than the Roman theatre, baths, temple, etc. On the hill behind one can scramble up to the medieval walled defences. Proceeding further upstream one is struck by the large Lycian rock tombs cut deeply into the steep rock-face. The village has 3,000 inhabitants who are mostly cotton-growers and fishermen. Bread and fruit may be bought; a modest bar and restaurant are by the quay. Ice can be bought at the fish plant.

Rounding the tall Cape Dısı Bilmez, 7 miles southward, one comes to Baba Island (distinguished by a ruined pyramid) behind which is temporary anchorage on clear sand. Depths are now less than those charted. Close north-east the Dalaman River empties its waters from the western Taurus into the sea. Continuing S.E. and rounding the bold Cape Kurdoglu one enters the Gulf of Fethiye with its port and town at the head. **Skopea Limanı**, lining the west side of the gulf, consists of a 10-mile stretch of coast including many small inlets and islands, all wooded and hilly, with inviting sites for yachts to anchor. Unfortunately they are nearly all rather deep to be practical. One of the two large islands, Domuz Adası, belongs to Erol Sımavı (owner of Turkey's newspaper *Huriyet*); only his residence, but no inhabitants or anchorage.

The most secure and attractive anchorage lies at the northern end of the mainland coast:

Köçek. Chart 1886, plan. The southern corner of the bay is surrounded by thick wooded scenery, but on the N.W. side is Paterson's Wharf (owned by Turkish Chrome Company) for loading large ships with local ores.

Anchorage is in S.W. corner with a warp ashore.

Anchorages among the islands are:

Tersane Adası, a well-sheltered inlet on the N.W. side.

Anchorage is in $3\frac{1}{2}$ fathoms at the point where the inlet opens into a basin. There is room for a small to medium-sized yacht to swing in almost all-round shelter.

At the side of the basin are the ruined houses of a hamlet. Only a couple of cottages were occupied recently by shepherds who keep a small herd of cows.

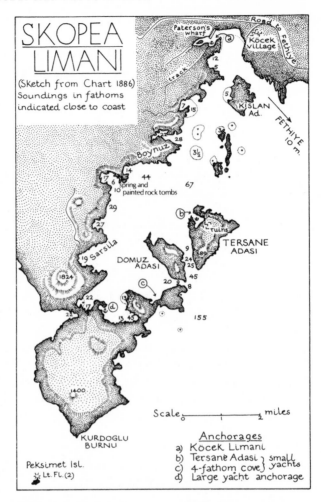

SKOPEA
LIMANI

(Sketch from Chart 1886)
Soundings in fathoms
indicated close to coast

Paterson's
wharf

Köcek
village

Road to Fethiye

track

12
5

KISLAN
Ad.

5

FETHIYE
10 m.

7 15

28

3½

Boynuz

17 6
10
spring and
painted rock tombs

44

67

29

27

b
ruins

TERSANE
ADASI

19 Sarsila

DOMUZ
ADASI

9
89

24
25

1824

c
20

45
8

22

d

1315

21

155

1400

Scale
0   1   2 miles

KURDOGLU
BURNU

Peksimet Isl.
Lt. Fl. (2)

Anchorages
a) Köcek Limani
b) Tersane Adasi ⎫ small
c) 4-fathom cove ⎬ yachts
d) Large yacht anchorage

'Four-Fathom Cove' is suitable only for small yachts.

> **Anchorage.** Let go in the centre on a patch of shingle (4 fathoms) and run out a line to the western shore. The wooded hills are low and gusts of wind mild. Holding not entirely dependable, but the water being clear one can choose the best position for letting go the anchor.

Ashore can be seen a few stone huts with arched roofs. There are also some ruins under water, remains of a mole and some vaulting.

'Twenty-Two-Fathom Cove', which is 1½ miles west of 'Four-Fathom Cove', is suitable for larger yachts in two delightful anchorages in wooded surroundings.

25 Selimiye (Side), with the Roman theatre and the sandy coastline beyond

26　Girne (Kyrenia): a delightful little yacht harbour. The photograph shows the old entrance being sealed: the present entrance is beyond the left edge of the picture

Anchorage. Let go in deep water and run out a warp ashore. Similar to the 'Four-Fathom Cove' but larger and deeper.

From the S.W. corner a track crosses a narrow isthmus to the ruins of Lydai.

Lycia

Fethiye is a small commercial port with a growing town of 13,000 people. It lies in the heart of a steep mountainous setting at the foot of the Taurus ranges.

Approach. Chart 1886. See plans below. Fethiye Island, now a mixture of ruins and modern villas, can be passed on either side. One should then head southwards for the extremity of the deep water stone pier where steamers berth. The yacht quay is immediately S. of it, extending from the root.

Berth off the quay in 2-fathom depths.

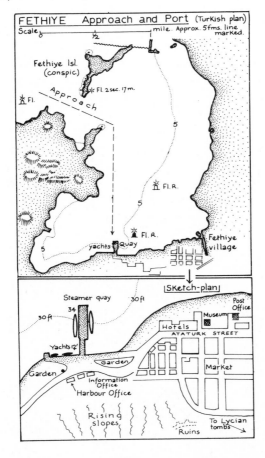

Officials. A Port of Entry with Immigration, Harbour and Health officials.

Facilities. Water by hydrant at the pier, fuel from garage, many shops, hotels, restaurants, bus communications with coastal towns, mail steamer every fortnight in summer. Bathing at Deniz, 6 miles distant.

The narrow island of Fethiye, formerly known as Snake Island, was famous in antiquity for 'snake men' who foretold the future. Aristander, soothsayer to Alexander the Great, came from here and it was here that Gordias sought the interpretation of his strange dream.

Fethiye is the centre of a large agricultural area and an exporting point for manganese and chrome ore. Apart from the Lycian tombs on the hillside and the Venetian walls, the town is quite pleasant; it is also a convenient centre for exploring the country. Hiring a car one may drive through rich, cultivated valleys with flowing rivers and wooded hillsides to Xanthus the ancient Lycian capital and its seaport at Patara. Neither city has been excavated to any extent; but by far the most remarkable edifice of Xanthus is the Nereid monument, excavated by the archaeologist Fellows, and shipped to London in the last century. Only recently has this magnificent temple been re-erected in a hall of its own in the British Museum; less remarkable, but also of interest is another memorial from Xanthus – the so-called Tomb of the Harpies.

A century ago Fethiye was a port of call for 'Government expresses and travellers from Constantinople embarking for Egypt'. Small British warships, brigs and sloops sometimes put in for shelter, their captains complaining of the ill effects of this 'mean little port' on the men's health. Malaria was then the scourge.

Of ancient Telmessus (Fethiye's name in classical times) there now survive only a few rock tombs, for during the recent centuries much of the ancient remains have been quarried for building and even the theatre has been plundered.

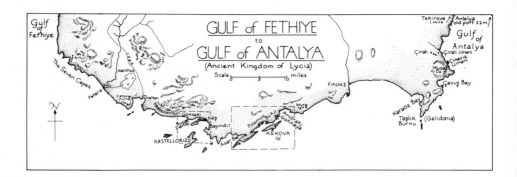

The Gulf of Fethiye to Gulf of Antalya

The Lycian Coast, which begins at Fethiye, is mountainous and inhospitable; its green wooded slopes reach steeply to the high ranges which stand only a few miles back overlooking the sea – only in the occasional valley where a river may water the land does one find a small primitive populace. There are almost no fishing boats or signs of sea communication. Many valleys are remarkable for the ruins of the ancient Lycians, especially their tombs, as well as some Greek and Roman remains. Timber has been Lycia's only trade for centuries, shipments of pinewood and Valona oak having been sent to Egypt and the Levant until very recent years.

This coast was first accurately shown on the charts at the beginning of the last century when Captain Beaufort, hydrographer and archaeologist, moved along the shores and into the hinterland, recording, surveying, and identifying all he saw. It was not always easy to determine the backgrounds of each ruined site, for names had changed throughout the centuries, and the illiterate Turks whose tribes have been settled near these ancient places since the twelfth century had no knowledge to impart.

Lycian tombs are to be seen everywhere. The rock tomb, often fronted with marble pillars and Ionic capitals, and having panels with pediments and lintels, is usually found cut in the mountainside near an ancient site. The sarcophagus, also carved with panels and lintels, has protruding trunnions for the heavy stone lid.

The sarcophagi generally lie in groups, occasionally alone and often at an inclined angle, the supporting earth evidently having been washed away during the centuries. All tombs have been broken into at some period.

After leaving Fethiye and following the indented coast in a S.E. direction one comes to two small islands close off the peninsula of Ilbiz Burnu: **Gemile** and **Karaça Ören**, both closely packed with ruined medieval buildings. Neither island has an anchorage, although close N.W. of Gemile is a pleasant cove suitable for a medium-sized yacht to bring up for the night. Here are submerged ruins, possibly Byzantine period.

Yorgun Köyü is a place of great beauty. Except for a couple of fishing boats and the many tourists who flock here in summer the shores are unspoilt. A hotel and restaurant on the beach.

> **Anchorage.** Passing the rock to port a yacht can find anchorage off the nearby sandy shore and run out a stern warp to a tree. The other end of the lake can also be used for anchoring, but here also it is advisable to take a warp to a stone ashore.

> **Facilities.** A small house with a jetty which sells fish, eggs and vegetables, also drinks.

Following the coast to the S.E. past the Seven Capes you come to Patara, the ancient port for Xanthus, one of whose lovely temples, perfectly restored, stands in the British Museum.

Patara is now entirely silted, the old port being no longer recognizable. From seaward one can see only a few ruined buildings, the most noticeable being Vespasian's city gate. In calm weather a yacht may anchor off the beach and land by dinghy, but everything is covered by mountains of sand blown up by the winter gales in the course of centuries. Even the theatre is half filled with sand. The ruins of Xanthus standing on the hill a few miles up the valley are scarcely visible, but its substantial river still flows into the sea at Patara, some of it springing up under the sea a few hundred yards offshore.

It was at Patara that St Paul, having made a fast passage down the Aegean, found a ship crossing to Phoenicia, went on board and set sail.

Kalkan, a large bay exposed to south, at the head of which is a growing village with a small well-sheltered harbour formed recently by a rough mole.

> **Anchorage** is off the village inside the mole in 3-fathom depths on sand with a stern warp to a

boulder on the waterfront. Land in dinghy at a short stretch of quay. A fresh water spring bubbles up under the sea.

Facilities. Restaurants, a pension, provision shops, and water by can nearby. Main road to Fethiye passes above. Taxis available for visiting Patara and Xanthus.

The village was rebuilt after the 1968 earthquake and is extending up the hillside. The port can be useful as a night anchorage when beating against the westerlies towards Fethiye.

There is also sheltered anchorage of the W. shore of the bay.

Kastellórizo is an outpost of Greece close off the Turkish Anatolian coast – a scorched, barren, little island with a little-used port affording good protection for a yacht. Close off are some islets no longer inhabited, but also under Greek sovereignty.

Approach. Chart 2188, with harbour plan, shows the entry clearly, as well as a suitable outside anchorage. On entering the port, anchor off the yacht station and haul in the stern to the quay.

Facilities. Ample provisions including frozen meat can be bought at the two stores. Fresh water is very limited, and is collected in private cisterns. A small hotel. Fuel, out of bond, may be available at the yacht station. There is no airstrip but there is air mail and occasional steamer connection with Rhodes.

161

Although it has an appeal, the little town, tucked under the eastern arm of the bay, is largely deserted. It was damaged by fire during British occupation in the Second World War, but it is the lack of trade that has driven away the inhabitants.

Formerly 'Castel Rosso' of the Genoese, it is known as Meis by the Turks today. Before the First World War, when it was part of Turkey, this small island had a population of nearly 20,000 Greeks, and at one time its trade was of sufficient importance to merit 'more than one European consul'. Only a few hundred people live here today and many of them are looking forward to emigrating to the United States and Australia.

On the hill slope overlooking the harbour is the large white church with Corinthian columns, brought in some past epoch from an ancient Greek temple at Patara, and close to the church is a Greek school, also far too large for present requirements. Both these buildings are a reminder of the island's more prosperous days. On the summit are still some ruins of a fortress, probably erected originally by the Knights of Rhodes who held the island until 1440. On the east coast is a remarkable Blue Grotto, best approached by local boat – $1\frac{1}{2}$ hours; the morning sun shows it to best advantage.

Until the end of the last century Kastellórizo was an important pilot station, many vessels at this time being engaged in the firewood trade with Egyptian and Syrian ports, while others sometimes put in for provisions and water. This privileged position ended with the Turco–Italian war when so many ships were sunk that Kastellórizo lost control of the trade.

Kastellórizo's only connection with the outside world is with Rhodes. This 65-mile voyage is the town's lifeline, yet within hailing distance are the green shores of Turkey with their richly timbered hinterland which, until recent years, provided valuable commerce for both Greek and Turk alike.

On the Turkish coast immediately opposite lies a choice of anchorage:

Buçak Denizi, or Port Vathí, a long steep-to gulf with a sandy shore and depths of 7 fathoms at its head. Here occasional Turkish caiques bring up to load their cargoes. Violent gusts sometimes come off the mountains with N.E. winds during the autumn months. The water is often muddy due to cold water springs.

In the Second World War British destroyers used this anchorage for operations against German-held Kastellórizo.

'Port' Longos affords a good lee from the west, but is inconveniently deep as an anchorage. (The term 'Port' is misleading; the anchorage is open.) It can be useful to a yacht needing temporary shelter from the Westerlies.

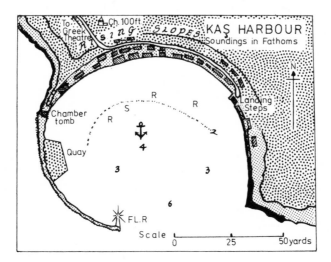

Kaş (formerly Andípholo), a growing village of about 1,500 people, lies in a mountainous setting with a small harbour formed by a recently built breakwater.

Approach. The port may be recognized by the cluster of white houses and by the Greek theatre on the hill to the northward. The entrance is marked by a light-tower (Fl.R) on the breakwater extremity, and is 50 yds wide with depths of 4–5 fathoms. The harbour can be disturbed with fresh W. winds.

Berth at the west side of the harbour, stern to the new quay, fitted with rings. The depths are irregular and holding poor. A Lycian sarcophagus has recently been salved and mounted near the root of the breakwater.

Officials. A Port of Entry. Harbour Master, Health, Customs, Police.

Facilities. Water at the quay, provision shops, modest restaurants, hotel, fuel at a garage. A new Corniche road now connects with Fethiye, Finike and Antalya. A small motor boat may be hired to visit Kastellórizo (Meis).

Beyond the village is a very well-preserved Greek theatre, all that is left of ancient Antiphellus, with twenty-six tiers of seats facing southward affording a fine view over the fjords: a number of Lycian tombs outside the village, as well as others on the cliff above, are now largely destroyed. From the northern side of this ridge there is a commanding view of the long, sheltered fjord, Buçak Denizi.

The village is slowly recovering from a period of decline at the beginning of the century when the brisk trade in cedar and firewood to Egyptian ports suddenly ceased at the end of the Turco–Italian war.

Bayındır (Port Sevedo), a spacious and completely deserted anchorage with high, steep-to cliffs and fair shelter but, except in the far corner, very deep. Better shelter than Kaş in W. winds.

> **Approach.** Chart 2188 and *Sailing Directions* are sufficient for a daylight approach. The ledge, which extends underwater from the northern point of the entrance, was evidently a substantial breakwater in the early nineteenth century, and Captain Beaufort, after his survey, describes it as suitable for 'heaving down ships of the line'. The point is now marked by a small light structure exhibiting a L Fl.

> **Anchorage.** There are 5 to 6 fathoms in the S.E. corner of they bay with barely room to swing. It is well to run a warp from the stern to the rocks. The holding is mud, and the shelter from southerly and westerly winds is good – a slight swell enters.

The tall brown cliffs, honeycombed with Lycian tombs, look very fine in the evening light. There is no habitation on the shores of the bay. Wild boar sometimes come down at night seeking water by the dried-up torrent.

The coast now continues rocky and steep-to for the next few miles until beyond Kekova Island.

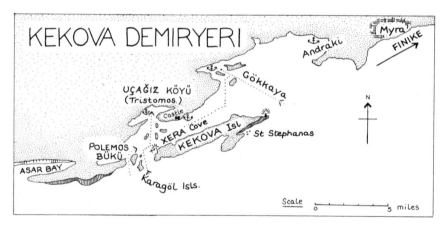

(Coastline west of Karagol Islets is not from Beaufort's Survey)

Asar Bay lies on the N. side of the peninsula of Sıcak Yarımadası. This anchorage has previously been avoided by yachts owing to its irregular rocky bottom. This has recently been examined by the American yachtsman Robert Carter who found in 7-ft depths the clearly defined quay of an ancient port with walls leading from the sea up the hillside. This has now been identified as the ancient city of Aperlae flourishing from the third century B.C. to the seventh century.

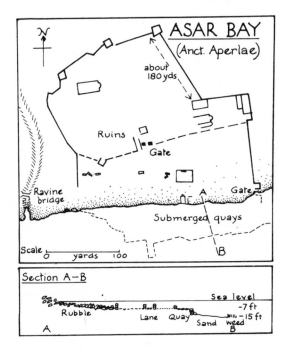

Approach. Head up towards the head of the bay keeping slightly southward of centre.

Anchorage. Opposite city walls in 2½ fathoms; weed on sand. The afternoon breeze can make this anchorage uncomfortable, although towards evening, calm conditions usually prevail.

Continuing eastwards one reaches the spectacular Kekova Roads.

Kekova Demiryeri. These Roads, sheltered by Kekova Island, provide some pleasant remote anchorages; they can be approached only by day.

Approach. Chart 241 and *Sailing Directions.* One can enter by the western approach passing either side of the islets, but care is needed to avoid an underwater rock (4-ft depth) lying 200 yds N. of the western tip of Kekova Island. The eastern entrance for Gökkaya is straightforward.

The following anchorages are at the western end of Kekova Roads:

Ucağiz Köyü (Tristomos) lies northward from the western approach and requires care in negotiating the underwater rocks immediately inside the entrance and the small islets. There is good shelter and holding off a dull little village; this is the safest place to make for in event of bad weather.

Crossing Kekova Roads on a northwesterly course from the westernmost

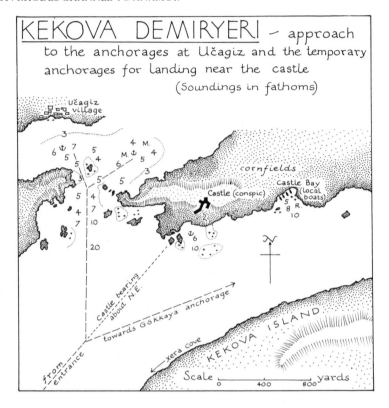

KEKOVA DEMIRYERI – approach to the anchorages at Učagiz and the temporary anchorages for landing near the castle

(Soundings in fathoms)

entrance, one can find shelter by the north shore behind two flat islets in 5 or 6 fathoms on sand. There is also complete protection at the western end of Kekova Roads, where it narrows and gradually shoals to its head. Anchor in 2 fathoms or less in very sticky mud, for which reason a warp is preferable to chain.

Xera Cove is suitable only for a small yacht at the mouth of the cove – sandy bottom, 3–5 fathoms. A good day anchorage cooled by the breeze. The ruined early Christian church is of interest.

Castle Anchorage should be treated with caution, the bottom being very irregular. A quay has now been built where a yacht may be moored temporarily if visiting the castle which stands on the rocky spur above. Two simple restaurants nearby.

With its Ghibelline battlements dramatically projected against the mountainous background the castle is a fine sight. Climbing up from the anchorage (shown on the map) takes 20 minutes; inside its walls one is astonished to find a minute Greek theatre.

From here one may look over the ramparts across the great sheltered fjord. To the S.W. is the narrow entrance, and as the eye follows along the lengthy Kekova Island there is the small Xera Cove with the ruined Christian church and the remains of houses and cisterns; beneath the ramparts in the near foreground more than one stone sarcophagus lies submerged under the clear waters of the fjord. Around the steep hill, inclined at varying angles like drunken sentry boxes, lie the Lycian sarcophagi; obviously they had originally been placed on soil, probably beside a roadway long since eroded away.

The present-day Turkish peasants living in hovels around the foothills appear to contrast strangely with the ancient Lycians, whom one supposes to have been a civilized people, having had not only time to prepare monuments for the safekeeping of their bodies after death, but who enjoyed a high standard of living among these delightful surroundings. According to the *Iliad*, their forebears were 'a powerful war-like nation'; these tombs were long after Homer's day and quite possibly just before the period of Alexander. It is interesting to note on the island that the steps cut into the rock leading up from the sea to the ruined houses (probably medieval) are now several feet underwater. On the mainland behind the hills are cornfields, where the peasants, guarding the crops, build themselves small two-decker grass huts; open at the sides, these provide shade and a place to rest during the hot summer months until their occupants again return to their distant villages.

At the eastern end of Kekova Island is the open approach to

Gökkaya (see plan on Chart 241). This is a charming place, completely deserted, with convenient depths in uncertain holding. Swinging room for three or four yachts in wild rocky surroundings. A track leads to the Hayitle ruins.

St Stephanos is a deserted cove on the S.E. side of Kekova Island, useful to a yacht for a night's shelter when beating against the westerlies.

The entrance can be recognized by three off-lying islets; the sheltered anchorage is in the northern corner in depths of 5 fathoms with a warp to a rock on the wooded shore.

Andraki Bay lies at the mouth of the Andraki River, which led to the ancient port of Myra. A pleasant anchorage in the forenoon before the day breeze sets in. (The river's local name is Kokas.) At either end of Andraki Beach is the outflow

167

of the river. At the eastern end is a taverna and a number of beach shacks but the western end with a pretty village is otherwise deserted.

> **Anchorage** is off the river mouth in depths of 3–4 fathoms, sandy bottom, open only to the south-west. A restaurant is nearby. A fine bathing beach.

To visit the ruins of Myra one may row across the bar of the river (depth 1 ft) and continue in deep water for nearly 2 miles upstream. On either bank are Lycian sarcophagi and ruined Roman buildings. After passing the Roman granary one reaches a landing place where transport is available to the modern village of Kale. Close above it on the steep slopes are the ruins of Myra but much of it is buried by the silt of the river. Here are splendid rock tombs cut into the vertical hillside, and beside them is the large Roman theatre still well preserved. The church of St Nicholas, of Byzantine origin and now largely excavated and repaired, is also well worth a visit. From above one has a fine view across the plain: where the Demre Çay flowed into the sea is now a sandbar which during the centuries has caused the silt to build up a rich agricultural plain. Here a large number of peasants can usually be seen working on the cotton-fields and market gardens.

It was at Andraki where St Paul trans-shipped to a Roman corn freighter on the last part of the voyage to his trial at Rome. During Diocletian's reign the city became famous for its Bishop Nicholas (Father Christmas) who, after persecution by the emperor, was later canonized, becoming the patron saint of sailors, virgins, pawnbrokers and children; in more modern times he was adopted by Russia. Most of his bones were carried off to Bari during the eleventh century, and shortly afterwards more were taken to Venice; early in the last century a Russian frigate got away with what was left and took them to St Petersburg. In England nearly 300 churches are dedicated to St Nicholas.

Finike (ancient Phoenicus) is a small artificial port at the foot of a lush green valley.

> **Approach.** Chart 236. A breakwater extends in a N.E. direction from the lighthouse, and together with a short mole from the north shore provides complete protection within. A yacht may anchor close off in 3 fathoms or berth stern to the quay which has been extended with depths of 2 fathoms alongside.

> **Officials.** Not a Port of Entry, having only Health, Customs, Harbour master.

> **Facilities.** Water and fuel conveniently supplied at the quay. Small market for fresh provisions, a couple of restaurants and hotels. The Istanbul steamer calls every two weeks in summer. Road communications with Marmaris and Antalya.

Finike, with a population of 5,000, lies in the centre of a rich agricultural area.

Oranges, lemons, market garden products and cotton are shipped away in small coasters which berth at the pier. Interesting motor excursions can be made from here to visit Myra (half an hour), Limyra 20 miles and Termessus 21 miles, the most magnificent of all.

Karaöz. Chart 237. This wide sandy bay lying on the W. side of the Taşlik Burnu Peninsula and two miles N. of the Cape, is a useful summer anchorage and well sheltered from easterly winds. From seaward the cliffs on the W. side of the bay resemble fortifications. The holding is sand and the depths convenient for any size of yacht. On the S. side of the bay where cliffs extend from the wooded shore is shelter from S., but the bottom is partially rocky. Under normal conditions the best anchorage is off the beach opposite a farmstead – the only habitation near the shore.

Taşlik Burnu (Cape Gelidonya) the western point of the Gulf of Antalya, is steep-to, lying at the tip of a mountainous promontory rising to over 3,000 ft some 4 miles N.N.E. A west-going current is sometimes experienced, running at over 1 knot, but with the Meltemi blowing out of the Aegean along the coast an

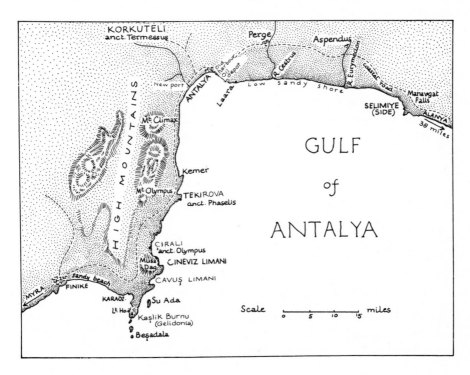

east-going current is often induced. The five barren islets were known in earliest times as Chelidonae (Swallow Islands). Pliny describes them 'as being fraught with disaster for passing vessels'. Today they are without interest, there being no coves suitable for any type of yacht to shelter; although apart from a few eagles there is no bird life, the waters around the cape sometimes abound with fish; many dolphins are often to be seen.

In 1960 the underwater expedition sponsored by the University of Pennsylvania located a bronze-age wreck close off the nearest islet by the cape. They recovered many interesting pieces of her cargo: bronze ingots, bronze tools, amphorae, etc., which are now imaginatively displayed in the small museum in Bodrum Castle.

On rounding the cape one enters the broad Gulf of Antalya; its wild and wooded mountain slopes continue for 50 miles until reaching the Plain of Antalya.

Gulf of Antalya – Western Shores

Winds. On summer mornings a fresh north wind often sweeps down from the mountains and blows along the shore out of the gulf, stirring up a short sea with subsequent swell some miles to seaward. About midday a light sea breeze is drawn in, dying away at sunset.

Su Ada or **Sulu Ada.** In an open cove opposite the island of Su Ada is temporary anchorage for a small yacht. The American caique used it as a base during the summer months of 1960 when working on the Gelidonya wreck. The beach rises steeply with 8-ft depths close off – a freshwater spring rises in the corner of the cove.

Çavuş Bay, lying about 7 miles N.N.E. of Taşlik Burnu, has a long sandy beach with a few small houses standing on a green plain.

> **Anchorage.** Room for several yachts to anchor in convenient depths off the beach, sandy bottom, open to E. The headland which is lit, has a small cove in its western side with space for a medium-sized yacht to anchor; this is open only to N.E., but during the autumn months strong mountain gusts sometimes cause an uncomfotable swell to enter the bay.

Cineviz Limani (Port Genovese), Chart 241, is a sheltered cove, bordered by steep wooded slopes, affording good anchorage for any size of yacht. The place is entirely deserted. During the day strong gusts sweep down from the tall Musa

Dağ. The adjoining cove close eastward is also a good anchorage. In the event of a northerly blow good shelter may be found in the bay immediately N. of the Cape.

Deliktaş. Lying little more than a mile northward from Cineviz, Deliktaş now has a substantial number of huts and restaurants along the beach and a motor camp.

With the building of the coastal highway there has been a rapid opening of this coast to tourism. There is temporary anchorage off the open shore before the afternoon breeze sets in. The dinghy must be carried across the silted river mouth to the stream the other side. Here are the remains of the old quay and nearby the unexcavated and very overgrown ruins of ancient Olympus. An hour's walk from here and lying on the slope of a hill is a minute 'volcano' – the Chimaera of the ancients where, according to *Sailing Directions*, 'a bright and constant flame can be seen from some distance'. Pliny called it 'the flame that does not die by day or night'. This phenomenon can be simply explained as being the result of a shallow stream of sulphurous water flowing over rocks from whose crevices rises an inflammable gas. Nowadays it is not an impressive sight; but in the summer months a motor-boat can usually be hired both at Antalya and Finike to make the excursion to Olympus. It can also be visited by the road from both these places. At the café a tractor and a guide can be hired. He will take one along the beach for half an hour, then climb half an hour up the hill.

Heading up the Gulf of Antalya in the summer a yacht is nearly always blown by the day breeze and helped by the current which is liable to set one towards the shore. The two coves, very green but lined with cliffs, immediately after Deliktaş look inviting as an anchorage but they are encumbered with rocks. The wooded mountains rise from the coast; Solyma and Climax can be identified, and after 9 miles one reaches Tekirova, some of whose ruins can be distinguished 3 or 4 miles off.

Tekirova, ancient Phaselis – 'A noteworthy city with three harbours and a lake' (Strabo). Plan on Chart 241 is no longer entirely accurate, but see p. 172.

> **Anchorage.** As one approaches the harbours caution is necessary with regard to submerged moles and underwater obstructions. Most yachts anchor off the S.W. port in about 4 fathoms, being careful to clear the submerged mole which extends for about 80 yds mostly underwater. Other yachts have preferred to anchor off the N.E. port in depths of 3 or 4 fathoms within the perimeter of the sunken mole which formerly protected the outer anchorage. The very small N.E. port has largely silted, but can be useful for boatwork.

The ruins, mostly Roman, have been partially cleared of scrub and it is possible

171

to land at the isthmus by the S.W. port and find the paved avenue which connects it with the small N.E. port. Although obstructed by vegetation one can see the ancient buildings – theatre, agora, aqueduct, etc., which border the former broad avenue. There are traces of a shipyard in the corner of the small silted port. The whole site has now been acquired by the government and has a guard.

History. Phaselis is of interest for its association with Alexander. When making his way eastward in 333 B.C. his next destination was Perge, but the mountain route was difficult. Plutarch describes how one division, led by Alexander himself, marched eastwards through the sea by the 'straits called Ladders' to the foot of Mount Climax. This involved wading through water chest deep as they could not march over the cliffs but 'round which men could readily pass by wading through water'.

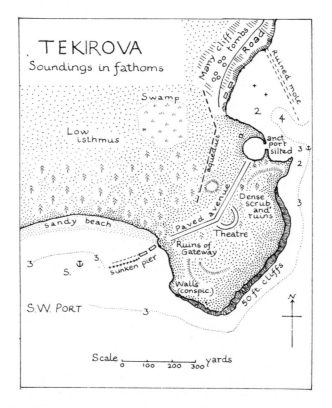

Kemer Bay, protected by a small peninsula in its N.E. corner, provides reasonable shelter for a yacht anchorage. (See plan p. 173.)

Approach. Charts 236 and 237 being on a small scale make the entry look difficult on account

27 Paphos harbour: an aerial view before the breakwaters were improved

28 Alanya pier, overlooked by
the Red Tower

29 Anamur Castle, evacuated
finally by the Lusignan kings
before embarking for Cyprus

of off-lying rocks. A large submerged rocky outcrop lies N.N.E. of the bay, but by rounding the cape of Ak Burnu a cable distant all dangers can be avoided.

Anchorage is in the N.E. corner of the bay where the small wooded peninsula projects. In 1981 a small marina was under construction with a rough stone breakwater extending from the point in a N.N.E. direction. Local craft prefer the anchorage to Çavuş and Cineviz, although in fresh N.E. winds it is uncomfortable.

Facilities. The hamlet is a mile distant where fresh provisions can be obtained. The southern part of the bay is much developed, closely packed houses forming a summer holiday resort with many restaurants.

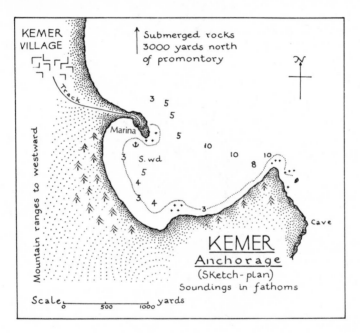

Pamphylia

And when they had preached the word in Perga, they went down into Attalia.

Acts 14: 25

Antalya (formerly **Adalia** or **Attalia)** has a very small ancient port suitable for a yacht beside a growing tourist-minded town. A modern commercial port 5 miles S.W. of the town has recently been completed, but it serves no purpose for a yacht. There is also an oil installation S.E. of the old port where tankers occasionally moor off, but this is of no hindrance.

Approach. Chart 241 has a plan dated 1810, but see sketch below. This little harbour lying close beneath the town has great attraction. The columns of cascading water formerly seen against the cliffs S.E. of the harbour have now been diverted into the harbour to keep it clean. They were known by the early Greeks as *Cataractes* and described by Strabo as 'dashing down in such volume and so impetuously that the noise could be heard from afar'.

Berth. The recent addition of a short mole and another short extension within the harbour now provides a small boat camber (not shown in sketch). All but very small yachts now berth alongside the quay of this new mole, but they claim that shelter from southerly gales is not improved.

The harbour is usually crowded, but yachts can berth stern-to leaving little space in the event of bad weather. Except in the actual entrance, the bottom is irregular, but recently many boulders have been cleared away making more space available at the sides. The day-breeze between S.W. and S.E. is apt to bring up a swell, some of which penetrates the harbour. The sea level may vary as much as 2 ft.

Officials. A Port of Entry. Customs and Police have their offices at the 'Landing Place': the Harbour Office east of Customs. (Change of crew may be forbidden unless clearing for 'Foreign'). The Health Office is in a conspicuous building on the east side of the harbour.

Facilities. Water by hydrant; the water is hard but safe to drink. In the town, 15 minutes' walk from the landing, there is a market and a number of shops where a variety of provisions may be bought. There are many hotels, and restaurants.

In the port it is possible to buy ice and some fruit. A steamer from Izmir calls weekly. There is a thrice-weekly air-service to Istanbul and Izmir. It is also possible to drive by car to Istanbul in a little over 12 hours.

Antalya former capital of Pamphylia, has an expanding population of 80,000, mainly occupied in agriculture and working in the port. The town has been much advertised as a tourist resort – hence the hotels. Part of the old walls, Hadrian's gate and two mosques are the only parts of the old town remaining. A very new broad boulevard now encircles the modern town, and concrete buildings are slowly replacing all that is old. The Byzantine church near the 'grooved minaret' was formerly the museum. A fine new museum has now been built to the west of the town.

The harshness of the modern surroundings is somewhat alleviated by groups of poplars and sub-tropical flowers and in the spring by the smell of orange blossom. At the end of the long boulevard lined with acacias is a modern park overlooking the ancient bastions. A few years ago the houses in the town were remarkable for their flowers and fruit trees. These are no longer apparent, and one must go to the well-irrigated countryside beyond the cotton fields to see the many cypresses; towards the mountains are oak forests, poplars, date-palms and oleanders.

History. The whole province of Pamphylia had long been prosperous even before the Romans came, when it was already called Attalia – named after its successful ruler Attalus, King of Pergamum. Under the Romans it continued to prosper and not until Byzantine rule did the decline set in.

Among the early visitors here were St Paul and St Barnabas, and later the Emperor Hadrian, whose visit in A.D. 130 was commemorated by the building of the arch. Some centuries afterwards the Crusaders used the port when embarking for the Levant, thus avoiding Seljuk territory. King Louis, setting off for Antioch on the second Crusade, is said to have abandoned 7,000 infantry here to become Moslems and never to return to their homes. In those days the town was still called Attalia; later it became Adalia and, only in recent centuries, Antalya.

The last occasion where an uninvited armed force landed at Antalya was in 1921 when an Italian army, taking advantage of the unhappy defeated state of Turkey, disembarked with the object of obtaining a foothold in the territory near Smyrna. Later good sense prevailed and the invading force was evacuated.

The following interesting excursions to Graeco–Roman cities are within easy reach by car:

Belkis, the ancient Aspendus, 31 miles east of Antalya. The ruins are extensive and the Roman theatre, with its immense stage building, is quite remarkable. Occasionally Greek plays and Shakespeare are produced in the Turkish language.

This ancient Greek city, perhaps the largest in Pamphylia, was, at the time of Strabo, approached up the River Eurymedon, the modern Köpru, which was then large enough to accommodate sizeable fleets.

Korkuteli, lying in a dramatic mountainous setting, is the modern village near the ancient Termessus, 20 miles N.W. of Antalya. A former stronghold, it was once a thorn in the flesh of Alexander on his march to the Issus. Covering a large area the remains of Termessus are worth a visit as much for the city's position as for the ruins themselves.

Perge, still being excavated in 1980, lies only 12 miles east of Antalya. The ruins are extensive and well worth a visit – the unusual city gate, the stoa, stadium, theatre and remarkable defensive walls with towers still standing. Perge was previously approached from the sea by its port on the Cestrus (Aksu) River, and it was here that St Paul and St Barnabas landed after crossing from Cyprus. Karucucak reached via the Selcuk bridge over the Köprü river, is famous for its own peculiar brand of wrestling.

The coast from Antalya stretches along the Pamphylian Plain towards Cape Anamur – 100 miles distant. After nearly 50 miles the plain gradually narrows as the Taurus foothills encroach upon the coast. The shores then become steep with occasional green valleys until finally towards Anamur inhospitable cliffs rise abruptly from the sea with high mountain ranges close behind. Along this coast are a few minor anchorages sheltered from west winds as well as the better sheltered port of Alanya, half-way to Anamur.

During settled summer weather the winds off this stretch of coast are regular. Beginning with a land breeze about dawn, there follows a sea-breeze starting in the forenoon and blowing between N.W. and S.W. with a strength of Force 2–3.

Leaving Antalya you first come to high overhanging cliffs where formerly cascades of river water were tumbling into the sea. The most impressive one is Duden Çay (ancient *Cataractes*), about one mile E. of Baba Burnu. A mile beyond this is the ancient port of Magydus, now called **Laara**. Its moles can be seen disappearing under water; the place has silted but recent depths have not been checked.

Following the Pamphylian Plain for nearly 30 miles you come to a low-lying peninsula now named Selimiye. This was the former Roman city of Side whose large theatre can be seen for many miles to seaward.

Selimiye (Side), which has recently been excavated, is deserving of a visit, although it has only an open anchorage.

Approach and Anchorage. See plan p. 177. When closing the shore run on a S.E. course towards the theatre and anchor where the 'pier of hewn stones' bears about S.W. The depth should be about 2½ fathoms, the bottom sand. A kedge anchor may be helpful in keeping the yacht head-on to the swell caused by the day breeze. Small yachts claim to have found better shelter off the cove on the S. side, but both anchorages are for fair weather only.

Officials. A Customs Post.

Facilities. Provision shops, many restaurants, hotels, pensions, tourist boutiques. Selimiye has now been so completely given over to tourism that a café has even been opened in the ruins themselves and discotheques on the beach. On the N. shore is a short stone pier where one may land and haul out the dinghy; close S.W. of it is a light Fl.R.

After recent excavation by Istanbul University the site has been considerably cleaned up. In Roman times it covered an extensive area; the large theatre with forty-nine rows of seats is estimated to have held nearly 25,000 people; the two temples reached by a colonnaded street leading from the theatre were, until recently, buried in sand as are still parts of the S.E. end of the city. Like the silted ports they are likely to remain under sand. Its early history is unknown, but it surrendered to Alexander and in Roman times a great naval battle against Hannibal was fought off it. Later it became a famous pirate stronghold and was important during all the Byzantine period until the time of Arab and Turkish invasions when it was abandoned altogether; the surviving inhabitants then found refuge in Antalya, their old city being then referred to as Eski Antalya (Old Antalya), a name it retained until recent years. The present village built among the ruins was settled in 1923 by Turkish refugees from Crete and called after their home village, Selimye. It now has a population of 800. There is an exceptionally well-planned museum in one of the Roman baths.

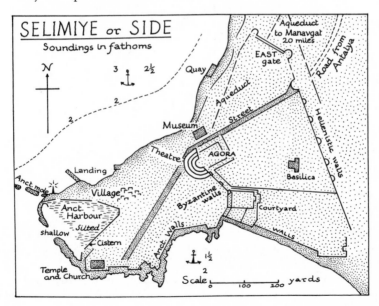

A pleasant excursion from Selimiye leads one to the small market town and waterfalls of Manavgat some 5 miles eastward. The Manavgat River (Melas) formerly renowned for its trout, no longer flows into the sea, its mouth being almost closed by a bar. It is navigable by dinghy for about 4 miles passing close to a ruined castle. Above the falls the Turks have now built a power station to serve the factories near Konya.

Fiğla (Chart 241) is a small sandy bay with a curved rocky headland protecting it from S.W. Close by once stood the ancient town of Ptolemais. Many of the stones which formed the ancient mole have buried themselves, but recent soundings are lacking. A summer hotel has been built on the shore near the anchorage.

Alanya, the most impressive place on the Pamphylian coast. A tall promontory with a medieval fortress and walled defences visible for many miles to seaward.

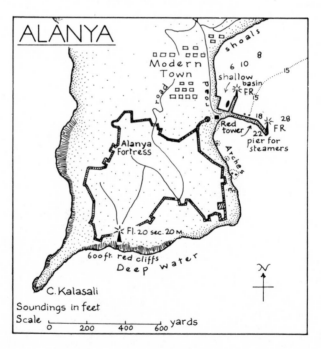

Anchorage. Chart 237 and plan (above). From the prominent Red Tower at the water's edge a pier for berthing steamers projects for 200 yds in an E.S.E. direction and then another 100 yds S.E. A yacht may berth off the inner pier on the N. side in 3–4 fathoms using, if necessary, a stern anchor to keep head-on to the swell which after southerly weather can be considerable.

Although open to S.E. it is seldom in summer that conditions are disturbing, and only in the autumn months are there mountain gusts at night. The harbour is often cooled by a local breeze from the peninsula.

A short rough mole was recently built extending from near the root of the pier for 70 yds in a N.N.E. direction. The extremity is lit, but the depths being barely 6 ft and the place often crowded with small fishing boats, only a small yacht can find shelter – close W. of molehead.

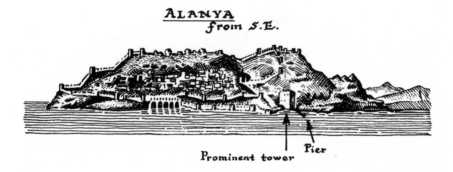

ALANYA
from S.E.

Prominent tower   Pier

Officials. This is a fully equipped Port of Entry. Customs House is by the root of the pier and Harbour Master 200 yds towards the town.

Facilities. Good water is laid on to the pier (weekdays). Fuel from garages. Bread, fresh provisions, and ice can be bought at the market or village shops. Several hotels, pensions, and restaurants in the village; the modern ones are outside where the main road skirts the sandy beach. Bus to Antalya – $2\frac{1}{2}$ hrs, hydrofoil to Kyrenia (Girne) $2\frac{1}{2}$ hrs (summer season).

Standing on the high peninsula is the former walled city of Coraceseum. With its existing thirteenth-century walled defences it is unique. One can hire a car to reach the heights and wander around Greek-Roman-Byzantine ruins, but it is more interesting to walk up by the old road.

History. The place has a long history. It was one of the towns given by Antony to Cleopatra. After the destruction of piracy by Pompey, Alanya gradually declined, becoming only a modest town in Byzantine days. In the thirteenth century after its capture by the Seljuk Turks the present fortress was begun; also the naval arsenal whose vaulting and arches still survive and where until the latter part of the last century the three-masted xebecs (called by the Turks kırlangıc) were built. The fine octagonal Red Tower of Kızıl Kule at the junction of the two city walls was built of red-coloured stone by Alaadin Kekubad in 1225, and is in a surprisingly good state of preservation. In the morning and evening light it is an enchanting sight, the golden-red tower standing out against steep honeycombed background of ruins and fortifications.

The town with a population of 18,000 now has a number of modern hotels close to the long sandy beaches which extend either side of the isthmus. Silk weaving, introduced by the Selcuks, continues today, raw silk sashes now being

179

made in the old quarter of the town. Ruins of a Byzantine monastery on the peninsula.

A number of modern hotels have grown up close to the long sandy beaches which extend either side of the isthmus beyond the somewhat primitive village. The countryside rising towards the foothills is attractive. There are green fields with cotton and tobacco, orange groves, banana plantations, some well-built farmhouses and the occasional minaret.

For those interested in stalactite caves, one may walk to the small Cave of Damlataş, which is now visited by sufferers from rheumatism, asthma and lung complaints. There is no sign of steam in the cave, but its humidity may rise to 98 per cent. This together with some radium activity is claimed to produce beneficial results.

Alanya is a port of call for the Istanbul steamer, but with the excellent coastal road most visitors prefer to use land transport.

Following the mountainous coast to the S.E., you first come to small indentations with green valleys ascending to the tall hinterland. The coast then becomes steep-to with scrub-covered slopes rising abruptly from the sea, interspersed here and there with banana plantations and clusters of pink oleander shrubs. Cape Anamur lies fifty miles distant and along the route are only two suitable night anchorages sheltered from west winds. In each case a kedge anchor is helpful in keeping a yacht head-on to the swell:

Aydap, ancient Hamaxia. Chart 241, plan. This is a poor little anchorage very shut in by its steep rocky sides on which are many closely packed ruins. Though sheltered from W., the bottom is rocky and the restricted space does not permit any yacht larger than a motor-boat to berth here in safety.

Gazı Paşa (ancient Silinti or Trajanopolis). A tall steep-to promontory crowned by a ruined castle with open anchorage off a sandy beach.

> **Anchorage.** Chart 241, plan. Beaufort's soundings of 1810 are still correct today. Anchor two cables N.W. of the river mouth in $3\frac{1}{2}$ fathoms, firm sand. Sheltered partially from S. The west-going stream from the river mouth usually makes a yacht lie broadside-on to the swell from the day breeze.

Landing may be made in the dinghy, passing over the bar (1-ft depth) and up the stream for a few hundred yards towards the mausoleum of Trajan who died here on his way to Palestine. It is concealed by trees and no longer the significant building described by Beaufort. The hundred columns which once stood on the perimeter of a fine courtyard have all gone; even the plinths of the columns now seem to be in process of destruction by local peasants. The whole site has been plundered and although very little of the theatre remains several arches of the aqueduct still stand. Bananas have recently been introduced.

Some miles further along the coast is a high pinnacle on the summit of which can be seen the crowded ruins of one of the many Antiochs. On the mountain ridge above is a large gateway and a ruined church.   ·

Yakacik (Kalıdıran; ancient Charadus) is a pleasant bay at the mouth of a valley facing south.

> **Anchorage** is close to the western shore near a small house. The bottom is sand, the depths 3–4 fathoms, and there is protection from W. and N.W. winds. A swell rolls in after the day breeze.

There are four small houses near the shore and a little shelter for a couple of fishing boats. In Roman times, according to Strabo, it had a harbour protected by a fort. Only the sunken mole of the harbour can now be seen.

Karataş (ancient Melissa), which affords similar, but inferior, shelter to Yakacik, is only 6 miles from Cape Anamur. The coastal road sweeps round the bay, at the side of which is a police post.

> **Anchorage.** Though well protected by a rocky ledge from winds between N. and S.W. the bottom is rock and stone with patches of sand usually distinguishable underwater. Anchor 100 yds offshore with the road-bridge bearing 340°. The shore shoals out for at least 30 yds. With a westerly swell this anchorage can be uncomfortable.

Anamur Burnu Chart 241 (plan). The cape is bold and steep-to and the anchorage close eastward usually well-sheltered in summer. One can anchor close off the cape, 70 yds from shore in 4 fathoms on a sandy bottom. Open to S. and E.

If wishing to obtain clearance for Greek Cyprus it is necessary to ʿollow the coast N.E. for $4\frac{1}{2}$ miles to the pile pier at Eski Anamur. Here one can land with the necessary papers for the officials whose offices are close to the pier.

Winds off Cape Anamur. In summer after the day breeze has died there is usually a calm, after the sun has set a westerly wind often springs up and offers a sailing yacht the chance of a fast passage to Cyprus. Half-way across the night breeze from the Troodos Mountains augments the west wind and one may thus hope for a favourable breeze to continue until sunrise.

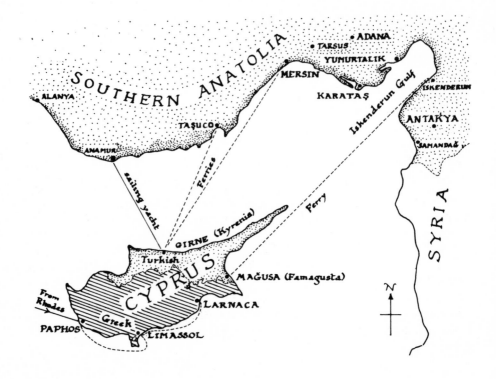

CYPRUS
    Kyrenia (Girne)
    Larnaca

8

Cyprus

Until 1974 many yachts used to visit the delightful island of Cyprus. Since the attempted murder of Archbishop Makarios and the subsequent invasion of the northern half of the island by Turkey, the political situation has been tense.

A visit to Kyrenia (Girne) is a pleasant and easy excursion for a yacht which may have reached Anamur; but owing to military restrictions one may not use Kyrenia as a base for visiting coastal anchorages in this island.

Therefore, only Kyrenia is described as a cruising objective in Turkish Cyprus.

In Greek Cyprus the port of Larnaca is in detail because a number of yachts like to winter there in the marina.

Procedure for Entry of Yachts. Yachts may cross from Turkey into Turkish Cyprus or to Greek Cyprus and vice versa, but *not* from Turkish Cyprus to Greek Cyprus. A Turkish Cypriot entry stamp is not welcomed in Greece. In Girne (Kyrenia) the authorities will issue a separate card to avoid stamping passports.

Communications with Cyprus

Turkish Cyprus. Ferry: Alanya, Taşuco and Mersin or by air to Istanbul.

Greek Cyprus. Ferry to Greece; air to Athens.

Note. One should ascertain that the insurance company will cover the yacht during its period in Cypriot waters.

Kyrenia or **Girne** (its Turkish name). Chart 847 (plan). A delightful small harbour with all-round shelter. Well worth making the excursion from the Turkish coast, but bearing in mind the restrictions on movement to other anchorages.

Approach. Coming from the Turkish coast, a yacht often makes a landfall off the tall mountains of the Karpas Peninsula. Taking advantage of the favourable wind during the night

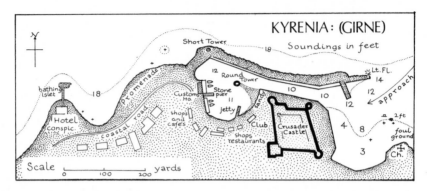

it usually means an early morning approach, and the unforgettable sight of the steep peaks like a high frieze hanging over Kyrenia, silhouetted against the dawn sky.

The Crusader castle by the harbour can be recognized by day, and one may not enter by night. Recently the depths were fully 2 fathoms, but the entrance to the port is liable to silt.

Berth. A quay has been constructed on the west side of the harbour where a few yachts can berth stern-to, four berths being reserved for visting yachts. The harbour is safe under all conditions; only in strong S.E. winds does a slight swell enter the port.

Officials. As for Port of Entry, but yachts must report to the Military outpost on entry.

Facilities. Water and electricity are laid on at the quay. Fuel is difficult to obtain. Provisions can be obtained. Some good hotels (with bathing facilities) and restaurants are close by the port. There is only a small slipway. The airport at Nicosia is half an hour's drive; taxis available.

Kyrenia had grown enormously during the last thirty years and until its recent occupation by Turkey had a population of nearly 5,000; but it remains in essence a small place and the old buildings around the harbour-front, where a Crusader castle dominates the port, are unchanged. It is now a popular resort for Turkish tourists.

The castle should be visited, not only for its interest as a medieval fortress, but because within its walls can be seen the recently reconstructed hull of a small Greek merchant ship of the period of Alexander the Great. Discovered originally by the late Andreas Cariolou, well known in Cyprus as a diver with archaeological interests, the wreck was located one mile offshore in a depth of 15 fathoms; the water is very clear. In 1967 and the following years an enthusiastic team sponsored by Pennsylvania University and led by Michael Katzev carried out diving operations from a raft moored above the wreck.

The setting of Kyrenia is probably one of the most appealing in the Mediterranean – a dramatic skyline of mountains on whose crags can be seen the Lusignan castles of St Hilarion and Buffavento. On one of these hills directly above Kyrenia stands the ruined Byzantine monastery of Bellapais, one of the most beautiful monuments of the Latin East; from here and also from the high peaks are breathtaking views along the coast.

At St Hilarion a ruined Gothic window frames a superb view. Richard Coeur de Lion and his queen Berengaria are reputed to have spent their honeymoon there.

As regards prohibited areas, conditions resemble those of the Turkish mainland a few years ago. From the west end of the north coast these are:

(a) From the Greek/Turkish boundary to $\frac{1}{2}$ mile W. of C. Kormakiki.

(b) The vicinity of Snake Island.

(c) From a point 4 miles E. of Girne to 8 miles further E.

(d) From 12 miles E. of Girne to Karpas.

(e) The eastern shores of the island.

(f) South coast: from Famagusta as far as bathing beaches.

These areas may be changed from time to time.

· To sum up: only the ports of Girne and the less attractive Famagusta are at present available for a visiting yacht in Turkish Cyprus.

Larnaca (Greek Cyprus), an agreeable small town is remarkable today for its yacht harbour with a well equipped marina, safe in all weather. In 1981 the marina was completely booked a year ahead. (See plan overleaf.)

Approach. The yacht harbour lies southward of the commercial port and is entered on a S.W. course. The extremity of the mole is lit (Lt.Occ.) and the short mole has a Lt.Fl.(G). The depths at the head of the marina berths are $2\frac{1}{2}$ fathoms (min.). Bottom is mud.

The Marina can accommodate altogether about 200 yachts, afloat and on the hard (max. 100 of 10 m.l.o.). About one-third of the afloat area is occupied by fishing craft, but they are likely to be moved in future to a small harbour now under construction. A travel-hoist can lift up to 40 tons (max. L.O.A. 17 m beam 4.8 m); the charge for being paid up 'on the dry' is the same as the cost afloat. Repairs ashore can be undertaken at reasonable cost by Neptune Yard (Hillyar).

Water and electricity are supplied at each berth, shipwright and mechanical repairs are available – fuel on request, showers and laundry are provided. Telephone and TV connection are being arranged. Provision shops are close outside main gates, and restaurants nearby.

The marina is well lit and well guarded. In 1980, prices were less than in Greece and yachts were satisfied with conditions. The airport is just outside the town.

The small town of Larnaca has extended in recent years due to tourism and today there are some first grade hotels and restaurants on the sea front.

Winds between S.E. to S. prevail, and in winter one expects to find temperatures in the lower sixties.

In the early part of the year pink flamingos may be seen on the salt lake near the airport.

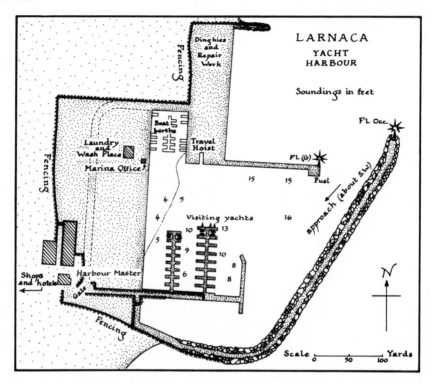

History. Standing within sight of the sea near the large lake is the Mosque of Hala Sultan Tekke, a holy place revered by all Muslims, and at one time saluted by every passing vessel flying the Ottoman flag.

Within the mosque is a tomb with the following history: in A.D. 649 one of many Arab invasions of Cyprus was led by the Governor of Syria. He brought with him in the expedition one Samit, a companion of the Prophet and his wife Umm Harem, a kinswoman of Muhammad and, according to some authorities, his fostermother.

Landing with the expedition near Larnaca, the holy woman then mounted a mule and reached the place where the mosque now stands. Here they were attacked by Genoese infidels. Falling from her mule she broke her neck and died, and was buried at once on the spot. Her tomb is a prehistoric-looking structure of three enormous stones, two being upright and supporting a third across.

Ports of call when approaching from the west towards Larnaca

If coming from the direction of Rhodes, there is Kastellórizo, (see p. 161) and in Cyprus, Paphos and Limassol, both Ports of Entry.

Paphos is a shallow, but sheltered little harbour with the small town of Ktima close by. A number of ancient Greek and Roman sites are worthy of a visit.

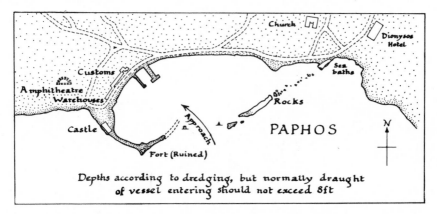

Approach. Chart 846, but beware of changing depths. Recently there was a minimum of 2 fathoms in the approach channel as far as an elbow buoy, after which there is a 9½-ft basin, as indicated on the chart, but dredging sometimes takes place. The two approach buoys lead one into the channel along a line midway between the pier and lighthouse. The ancient mole to the N.E. of the entrance shows well above water; the other one does not. A yacht drawing more than 8 ft should not attempt to enter the port. The breakwaters are built upon the Phoenician foundations, and the defending castle is of Genoese origin with Turkish modifications.

Berth. Lay out anchor to S.E. and pass a long warp towards a long building on shore. The bottom is small rocks, boulders and patches of sand. Shelter is good except from S.E. when a swell comes in with fresh winds.

Officials. As for a Port of Entry with Customs, Health and Police, whose offices are close by.

Facilities. Land in the dinghy at steps N.E. side of the pier where there is a water tap. Facilities are limited, but there is a Customs Agent in the port who can be helpful. A small yacht club. Restaurants; taxis to Ktima (distant 2 miles) for shopping where there is also a pleasant hotel and restaurants.

Paphos, now united with Ktima, has a population of about 12,000. There are interesting Greek and Roman sites nearby: The Hellenic 'Tombs of the Kings' – half an hour's walk – are palatial burial places. The early Christian church of Chrysopolítissa built on the site of St Paul's scourging; also the mosaic flooring of a Roman palace.

Limassol. An important commercial port with a basin adjoining a town of 80,000 people. See plan on Chart 846. There is good anchorage near the head of the Akrotíri Peninsula 3 cables N.W. of C. Gáta in a basin behind a mole with 7-ft depths: Chart 846 and plan on 850.

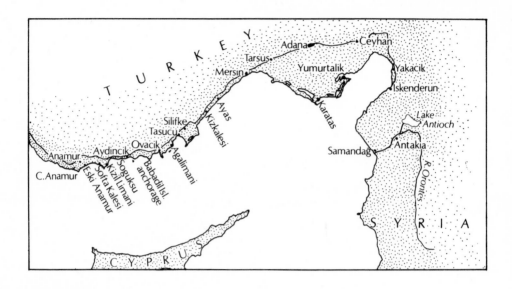

ICEL (Ancient Cilicia)
  Eski Anamur
  Anamur Castle (Kalesi)
  Softa Kalesi
  Kızıl Limanı
  Soğuksu Limanı
  Aydıncık (Celendris)
  Babadil Isl. Anchorage
  Karğıncık Borğasi
  Ovacık
  Dana Ada
  Ağalimanı (Bağsak)
  Taşucu (Silifke)
  Susanoğlu
  Narlıkuyu
  Kızkalesi
  Ayas
  Limonlu
  Vıranşehir

MERSIN
  Port of Mersin (Tarsus & Adana)

HATAY (Sancak of Iskenderun)
  Karataş
  Yumurtalık Limanı
  Ayas
  Ceyhan Limanı
  Yakacık

ISKENDERUN (Alexandretta)
  Ulcinar (Arsuz)
  Samandağ (Seleucia)
  Orontes River (Asi Nehri)

30 Gilindire: an important Turkish official being embarked in the mail brig for Cyprus, about 1800

31 A typical Turkish *takah* under way between Ereğli and Zonguldak

32 Orontes River: the great water-wheels at Hama

9
Turkey (contd)

PART II
ANAMUR TO THE SYRIAN FRONTIER

Following the sandy shore from the cape to the pier at Eski Anamur one passes terraces of tombs on the hillslopes which Turkish archaeologists are in the process of restoring. These are some of the ruins of the ancient city mentioned by Pliny with theatre, many tombs and vaults. Formerly a Hellenistic colony and originally Phoenician, here are also buildings of a later period with medieval walls climbing the hillside.

The modern **Anamur** is a scattered village with a population of about 22,000; it stands inland on rising ground N.E. of the ruins. On the surrounding countryside there is much cultivation and banana plantations.

> **Anchorage** is off the pierhead in 3 fathoms. The bottom, which rises appreciably as one nears the shore, is sand. The anchorage should be regarded as temporary. Sometimes a strong E. going current.

> **Officials.** Harbour office and Customs are at the root of the mole. Immigration office is at Anamur village to where one is sometimes made to go by taxi to complete formalities; at the root of the pier is a meteorological station, some villas and a motel.

Anamur Kalesi consists of a castle on the open sandy beach six miles eastward of Cape Anamur. (See Plate 29 and plan p. 190.)

> **Approach and Anchorage.** Even small vessels should approach the beach with caution on account of the reefs between the small rocky islet to the east and the rocks on the west. Fifty yards off there are depths of 8 ft on a sandy bottom.
> A yacht should time her stay here between the hours of 0700 and noon, since the westerly winds then begin to set in freshly, making the anchorage most uncomfortable.

The castle, with walls intact and three wards and thirty-six towers still standing, was originally a Roman fortress, later built on by Lusignan kings who, driven from their own country, overran the mountainous coast of Cilicia which they subsequently controlled by building castles at strategic points. Anamur,

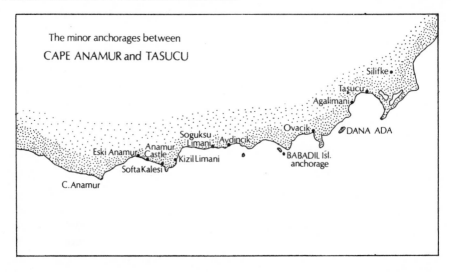

The minor anchorages between
CAPE ANAMUR and TASUCU

Silifke•
Taşucu•
Agalimani•
DANA ADA
Ovacik•
Soguksu
Limani• Aydincik•
BABADIL İsl.
anchorage
Anamur
Eski Anamur• Castle• KizilLimani
SoftaKalesi
C.Anamur

later occupied by Crusaders, became their embarkation point when they finally abandoned Cilicia and set forth for Cyprus.

At one time surrounded by a moat, the castle had it main entrance on the north or landward side with smaller exits to the sea. The mosque, baths and fountain in the middle of the inner structure were added by the Karamans when they in their turn captured the castle. The garrison at this time was reputed to have had an efficient distant signal system to summon help in event of attack from the sea.

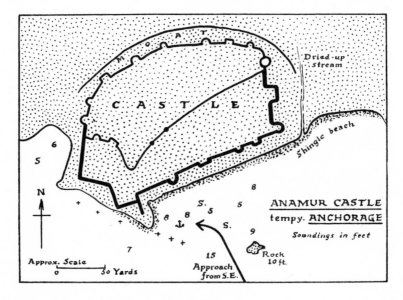

Dried-up stream

C A S T L E

Shingle beach

ANAMUR CASTLE
tempy. **ANCHORAGE**
Soundings in feet

Rock
10 ft.

N

Approx. Scale
0   50 Yards

Approach
from S.E.

Softa Kalesi, a small sandy bay lying nearly 2 miles S.S.E. of a fine Armenian castle standing on the hilltop – 650 ft up.

> **Anchorage.** Approaching the bay from S.E. a yacht should keep towards the northern shore in order to avoid the rocky bottom on the west side. There is also a dangerous rock in the centre of the bay 4 ft underwater. Anchor should be let go in about 3 fathoms on a sandy bottom where there is room for a medium-sized yacht to swing.

Some small farms by the shore can sometimes supply vegetables. The countryside around is well cultivated with market garden produce and banana plantations. Some scattered ruins nearby are those of the ancient city of Arsinoe whose port this once was. The Crusader castle standing prominently on the summit was once used by the Crusaders for accommodating raiding forces on Muslim ports. It was captured by the Venetians in the fifteenth century: from its splendidly isolated position it has a wonderful view.

After Softa Kalesi the Taurus ranges begin rising steeply from the sea. Some 50 miles further, after reaching Silifke, they again recede from the coast giving way to cultivated plains watered by continuously flowing rivers. This mountainous section of the Cilician coast is of interest mostly for its medieval ruins – Byzantine, Armenian and Crusader castles. The small deserted anchorages protected from S.W. winds enable the small- or medium-sized yacht to bring up and visit these places. The occasional hamlets are small and primitive; but the new coast road has already begun to attract the inhabitants back to abandoned places, and one notices that bars and modest restaurants have recently sprung up by the roadside.

Chart 237 from surveys by Beaufort in 1811 are more useful than a modern chart for recognizing the topography of the coast, although plans and descriptions in *Sailing Directions* have sometimes become outdated by circumstances such as coastal erosion, silting, collapse or plundering of ruins.

Kızıl Limanı. Close eastward of the bold cape Kızıl Burnu (633 ft) are some deserted steep-to rocky inlets. Among them only one, lying three miles N.E. of the cape, can be called a reasonably safe place for a medium-sized yacht to anchor in settled weather.

> **Anchorage.** Approach the high steep-to shingle beach and let go when 50 yds off. Bottom is sand. Sheltered from winds in the western quadrant as far as south.

Soğuksu Limanı (ancient Melania), 10 miles E. of Kızıl Burnu, is a horseshoe-shaped cove providing excellent shelter especially for a small yacht.

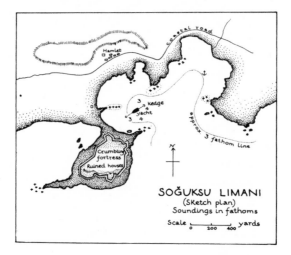

SOĞUKSU LIMANI
(Sketch plan)
Soundings in fathoms

Anchorage. See plan above, and note that plan on Chart 241 is no longer correct.

Let go in 4 fathoms on a sandy bottom with the fortress wall bearing about S. The water is clear and rocky patches can be avoided. Protected from W. and S.W. winds. There is insufficient room to swing and a kedge anchor should be laid out to N.E. to hold up the yacht when the land breeze sets in at night. A small yacht can get inside the cove and thus gain full protection. Alternatively, in event of easterly weather, the N.E. corner affords good holding.

Most of the fortress walls shown on the survey of 1812 have crumbled away and a modern hamlet has appeared above the coastal road in the area formerly marked on the chart as 'Tombs'.

Aydınçık (ancient Celendris), lying only 1 mile E. of Soğuksu, provides a similar type of anchorage with good shelter in 3 fathoms, but Soğuksu and Ovacik are better.

Anchorage. Let go in 3 fathoms when the light structure bears about S. The water is clear and a sandy patch can be selected, but holding is uncertain as the sand, in places, lies thinly on smooth rock interspersed with boulders. Sheltered from W. and S.W. winds. A small yacht can get inside and run out a warp to a damaged stone pier; but she must carefully avoid an overhead cable which passes only 25 ft above the sea. Note that the tower referred to in *Sailing Directions* is no longer standing. Its rubble has been used to build a short mole which is now submerged. The fortress is hardly recognisable from seaward as the walls have mostly collapsed. A light is now exhibited on the S. point of entrance.

Facilities. Simple restaurant, limited provisions, bank. The coastal road passes by the hamlet which has recently expanded, some new houses having been built overlooking the seafront; the old buildings in the port have been disbanded. Of no importance today, Aydıncık in the last century was maintained as a terminal for the sea-packet service to Cyprus.

Babadıl Islands anchorage. There is no convenient anchorage for a yacht by the

192

islands, but a suitable and pleasant anchorage can be found in an inlet about one mile north of them:

> **Kargıncık Borğasi anchorage.** Proceed into the inlet and when about 150 yds from its head let go anchor in about 3 fathoms on a sandy bottom. Open to W., but only through an arc of about 30 degrees.

The mountain slopes are green and wooded. A few farmsteads can be seen but there is no sign of life near the shore.

After rounding Ada Burnu comes the site of ancient Aphrodisias, but there are no ruins visible from seaward. Thence comes the prominent Cape Ovacik with its anchorage beyond.

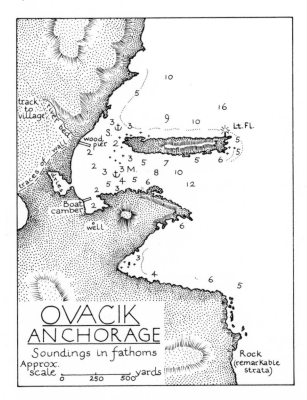

Ovacık, formerly Cavalière, is the name of the prominent cape, now called Bölükada Burnu, at the extremity of a tall rocky peninsula; also the name of the sheltered anchorage tucked into the eastern side of the isthmus. The cape is a prominent objective for a landfall when crossing from Cyprus, and the anchorage is the best sheltered for all weather on this stretch of coast. It has been used by sailing craft throughout the centuries. A west-going current is often apparent both at the cape and at the anchorage. Plan on Chart 241 omits some recent changes.

> **Anchorage.** A yacht must avoid a line of underwater rocks extending west of the island, and anchor as convenient in 2–5 fathoms on mud or sand. Good holding, excellent shelter. Room for three or four yachts to swing. Heavy swell in an easterly.

> **Facilities.** A wooden pier projects from the centre of the bay and a boat camber has been made in the southern corner.

Only one or two little cottages are near the shore; the village of Ovacık lies on the west side of the isthmus and nearby are some scattered ruins of ancient Gerga and an exceptionally beautiful Roman mosaic. Silica was quarried here until recently but now there is no activity.

> **History.** According to Homer it was here that the Sarpedonians landed their army in support of the Lycians during the Trojan war. In the later centuries this island, with Dana Ada, and the peninsula behind the little cove (then known as Cavalière because they were governed by knights from the tongue of Provence) became part of the Kingdom of Armenia. When that country recognised the Latin Church the Pope gave these islands to the Knights of St John so that they might become outposts of Christianity and serve as a place of refuge for escaping Christian slaves. Both islands have a few ruins, but are uninhabited today. The privately owned mine here produces manganese and emery and should it turn out to be prolific a mole will be built between the mainland and the island. Camels winter here, cared for by ten families of nomads from Konya. There is no fishery.

Dana Ada (Provençal), a comparatively long island lying 4 miles E.N.E. of Ovacık, sometimes provides a lee for steam vessels seeking shelter from strong S. and S.E. winds. The anchorage between the island and the mainland being so deep they sometimes prefer to keep under way rather than anchor. A Lt. Fl. on the N.E. extremity.

Ashore are the ruins of Roman and medieval dwellings, fragments of glass, pottery and mosaic. Also an occasional stairway cut in the rockside, partly submerged.

Ağalimanı (Bağsak) Chart 241. This is the sheltered anchorage for the village of Silifke.

> **Anchorage.** The plan shows the best place to anchor, i.e. 70 yds off the sandy beach opposite the new motel in 3–4 fathoms, open only to E. There are sometimes gusts from the High Taurus at night during the autumn months: yachts have experienced winds of Force 9–10 from the N.W.

> **Facilities.** The motel can provide meals, and also sells bread, fish and ice to a visiting yacht.

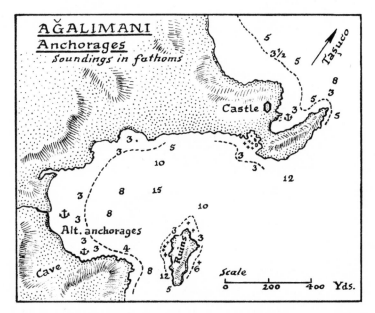

Castle Cove, the anchorage under the castle, should be regarded as temporary as the holding is unsure. There are sandy patches in 3-fathom depths.

The castle and the islet both contributed to the defence of the anchorage. The castle, originally Armenian, was strengthened in the 14th century, and with the help of the Pisans was still a Christian stronghold as late as the 16th century. Much of it is still in fair condition. Across the highway is an early Christian rock-hewn church.

Taşucu. A small Port of Entry and the main ferry port for Girne (Kyrenia), Turkish Cyprus. A new unfinished harbour, entered from E., offers the best shelter between Antalya and Mersin. (Plan overleaf.)

Anchorage. Anchor in centre of the harbour in 2 fathoms (on mud). Keep well clear of the ferry boat entry route and hydrofoil mooring.

Officials. Harbour master, Customs and Immigration in the village.

Facilities. Water on quay. Fuel from garage (2 miles on Mersin road). Basic provisions, bank, post office, currency exchange, small hotel, simple restaurants. Bus, hourly to Silifke. Daily ferry and hydrofoil (summer) to Girne (Kyrenia).

Half an hour's drive by bus brings one to Silifke, an unexciting town of 15,000 people. It lies close to the site of the original city founded by Seleucas I (the

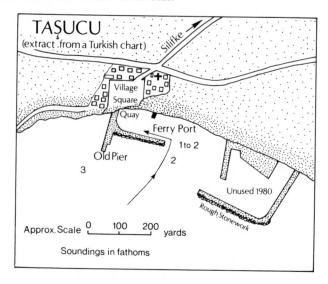

TAŞUCU
(extract from a Turkish chart)   Silifke

Village
Square
Quay
Ferry Port
1 to 2
Old Pier   2
3

Unused 1980
Rough Stonework

Approx. Scale 0   100   200 yards

Soundings in fathoms

Victor) when its port then lay four miles from the mouth of the River Göksu. It was here that Frederick Barbarossa, leader of the German contingent of the Third Crusade, was drowned, thus ending further progress of the Crusade.

From a small restaurant beyond Silifke village there is a view of the fine medieval castle with its twenty-three towers and turrets standing on a pinnacle overlooking the River Göksu. Following the road for some 30 km by the slopes of the Taurus you reach the remains of ancient Olba. Against a background of pinewoods are the ruins of a temple.

The eastern side of Taşucu Bay has a large lagoon full of fisheries and bounded by low, sandy dunes reaching as far as Cape Incekum. These extensive shallows are caused by the silt of the Göksu River, the discoloured water of which is encountered some miles to seaward. Recently its mouth, unmarked, was about 6 miles S.E. of the cape, and the 3-fathom line about one mile off. Beyond the cape the sandy shores bend away northwards for 6 miles until reaching the rocky coastline of the bay of Susanoğlu.

Susanoğlu is the quay at the head of an open bay forming a port for Persenti. Though exposed to the day breeze, small trading vessels sometimes berth here, but it is quite unsuitable for a yacht. Between here and Kızkalesi are 3 miles of rocky shore with one or two inlets. The best of these is **Narlıkuyu**, a small cove with an L-bend turning to the south. It lies half-way along this stretch of coast and is unnamed on the British chart.

Approach. The cove may be recognized by a couple of small houses and some poplars at the head of the creek.

Anchorage. There are depths of 2–3 fathoms about 100 yds from the landing place, where the bottom is sand. Perfect shelter from the day breeze, but open between N.E. and E., i.e. to the night breeze. It might be dangerous by night in August and later.

Officials. A Customs guard with a house by the poplars.

Facilities. There is fresh water from a spring and two fish restaurants. The coastal road passes close above with a turning-off to the famous potholes of Cennet and Cehennem (Heaven and Hell) 2 km away.

This cove is sometimes used by small trawlers and one or two local fishermen. It is a pleasant night anchorage, and the cold water lying on the surface of the sea makes bathing very refreshing.

Kızkalesi, with an exposed beach and two Armenian castles, lies about 3 miles N.E. of Susanoğlu.

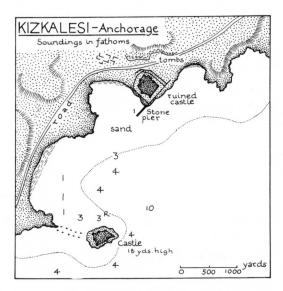

Approach. The castles are conspicuous many miles to seaward, and there is deep water until within the bay. See plan, Chart 241 and above.

Anchorage. There is no satisfactory shelter here. The day breeze which sets in from S.S.E. about 10.00 hours freshens later and sets up a short sea, making boatwork difficult.

To land and look at the sea castle a yacht should anchor temporarily close under its lee on the north side. Depth here is about 3 fathoms and the bottom rocks or sand. Inshore, the stone pier off the other castle has only 6-ft depth by its extremity, and inside the sand has built up a slowly shelving beach. There is no adequate lee, and a yacht should anchor off the molehead and land by dinghy at the rough stones on the N.W. side of the pier.

Facilities. Two characteristically Turkish motels have grown up on the edge of each sandy beach. Here spring water may be obtained and also a meal at the restaurant.

This place has been developed very recently for visitors and bathing parties from Mersin who come by the new coastal road; there are villas growing up around the bay.

History. Kızkalesi is the ancient Corycus so named from the saffron which grows here in abundance. It was Cicero's chosen place of residence when he was governor of Cilicia 52–50 B.C. The castles were built by the Armenian kings, one on the land, the other on an islet joined by a causeway to the mainland. (The causeway has been destroyed by the sea and now affords no shelter in the bay.) Later occupied by the Lusignan kings of Cyprus, the castles were eventually captured by the Karamans in 1375. Legend claims that the maiden after whom the castle is named was shut up there because it had been foretold that she would die of a snakebite; this she did when one was brought into her hidden in a bunch of grapes. The last Armenian king held out here until he could escape to exile in Paris.

The castle by the shore has double walls and a robust sea-gate, but the whole fabric is slowly crumbling away and is no longer so impressive to look at except in the evening light. In the vicinity are two ruined churches, and a mass of medieval structures lining the coast for some distance to the N.E. The Hittite and Phoenician ruins at Kanlıdivane are a short distance away by car.

The castle by the shore has double walls and a robust sea-gate, but the whole fabric is slowly crumbling away and is no longer so impressive to look at except in the evening light. In the near vicinity are two ruined churches, and a mass of medieval structures lining the coast for some distance to the N.E. Many of them have been substantial houses with stairways cut in the rock leading down to the sea. The seaward castle, whose walls and turrets are largely intact, still stands as a fine example of medieval fortification.

Ayas, 2 miles N.E. of Kızkalesi, was the Eleusa of Strabo. The ruined tower on the peninsula, originally an island, is conspicuous from seaward; it was formerly Cilician.

The peninsula has a sandy bay on either side where in calm weather one may anchor in 2-fathom depths and land in the dinghy; but it is very exposed, and of limited interest.

The ruins are mostly mausoleums, rock-cut tombs and Roman sarcophagi. Outstanding among them are the Roman aqueducts which, crossing the low-lying land, lead towards the Taurus mountains whence they formerly conveyed water to the town some 8 miles distant.

In describing the coast from here eastwards, Strabo records that the region was well adapted to piracy, both by land and by sea.

Limonlu is a very small artificial port about 6 miles further to N.E. It is the property of a marine research institute whose buildings are close by with a sentry on guard. It was being dredged in 1979.

Following the coast N.E., the hills recede, giving way to wooded and very green, cultivated plains reaching as far as Mersin. Here and there are steep valleys with small rivers flowing into the sea. The new motor road cuts close to the shore towards Mersin, passing en route a silted Greek port:

Vıranşehir (Soli or **Pompeiopulis)** is 5 miles S.W. of Mersin. Even before Beaufort's survey in 1812 the port had largely silted, but today it is barely recognisable and a large restaurant with a bathing beach has been built across its former entrance. It is approached from the main road by an avenue of Roman columns.

> *Do not bring up here, sailor; do not stow your sails because of me.*
> *The harbour you see is dry, I am but a tomb.*
>
> Greek Anthology

The stone blocks of the port are still there, and much of the Roman aqueduct which previously brought water for the ships in the port. The theatre and main roadway, with a few columns still standing along it, can be seen from the sea.

History. As one of the early Greek colonies it was known as Soli, but after its decline in the early Roman epoch it became one of the principal centres for the shipment of slaves. They were taken to Holy Delos, whose market provided most of the slaves for the Roman Empire.

When Pompey waged a campaign to destroy piracy Soli was devastated; but later it was rebuilt as Pompeiopulis and the prisoners rehabilitated. Meanwhile their use of the Greek language had become so corrupt that it could no longer be understood by others – the word 'solecism' was thereby coined, the stem of this word now being found in most languages.

Mersin, with a huge outer basin, is Turkey's new and principal port in the eastern Mediterranean; complered in 1962 it forms an outlet for the valuable produce from the rich agricultural Seyhan plain. The harbour is mainly busy handling exports of cotton, cereals and fruit according to the season; at other times it may be almost empty. It should, if possible, be avoided by yachts.

Approach. Chart 2188. Part of the breakwater may be seen a long way off, and in the distant background the tall ranges of the Taurus, which, even in mid-summer, are snowclad.

Berth. A yacht should berth alongside the new Customs House until the officials have been dealt with. This is not an agreeable berth, being open to the short sea of the day breeze coming across the large basin. At night a cool breeze comes off the mountains.

Officials. As for a Port of Entry. Formalities have been much accelerated since the recent concentration of officials all under one roof.

Facilities. There is water on the quay and fuel is easily made available. The town – 20 minutes' walk – has many hotels and some restaurants on the seafront. Several shops, buses to Antioch and Ankara. An airport.

The town of Mersin now has a population of 152,000 people, and a great many new buildings; it is still a dull place. Its commerce is dependent upon the prosperity of the adjoining inland towns of Adana and Tarsus and exports of cereals, copper, chrome, cotton, timber, flax, tobacco, sesame and citrus. It is famous for its orange liqueur.

Adana, now a modern commercial city with 350,000 people, is by far the larger and more important. Excavations have revealed its importance since Neolithic times and Hittites, Greeks, Romans, Byzantines and even Armenian kings have all left their traces in the western part of the town. The archaeological museum has the finds from Yumuktepe and Gozlukule and a splendid reconstruction of a nomad camp. Three or four mosques and a covered market. It is comparatively cool in summer, with a pleasant river front and gardens. It can be reached in an hour's drive from Mersin, and also by rail.

History. The Seyhan River, on which the town lies, is the Sarus of ancient time; where it enters the sea are many fish and turtles. In Roman days the emperor Hadrian had the Seyhan bridged – a lengthy structure of twenty-one arches of which fourteen of these, restored by Justinian, remain. In Crusader times Godefroy de Bouillon led his men across this bridge on their march towards Antioch. Today there is a sand bar at the river mouth, but the 12-ft depths inside enable boat traffic to reach Adana. Above here a barrage has been built to effect improvements in the irrigation of the cotton crop. Efforts have also been made to stamp out malaria, a scourge which hitherto has undermined the health of the peasants.

Adana administers the agricultural produce of this extensive and rich lowland plain. Its importance is similar to that of Izmir, although Adana, lying 25 miles from the sea, has to send its produce to Mersin for shipment. Adana also lies on Turkey's traditional communication route via the Cilician Gates to the East.

> ... *enquire in the house of Judas for one called Saul, of Tarsus.*
>
> Acts 9: II

Tarsus, lying 19 miles from the port of Mersin, was the birthplace of St Paul. Not only was Tarsus praised for its linen and cloth manufacture, but it was a city of culture. It lies 11 miles north of the mouth of the river which no longer serves any commercial purpose, but in Roman times was connected by canal with the sea.

Today the Tarsus Irmaği has no bar and is navigable for some considerable distance. 12-ft depth at the mouth.

The modern town, with a population of 33,000 people, has lost much of its importance since the departure of the Greek colony at the end of the First World War.

Although there are a few minor examples of Hittite, Hellenic and Roman remains, the remarkable double walls of the Middle Ages have all gone, and Tarsus now has little to show. Outside the town are some waterfalls and rapids; further inland is the small summer resort of Namrun at the foot of the Taurus.

It was across these sandhills from Tarsus to Issus that Alexander marched on his great eastern campaign. In 41 B.C. Cleopatra sailed up the Cyndus to meet Antony for the first time in Tarsus.

The low sandy shores of this large coastal delta are broken only by the bluff Cape Fener and its village of Karatas, has now become a bathing resort.

The Gulf of Iskenderun, nearly 20 miles wide, is spectacular along its S.E. shores where the green slopes of the steep Amanus Range rise steeply from the waters of the gulf.

Karataş (Chart 2188) lies on the eastern side of Cape Fener. The cape may be recognized by its white cliffs and by a white bungalow on which stands an inconspicuous structure supporting the light. The ruins of the ancient town of Megarsus, with its old harbour below, cannot be discerned from seaward. This was Alexander's first stop after Tarsus. Karataş village stands on the slope 2 miles beyond the cape, the shore being fringed by some low-lying rocky islets easily seen from seaward.

A motor road connects Karataş with Adana, whence in summer a number of visitors come by car to enjoy the bathing along this lengthy stretch of sandy beach. From seaward the place looks bare and uninviting.

> **Anchorage.** There is an anchorage 4 miles E.N.E. of Cape Fener near a place marked 'Landing' on the chart. A rocky spur extends eastwards· from the point and a sandy spit stretches northwards. This point is in fact the southern arm of a shallow sandy bay, and here temporary anchorage may be found, partially sheltered from the day breeze, in position 70 yds north of the sandy spit in $2\frac{1}{2}$ fathoms, but it cannot be recommended. The beacon shown on the chart cannot be discerned, but the lone tree is still there and makes a useful mark.

Yumurtalık Limanı (Chart 2188, plan) is the name now given to the large estuary originally formed by the Ceyhan Nehri, and is also the name of the small fishing hamlet lying on the northern shore. On early charts it was all called Ayas Bay. The sand bar is still extending southwards.

Standing above Ayas are the ruins of a castle built by Suleiman the Magnificent on an old Cilician settlement. The thirteenth-century castle of Yılandıkale lying 18 miles north of the village dominates the whole plain.

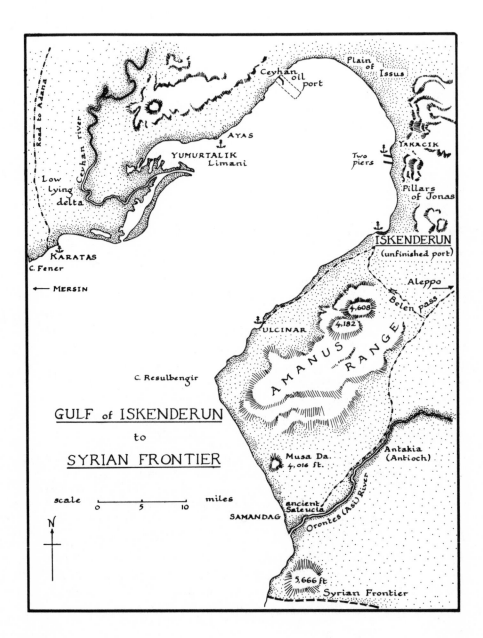

Approach and Anchorage. Chart 2188 shows the transit objects for approaching the most suitable small-vessel anchorage by day. It does not show the obelisks both on Bittern Point and on the uncultivated plain, nor the large radio station on the flat-topped mountain. The buoys, both navigational and mooring, being unlit, are dangerous at night. Though a huge expanse of water, it is considered to be a safe place to anchor in the summer months. There is no perceptible current flowing from the river today.

A group of five mooring buoys has been laid $1\frac{1}{4}$ miles south of the hamlet. Between the buoys and the shore to the N.W. is a prohibited anchorage.

Recent reports in 1980 confirm that there is very little traffic, almost no pollution and the anchorage quite suitable for a visiting yacht.

Ayas, the ancient Aegae, lying 3 miles E. of Yumurtalık hamlet is a small crumbling old Genoese port whose moles still afford shelter for small vessels.

Approach. A minaret shown on the plan is conspicuous. A course about W.N.W. pointing towards the minaret leads between the extremities of the two moles. These are clearly seen a few hundred yards off, and the passage between them is soon evident; it is about 50 yds wide. (Plan is based on a survey by Commander Brooker, 1858, still largely correct.)

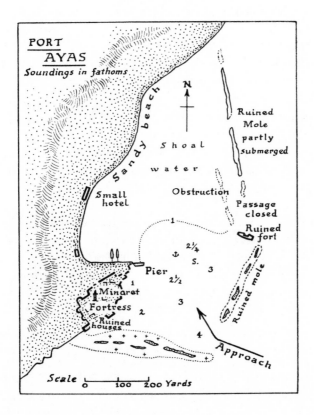

Anchorage. Let go eastward of the ruined stone pier in $2\frac{1}{2}$ fathoms. Sandy bottom. The shelter here is good. The village appears to be in a state of decay, the walls of the old houses having crumbled; the main village close to the westward also seems in a state of disrepair.

History. Until the Mameluke invasion in the middle of the fourteenth century, Ayas was the principal sea outlet for the eastern caravan trade with Mediterranean ports. This was largely the monopoly of the Genoese, who built two fortresses to protect both town and port. Only the outer walls and some turrets of the sea fortress now remain; the other has vanished.

At Port Ayas in 1812 when H.M.S. *Fredericksteen* was engaged in her survey work some Turkish guards opened fire on her boats. A midshipman was killed and Captain Beaufort so severely wounded that it was thought necessary to get him to Malta for medical attention as soon as possible. Fortunately for the hydrographic service he recovered and in later years became Hydrographer of the Navy, a post he held for a quarter of a century.

Except for some new building N.W. of the hamlet, there is no other sign of life nor is there any shipping.

The Ceyhan Nehri is the largest river in southern Anatolia. It formerly flowed into the sea by Karataş, but the huge quantities of sand brought down eventually blocked the river mouth and diverted it twenty miles eastward to Yumurtalık. A further change has now taken place, for some of the outflow has burst out via the large lake at the S.E. corner of the great delta, and its muddy waters may be seen extending many miles to seaward. This river, described by Cyrus on his long march eastwards, still abounds in fish and waterfowl, including swan, pelican, geese and duck; there are also turtles off the river mouth.

Ceyhan Limanı, the crude oil loading port 9 miles N.E. of Ayas, lies at the end of the 625 mile pipe-line from the Irak (Mosul) oilfields.

The loading jetties extend seawards for one mile and the port area extends 2 miles to seaward of that. The whole area known as BOTAS (the operating company) is prohibited to yachts.

Yakacık, an old Genoese port, is recognized by its ruined fortress and other fragments as well as the surviving moles of its original port. Today during settled weather it is pleasant to anchor temporarily off the sandy beach close to the ruins which form an attractive foreground to the rising slopes where, on many occasions, they have presented a natural defence against invading armies attempting to enter the Gates of Syria, known until recently as Payas.

History. When the Genoese were thrown out by the Turks at the end of the eighteenth century this was a prosperous place. It was Kuçuk Ali who made it a base for plundering the Aleppo convoys. He then turned his attention to the sea and one may find among the British Levant company records how in 1789 he seized the captain and part of the crew of one of the company's vessels which had gone to Jonah's Pillar to fill their water barrels. Only two years later a French schooner from Marseilles had imprudently anchored off the port having mistaken it for Alexandretta. The captain, having landed with some of his men to seek the company's consul and officials, was apprehended by this rogue and lured into accepting his hospitality. Whilst being entertained the Turks seized the schooner, landed the cargo and then destroyed the ship. Eventually the Turkish government at Constantinople was forced to send a strong expeditionary force against him. Yakacık was reduced to ruins from which it has never recovered.

Today it remains as a unique architectural complex consisting of a caravanserai, mosque, hamam and covered market built by the great Sinan, architect to Selim II.

Two miles further south is a new small port formed by a breakwater and two piers. Seven miles southward again is the new large port of Iskenderun. This should be approached with caution keeping at least one mile offshore to avoid lines of mooring buoys for oil tankers.

Iskenderun, formerly **Alexandretta** (Chart 2188), a vast new commercial port without berth or facilities for a yacht.

Approach. See warning about tanker mooring-buoys off eastern shore.

Berth. In 1979–80 there were quays only for berthing steamers. A newly arrived yacht should apply to Harbour Master.

Officials. As for a Port of Entry. The British consul now lives in Istanbul.

Facilities for a yacht did not exist in 1980, but there is water at the steamer quay and modern hotels and shops in the town. Buses to Antioch and Antalya; also rail connection with Turkish cities and Aleppo. An airfield.

The town, with a population of 107,000, is hot and very humid in summer, and during these months many local people migrate to the mountain villages close at hand. Although of no interest to a yacht, Iskenderun serves as a base for visiting some of the historical places by car. The road, ascending the Belen Pass (Gates of Syria), leads to Aleppo, Antakya (Antioch) and places on the Orontes Plain. Near the ridge of the wooded Amanus Mountains another road branching towards the S.W. leads to the small mountain resort Sogukoluk. These are day excursions by taxi and are well worth the visit.

History. Iskenderun was founded by Alexander in 33 B.C. and although about 23 miles from the scene of his famous victory at Issus, no town could have been better sited. It lies at the foot of the Belen Pass, the Gates of Syria, and is in fact the key to Asia Minor. The port until recently has been an open roadstead throughout the centuries.

It was the outlet of the great caravan routes from Bagdad and India, first exploited by the

Genoese and Venetians, and then by the French and British. The British Levant Company maintained a large mercantile base here for 200 years, only relinquishing their Middle East trade about the time of Queen Victoria's accession.

Ulcınar (Arsuz), 20 miles S.W. of Iskenderun, is a mediocre tourist resort and also a minor naval base. The short mole has been reconstructed, much improving the shelter: the village is close by the sandy beach and holiday camps have been set up.

> **Anchorage.** Useful when beating against the day breeze, but one must keep clear of two protruding rocky ledges (above water). Shallow water extends some distance offshore. Yachts are permitted to anchor outside the jetty (1979).

The prominent, tall headland of Resülhenzir separates the two gulfs of Iskenderun and Antioch. Before reaching this cape, when coming from Ulcınar, one sees the walls of a Crusader castle (once owned by Le Roche family), and standing immediately behind is the mountain of Kızılkağsak (5,268 ft) on the S.W. extremity of the Amanus range. From the cape to the Cyprus panhandle is 68 miles.

The wide and open Gulf of Antioch (Antakya today) affords no place of shelter, and there is none until reaching the Syrian port of Latakia nearly 60 miles from Ulucınar. But following this steep wooded coast S.S.E. for about 12 miles one comes to a prominent white islet with offlying rocks. This marks the northern boundary of the plain forming the wide mouth of the Orontes River. Close southward is Samandağ with the ruined port of ancient Seleucia, and here in fine weather there is anchorage off the open shore where one may sometimes land to explore the Orontes valley and the great Plain of Antioch.

> Two men, missionaries of the Holy Spirit,
> went down to Seleucia, and from there set sail for Cyprus.
>> Acts 13, v. 4

Samandağ (ancient Seleucia), the great Roman port for Antioch,* has been described by early historians, Josephus and others, as well as being mentioned in the Bible. Today its ruins are fragmentary and it is chiefly remarkable for two engineering feats – the port and the Rock Channel.

With the recent completion of a motor-road, these can be visited by land from Iskenderun more conveniently than by sea when anchored off the open coast.

---

* At that time, surpassed only by Rome and Alexandria, Antioch was the third greatest city in the world.

Approach. Chart 2632. About 4½ miles north of the charted outflow of the Orontes (Asi) River is a small white Customs House standing on a knoll. Cut into the hillside behind are a large number of tombs conspicuous from seaward.

Anchorage. An open sandy shore extends southward to the mouth of the river. Suitable depths for anchoring can be found; but one is completely exposed to the day breeze which makes boatwork on the shelving beach most unpleasant. A current sets northward along the shore.

Officials. Customs guards.

Facilities. A café close to the shore has warning notices against bathing owing to the strong undertow. A road leads to Antakya.

When Saints Paul, Barnabas and Mark, on their first missionary journey, embarked here for Cyprus in A.D. 45, they must have passed through the town as they descended into the port. On a clear day it is possible to see the Cypriot mountains from here. The present village lies inland from the ruins or about 3 miles from the coast.

The Ancient Port consisted of two outer moles whose stone blocks (about 20 ft × 6 ft × 4 ft fixed with cramps) shielded the mouth of a canal from winds and the north-going current. The canal led to a large basin where the Roman freighters were unloaded and their cargoes transhipped into lighters for towage 5 miles down the coast, across the Orontes bar and thence another 16 miles to Antioch. The port continued in use until the time of the great earthquake in the sixth century, although by then it had begun to silt with deposit brought along the coast by the current from the Orontes River.

Today the two moles are to be seen high and dry on the shore; the canal approach has disappeared, but the harbour basin can be traced.

The Rock Channel was a major engineering feat. By means of large tunnels and a channel cut

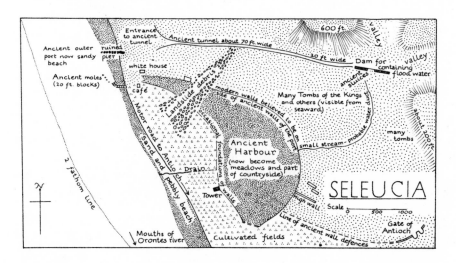

into the solid rock, it diverted a dangerous torrent from flooding the town and port.

A barrage was first built into the mountain side which diverted the torrent into two large sections of tunnelling (150 yds and 90 yds long respectively, 70 and 20 ft wide respectively and more than 30 ft high) and thence by a deep cutting into the sea. To follow this remarkable channel today it is best to enter from the outlet near the shore where the present road ends. The course is nearly a mile in length and, apart from some very slippery limestone and the occasional snake, there are no hazards. Near the tunnel mouth is an inscription referring to Vespasian and Titus, and another to indicate that the work was completed by a detachment of Syrian legions and teams of sailors.

The water which filled the reservoir behind the barrage also had another purpose. This was for use as a medium for scouring the inner harbour of the silt which gradually accrued, and unless removed would gradually make it too shallow for shipping. Other devices had been used in Phoenician ports such as collecting the 'wave water' in a header-tank and then releasing it with a sudden 'hoosh' through sluices. Seleucia, however, is the only known port where torrent water was collected and released by sluices to gush into the stagnant waters of the inner port, stir up the silt, and exhaust it seawards. This method appears to have been the means of maintaining the port in constant use for many centuries.

The **Orontes River**, the largest in the Levant, is 170 miles in length; it reaches the sea over a shallow bar five miles south of the ruins of Seleucia.

Though never well suited for navigation, the lower reaches of this river served for many centuries as an artery for east–west commerce – operated by the great city of Antioch 16 miles from the river mouth.

For nearly ten centuries there was a natural port at Poseidón on the coast, and soon after Alexander's time the large artificial port and city of Seleucia was founded. This flourished, especially in Roman times; but after eight centuries the great earthquake of A.D. 526 destroyed the port, the city and very largely Antioch itself, none of them ever to recover their former importance.

Attempts were made in Byzantine days to re-open the river trade, but after centuries of stagnation a new route to the east was opened by the Genoese at Ayas and at Payas, and in the sixteenth century by the French and British at Iskenderun; these ventures have long since come to nothing.

The lower reaches of the Orontes have served no commercial purpose for many centuries. Inside the river mouth are depths of about 3 fathoms most of the way to Antioch; a few fishing craft may be seen today, and boats under sail still ferry small cargoes from Antioch to places near the river mouth.

The Orontes River was a focal point of British interest early in the last century when the need for a fast overland route to the East Indies became an urgent requirement and an expedition was organized:

Colonel Chesney, an experienced Middle East explorer, received from the Duke of Wellington a letter dated 28 November 1834, appointing him to command an expedition to establish a link 'between the Mediterranean Sea and H.M. possessions in the East Indies by means of steamer communication on the River Euphrates'.

Colonel Chesney's plan was to acquire two small paddle-steamers and transport them in pieces to the Syrian coast. After landing at the mouth of the Orontes River he intended to assemble them and navigate upstream as far as possible. Then the steamers were to be dismantled, carried in pieces across the desert to the banks of the Euphrates where, after being reassembled, they were to proceed downstream to Bagdad.

For this purpose Mr Laird's yard at Liverpool constructed two small iron paddle-steamers:

For the Euphrates – 103 ft long, 19 ft beam with a 50 h.p. engine.

For the Tigris – 70 ft long, 16 ft beam and driven by a 20 h.p. engine.

The small combined services expedition, together with the two steamers in pieces, and all their carefully planned equipment (including such items as reflectors for night navigation, a diving bell, Congreve rockets, small calibre guns and small arms) were ready to leave England early 1835. On 1 February, the chartered vessel *George Canning*, having embarked the whole expedition, sailed for the Mediterranean and reached Malta, where a naval sloop was provided to tow them to the Levant. After calling at Larnaca (Cyprus) the expedition sailed for Syria and anchored in the northern corner of Antioch Bay off the old Roman port of Seleucia.

On landing they soon realized the difficulties that lay ahead: local governors and sheiks (Turkish and Egyptian) were unco-operative, and the shallow bar across the mouth of the river was difficult to negotiate by the small landing boats on account of the dangerous surf. However, the task of disembarking and landing everything at a temporary base inside the river-mouth was accomplished, and on 6 May they 'commenced setting up the Tigris steamer'.

By the end of three months she was completed and ready to ascend the river to Antioch. But great was their disappointment when they found her 20 h.p. engine inadequate to stem the 4-knot current. Dismantling her again into eight sections, arrangements were made to move everything by land transport for the 140-mile journey to the Euphrates. A small party went ahead to make a survey from the sea-coast to the Euphrates to ascertain the practicability of cutting a canal.

Sections of the vessels, boilers and heavy machinery were mounted on sledges with small wheels: 'sometimes forty pairs of oxen and 100 men could not move them on account of the sharp angles in the track and steep ascent. Anchors, tackles, drag ropes and sometimes jack-screws were used.'

Finally, the vessels were assembled and launched at 'Port William' on the Euphrates, and the voyage downstream begun. Their troubles were not yet over, and after more adventures, the unfortunate Tigris was lost in a storm; but on 2 January 1937, nearly two years after leaving England, the Euphrates steamed proudly into Bagdad.

An alternative excursion is to visit the historical city Antioch, now called Antakya, with a growing population of 77,000. It was described by travellers in the last century as a modern town with fruit gardens and mulberries, surrounded by 7 miles of walls and towers of surprising solidarity. But many centuries earlier when ruled by the Seleucid kings it was 'a seat of pleasure and third city of the habitable earth' with half a million inhabitants.

Today this has completely changed – very little is left of the old; but a new and not displeasing modern town is slowly taking shape. Outside the town, standing on the steep surrounding hills, are the remaining tall walls of the old city. In Roman times the life of the city centred around the gardens of Daphne 5 miles outside the city – 'a place of beauty, worship and pilgrimage'. Today, the waterfalls and cascades still flow and in the deep ravine amongst the tall plane trees and flowering shrubs there is an atmosphere of freshness and peace. The gardens have deteriorated; their patrons, no longer the wealthy, are drawn from the poorer classes who use them as a picnic ground at weekends.

In the higher reaches the river has scored its way well below the level of the adjacent land which, being short of water, called for much ingenuity to provide a means of irrigation. This was achieved many decades ago by the construction of *norias*, large water-wheels sometimes 70 ft in diameter which raise water from the river to the desired level. The wheel is revolved by the force of the river water acting on flaps attached to its circumference; this in turn raises the buckets, which have scooped up the water to the level above, where they automatically empty into a water-duct which conveys the water to the fields. One can usually hear the grinding noises of these wheels long before seeing them. At one time there was a prosperous fishing industry, and for many decades smoked eels were a popular diet all over Turkey; but in recent years the use of dynamite has brought about a decline.

The coast continues southward from the frontier of the Orontes River to become the somewhat straight and unexciting seaboard of the three Levant countries. The Turkish coast now left behind will be remembered for its varied contours, the striking mountains and plains, and the contrast of colourful settings. In the new guide-books it is sometimes referred to as the 'Turquoise Coast', but this title does not adequately give an idea of its variety and great appeal. Moreover to those interested in bringing to light the history of so many heterogeneous nations no country could provide such imprints of its historical past as southern Turkey, and there is still much research for archaeologists and historians. This charming coast is likely to continue as an attractive cruising area for yachts, but one must bear in mind the progress of tourism and that many places which attract us so much today are on the way to becoming the Rivieras of the near future.

> *And thence sailed to Antioch . . .*
> *And there they abode a long time with the disciples.*
> (St Paul and St Barnabas) *Acts* 14: 26, 28

Index

Main text references are in bold; numbers in italic refer to maps, plans or drawings; n refers to footnotes.